W9-ABZ-454

STEPHEN LANGTON

SEAL OF ARCHBISHOP STEPHEN LANGTON
FROM A CHARTER DATED 1226

On the reverse the martyrdom of
St. Thomas of Canterbury

British Museum, Harleian Charter 74 A. 14

STEPHEN LANGTON

BEING

THE FORD LECTURES

DELIVERED IN THE UNIVERSITY OF OXFORD

IN HILARY TERM 1927

BY

F. M. POWICKE

FELLOW OF THE BRITISH ACADEMY
PROFESSOR OF MEDIEVAL HISTORY IN THE
UNIVERSITY OF MANCHESTER

BARNES & NOBLE, INC. · NEW YORK

PUBLISHERS · BOOKSELLERS · SINCE 1873

Reprinted by permission of Oxford
University Press

PREFACE

WHEN I chose Stephen Langton as the subject of the Ford Lectures in the University of Oxford, some of my friends doubted whether I could find anything new to say about him. My first intention, indeed, was to concentrate upon his share in the fight for the Great Charter and upon his later activities, but when I came to examine his unpublished Lectures, I found that the subject began to have a different and greater significance in my mind. What I had thought of as a restatement, containing a few new suggestions, was changed into a tentative introduction to a fresh, almost unworked, field of study. A happy result of the change has been that I have been able to gather together a little group of students who will be able, I hope, to carry the discussion farther. One of these is at work upon Langton's *questiones*, another on his commentaries, a third on his contemporary at Paris, Robert Curzon. To them I have left inquiry into such problems as that discussed by Father Mandonnet in the introduction to his edition of the *Questiones disputatae* of St. Thomas (Paris, 1926), namely, the connexion between the exposition of the Scriptures in the schools and the development of the *questio* in general. Later, I hope to make more careful investigation with others into the matters suggested by the last lecture, on Langton as archbishop, and by the last appendix, on the archiepiscopal *familia*. In the meantime, the lectures are printed here very much as they were delivered.

Two considerations have forced themselves upon me. The first is that the close relation between academic discussion and practical issues in ecclesiastical administration has been unduly neglected. The second is that, in England, as doubtless elsewhere, the reorganization which followed the general Council of the Lateran in 1215–16 was probably the most important episode in the history of the Church between the days of Pope Gregory VII and the Reformation.

Although this is a short book, it owes very much to the kindness of others, and not least to the encouragement which I have received from some of my Oxford hearers. The Master and Fellows of St. John's College, Cambridge, have been good enough to deposit for my use in the John Rylands Library their manuscript of Langton's *questiones*. Canon C. W. Foster helped me to unravel the mystery of Langton's origin and provided me with copies of the deeds printed or cited in Appendix I. Mr. W. A. Pantin copied, from a manuscript in Magdalen College, Oxford, the list of sermons given in Appendix II, made some extracts from the sermons themselves, and prepared from a Bodleian manuscript the text of Langton's *Documenta Clericorum* (Appendix IV). I have also been able in frequent conversations to draw upon his store of apt learning. I am especially indebted to Miss Alys Gregory, who is mainly responsible for the description of the Cambridge manuscript, given in Appendix III, and has helped me throughout in the investigation of the *questiones*. Dr. M. Tyson has compiled the index. Monsieur Henri Omont and Monsieur Ch. V. Langlois kindly sent me notes upon manuscripts in the Bibliothèque Nationale and the French national archives. Mrs. Stenton gave me helpful criticism of Appendix V. To all these, as also to Mr. Kenneth Sisam and the very careful staff of the Clarendon Press, I give my grateful thanks.

F. M. P.

MANCHESTER,
January, 1928.

CONTENTS

BOYHOOD IN LINCOLNSHIRE

STEPHEN LANGTON is one of the best, and also one of the least known figures in English history. He is known as a leading theologian in the schools of Paris, and he has a definite, if not very conspicuous place in the history of Biblical study. He was a cardinal, a friend of pope and kings, and archbishop of Canterbury. He was the foremost figure in the most bitter of all the conflicts between the secular and the ecclesiastical powers, and in the most far-reaching of all the political disputes in medieval English history. We think of him at once when we think of the great Interdict, or of the great Charter. And finally, his legislation as archbishop became an integral part of ecclesiastical law, as applied in England, as, that is to say, the application of the principles of the canon law in the years after the fourth Lateran Council and the fruitful pontificate of Innocent III. Yet Stephen Langton has had no biographer—contemporary or modern. Historians are uncertain where he was born, and how old he was when he died. Nothing is known of his early years, and almost nothing of his life in Paris and Rome, and during his years of exile. His numerous writings, with the exception of a few letters and state papers, a sermon on St. Thomas of Canterbury, two or three religious poems, stray fragments of his lectures and, of course, his constitutions, have not been published or even adequately described. We know nothing about his appearance, and can form only tentative judgements on his character.

The story of Langton's public life, for which we have to rely especially upon the St. Albans chronicler, Roger of Wendover, has been told by Dean Hook, in his *Lives of the Archbishops of Canterbury*, and, in firmer outline, by Miss Norgate in the *Dictionary of National Biography*. Many years ago a preliminary survey of his writings appeared in the *Histoire Littéraire de la France*.[1] Feret devotes a few unsatisfactory pages to him in his book on the faculty of theology at Paris; Grabmann, a competent estimate of his academic significance in his history of scholastic method.[2] Enough scattered evidence remains to justify a more elaborate estimate of his career, and of the part which he played in the academic discussions, the political and ecclesiastical crises of his time. And, as we follow up the hints given by this scattered evidence, in the investigation of Langton's life from boyhood to elderly manhood, I dare to hope that my readers may now and then share with me the pleasure which can be found in the exercise of historical criticism.

I have said that there is no contemporary life of Langton. This statement requires some qualification, for the archbishop's life was the subject of a lost work by no less a person than Matthew Paris. In his edition of the *Historia Anglorum* Sir Frederick Madden established the fact that Matthew Paris wrote a life of Langton, and called attention to a fragment of it surviving in a Cottonian manuscript (Vesp. B. xiii).[3] Ten years later (1879) Liebermann published this fragment, together with two others, inserted in the Liber Additamentorum, or commonplace book of St. Albans (Cott. MS., Nero, D. i).[4] It is a remarkable fact that, although they appear in different places and compose only a small part of the original life, and, furthermore, are written on one side of isolated bits of parchment, these three fragments fit into each other— the Vespasian fragment between the other two—and give a continuous narrative. The chronicler wrote late in life, with a hagiographical intention. The surviving passages relate to the later years of the archbishop's life and consist

---

[1] xviii. 51–66.

[2] Feret, *La faculté de théologie de Paris*, i. 276–84; Grabmann, *Die Geschichte der Scholastischen Methode*, ii (1911), 497 ff.

[3] *Historia Anglorum*, ed. Madden (Rolls Series), iii (1869), p. lii note.

[4] Liebermann, *Ungedruckte Anglo-Normannische Geschichtsquellen* (Strassburg, 1879), 318–29.

of accounts of Langton's differences with Pope Innocent, of miracles, preaching tours, and the translation in 1220 of the body of St. Thomas of Canterbury. Interesting though they are in themselves, they are even more important as evidence on the attitude of St. Albans to the archbishop's problems, and as proof of the tenacity with which he was remembered.

Another Cottonian manuscript contains a fragmentary chronicle followed by a collection of forty-one letters 'relating to the events connected with the election of archbishop Langton to the see of Canterbury'.[1] This very important text was edited by Stubbs in 1880 as an appendix to the preface in the second volume of the historical works of Gervase of Canterbury. The brief chronicle contains the only definite allusion which has come down to us to Stephen's father, Henry Langton.

In the third place, Langton's *questiones* or Paris lectures, which survive in several manuscripts in various forms, are frequently of great help towards our understanding of his views on political and ecclesiastical matters. I have generally used the version in a manuscript now belonging to St. John's College, Cambridge.

Langton is a very obvious, a very common place-name, and hitherto historical students have not known from which English village of Langton Stephen took his name. The one definite indication of his origin occurs in the short Canterbury chronicle printed by Stubbs. The passage is as follows:

'In these days (i.e. the summer of 1207) Henry of Langton, the archbishop's father, fearing that he would incur danger from the public authorities on his son's account, left his lands and goods, and for some time hid himself in England, with a few members of his household. At last he reached Scotland by sea (*in Scotiam transfretans*) and found a refuge in the priory of St. Andrews, where he was honourably treated on account of the love and esteem in which the archbishop was held. In course of time he died there. The

---

[1] *The Historical Works of Gervase of Canterbury* (Rolls Series), II, liv–cxv, printed from the Cottonian manuscript, Cleopatra E. I, ff. 134–46ᵛ.

royal officials, when they heard of his flight and retirement, confiscated his property.'[1]

So far I have not been able to trace any confirmation of this story;[2] but it tells us enough to go on. Henry of Langton, we may presume, died in exile before the reconciliation between King and Church in 1213. As he sailed to St. Andrews after taking hiding, he presumably lived in the northern parts of England near the east coast. He was clearly a man of some position, a fact also emphasized by Pope Innocent. In a letter of 21 December 1206, written to the prior and convent of Canterbury, the pope, dealing with Stephen's fitness for his new position, describes him as 'de ipsius regis terra et genere fideli sibi ducens originem'.[3] And rather later, in a letter to King John of 26 May 1207, after referring to Stephen's career at Paris, he says:

'We are very surprised that a man of such distinction and a native of your kingdom could be unknown to you, and the more so, since after we had promoted him to the cardinalate, you wrote to him to express your pleasure that he had received such an honour, although you had designed to summon him to your own service. But you should have taken peculiar note of the fact [here the pope is referring to Stephen's election as archbishop] that he was born in England of faithful and loyal parentage, and that he had been given a prebend in the church of York, which is so much greater and more dignified than that of Paris.'[4]

If we turn to the official records of Henry III's reign, we find clear proof that Langton came from the northern parts of England. He was a native of Lincolnshire. In

[1] Op. cit., lxii, lxiii. My friend Mr. M. Tyson kindly searched the Lincolnshire sections of the Pipe Rolls for the years 1207–12, but failed to discover any reference to the alleged confiscation of Henry Langton's lands. This, needless to say, does not disprove the story. The chancery rolls for several of these years are lost.

[2] It is perhaps significant that the abbey of Lindores in Fife, which was south of the Tay and not very far from St. Andrews, possessed a copy of the letters written by Pope Innocent and Archbishop Stephen during the interdict. See Bernard, *Catalogi librorum MSS. Angliae et Hiberniae* (1697), ii. 41, no. 1578—Gray's Inn MS. 11.

[3] *Gervase of Canterbury*, lxix.   [4] Ibid. lxxii, lxxiii.

April 1236 a royal writ was issued on behalf of Master
Simon Langton, archdeacon of Canterbury, well known
as the late archbishop's brother. In this writ the judges
assigned *ad custodem Iudeorum* are ordered to see that
Aaron of York, who has demanded of Master Simon the
debts owing by Walter Langton, Simon's brother, whose
heir Simon is, appears before the king with his charters and
tallies.[1] Stephen and Simon, then, had a brother Walter
who had died before April 1236, owing money to a well-
known Jew of York. Walter was alive in 1230, for in that
year he went with his followers—of whom at least two
were sufficiently influential to secure letters of protection
—on the royal expedition to Brittany.[2] In the previous
year, 1229, the prior of Bullington in Lincolnshire guaranteed his *bona fides* in seeking a suit of novel disseisin
against Walter Langton 'de tenementis in Langeton'.
Now this is noted in the margin of the Patent Roll as a
Lincolnshire case.[3] We have, therefore, to seek the Langton family in Lincolnshire, and to look out particularly
for a Walter Langton and his father Henry.

Every reader of Boswell will remember Dr. Johnson's
young friend, the sprightly Mr. Bennet Langton, and the
pleasure which the Doctor took in his ancient family.
'Langton, Sir, has a grant of free warren from Henry the
Second, and Cardinal Stephen Langton, in King John's
reign, was of this family.' Mr. Bennet Langton came from
Langton by Spilsby in Lincolnshire, where Dr. Johnson
visited him in his father's fine house. But this is not the
Langton of Stephen and his brothers. In the early years
of the thirteenth century, the lords of this place were
Osbert and Gilbert, not Henry or Walter.[4] There are,

---

[1] Close Rolls, 1234–7, p. 256, 11 April 1236.

[2] Patent Rolls, 1225–32, pp. 358, 359, 360. The two named companions
of Walter Langton were Thomas de Buk' and Richard de Essendon.

[3] Ibid., p. 291 (cf. p. 278). The prior entered upon another suit 'ad
recognoscendum utrum unum toftum in Langeton est libera elemosina per-
tinens ad ecclesiam ipsius prioris de Langeton an laicum feodum predicti
Walteri'. See further in Appendix A.

[4] See Oswald Barron in *The Ancestor*, no. 7 (October 1903), 166–9.

however, two other Langtons in Lincolnshire, Langton by Horncastle, and Langton by Wragby. Wragby lies on the old road between Lincoln and Horncastle, and both these Langtons, therefore, are in the heart of the county. The priory of Bullington, to which reference has been made, was about three miles from Wragby on the way to Lincoln. At this stage in my investigations, I turned for help to my friend Canon Foster, whose knowledge of Lincolnshire deeds and Lincolnshire topography is unrivalled. From the numerous transcripts made by Canon Foster of contemporary deeds, it seemed at first that Walter and Simon, and, therefore, Stephen also, came from Langton by Horncastle, for a Henry Langton—and Henry was their father's name—is frequently found, the son of Alan of Woodhall or Woodall, close to Langton by Horncastle.[1] But this Henry of Langton was alive as late as 1222, to which year one of his charters can be ascribed; whereas, if the story in the Canterbury chronicle can be accepted, the Henry Langton, who was Stephen's father, died in St. Andrews, away from home, some years before this date. Again, Henry the son of Alan, cannot, at any rate as yet, be connected with a son Walter. We were accordingly forced back on the conclusion that our Henry and his three sons belonged to Langton by Wragby, nearer to Lincoln, and not far from Bullington. Further search by Canon Foster confirmed this view, for among the original charters in the British Museum relating to Langton by Wragby is one of Master Simon, son of Henry Langton, concerning a toft to the west of Langton church.[2] We may accordingly assert with confidence that Stephen, Simon, and Walter were the sons of Henry of Langton by Wragby.

In the year 1232 Walter Langton had as wife Denise of Anesty, the daughter of Nicholas of Anesty, a tenant in Essex and Hertfordshire of the great honour of Boulogne.[3]

[1] See Appendix I.
[2] Harleian Charters 52, I. 30 (*c.* 1230). See Appendix I.
[3] Close Rolls, 1231–4, p. 91; Farrer, *Honours and Knights' Fees*, iii. 266.

As the father of Denise was still a minor in 1212,[1] it is unlikely that she had married much earlier than 1232, and
as she was a widow in 1234, her married life was a short
one.[2] But during her brief union, she must have increased
considerably the wealth and status of her elderly husband,
and that Walter was able to win a bride of such high rank
is further evidence of his solid position in Lincolnshire, a
position strengthened no doubt by his relationship with
the late archbishop of Canterbury. Walter died without
children, for his heir was his brother, the archdeacon
Simon.[3] In later years his widow became a very great
lady. In 1235 she married Warin de Muntchenesy, the lord
of numerous manors, mainly held of the honour of Richmond in Yorkshire, Lincolnshire, and Norfolk. This baron
was of high family distinction. His grandmother had been
a Fitz John, his mother a sister of the earl of Arundel, his
first wife a daughter of the great William the Marshal,
earl of Pembroke, and his daughter, Denise's step-daughter,
was later to marry William de Valence, the half-brother of
King Henry III.[4] When Warin died in 1255, Matthew
Paris spoke of him as one of the wisest of the barons, a
pillar of the state, and burst into a lament over the gradual
disappearance of the nobility of England.[5] Denise was
henceforward one of the chief ladies in the land. Her son,
William de Muntchenesy, was one of the barons who held
out against the king in the siege of Kenilworth. He died
before his mother, who in 1288 had the custody of her
young granddaughter, another Denise. The old lady
lived until 1298.[6] She had survived the conflict between
Edward I and Archbishop Winchelsey. Perhaps in those
days she thought of her first husband, who had died more

---

[1] Book of Fees, p. 125. Robert fitz Walter, later the leader of the rebellious
barons in 1215, held Anstey and Little Hormead in Hertfordshire 'in custodia
cum herede Huberti de Anesti'. Cf. Farrer, op. cit., p. 271.

[2] Close Rolls, 1231–4, p. 508.   [3] Close Rolls, 1234–7, p. 256.

[4] See Farrer, op. cit., iii. 102–10 for the Muntchesny family.

[5] M. Paris, *Chronica maiora* (Rolls Series), v. 504.

[6] Farrer gives two different dates of her death (pp. 108, 266). The true
date is 1298 (*Calendar of Fine Rolls*, i. 404).

than sixty years ago and had been the brother of a still greater archbishop.

We must go back more than a hundred years to Stephen's boyhood in the house of his father, a country gentleman of modest standing in Lincolnshire. It is probable that he was the eldest brother, for he died in 1228—well advanced in years—and his other brothers outlived him.[1] Walter indeed, the layman, must have married after Stephen's death. In those days, as a German scholar has recently shown,[2] a man could be called old (*senex*) at any age between 50 and 70, and we cannot assume that Stephen was more than 60 when he died, or that he was born before the date of the Constitutions of Clarendon. Also, we must remember that his father, Henry, lived until the period of the Interdict (*c.* 1210). Let us assume, without any violence to chronology, that he was born about 1165. Of his mother, unhappily, we know nothing.

The family was not distinguished, but had a standing in the neighbourhood and in the courts. The use of a common place-name suggests that the Langtons were of Anglo-Danish, not of foreign stock, and had gradually accumulated some property, a small manor, in the neighbourhood of Wragby. Professor Stenton has told us how divided these Lincolnshire villages were, how tenacious the small landholders, or sokemen, were of their freedom, yet how easily the fortune of one family could be lost, of another won, in a land where the compact, highly organized manorial system of the south did not yet exist.[3] It is

---

[1] If this suggestion is correct, Stephen surrendered any claims to succeed to his father's lands, unless Walter succeeded him in 1228.

[2] Adolf Hofmeister, 'Puer, Iuvenis, Senex, zum Verständnis der mittelalterlichen Altersbezeichnungen', in *Papsttum und Kaisertum*, ... Paul Kehr dargebracht (Munich, 1926), pp. 287–316.

[3] See F. M. Stenton's introduction to documents illustrative of the social and economic history of the Danelaw (1920), especially pp. xcvii onwards. In his recent essay, 'The Free peasantry of the Northern Danelaw', in *Årsberättelse*, the bulletin published by the Royal Society of Letters, Lund (1925–6), Professor Stenton has summarized the conclusions reached in his various studies, and added a calendar of charters.

quite likely that Henry of Langton belonged to a family of flourishing freeholders who had risen somewhat in the social scale. His household was presumably pious and interested in learning, as two of his sons departed at an early age for Paris. They must have had some schooling, and have been dedicated to careers in the service of the Church. Perhaps the Langtons were friendly with the inmates of the neighbouring Gilbertine priory at Bullington, to which the church of Langton had been granted when the priory was founded (*c.* 1155).[1] Gilbert of Sempringham himself, the founder of the order, received the habit at Bullington and would often be there.[2]

We cannot say where Stephen learned his letters, but he must have come in contact with the clergy in the great cathedral church at Lincoln, some fifteen miles away. In Stephen's boyhood only part of the west front of the present cathedral existed—the Romanesque church was still standing. The supervision of all schools in the shire, as we learn from the later statutes, was the duty of the chancellor, who also directed the theological teaching at Lincoln itself.[3] While Stephen was at Paris, the theological school of Lincoln became famous under the direction of the learned chancellor, William of Leicester. William of Leicester first definitely appears as chancellor in 1191,[4] but if, as Gerald of Wales says, his nickname 'William of the Mount' (*de Monte*) was given him because he had taught in the Mont Ste-Geneviève near Paris,[5] he must

---

[1] See the foundation charter of Simon, son of William, in Stenton, *Transcripts of Charters relating to Gilbertine Houses* (Lincoln Record Society, vol. xviii, 1922), p. 91.

[2] *Monasticon*, vi. 2, p. xii (from the life in Cotton MS. Cleopatra B. 1); Rose Graham, *S. Gilbert of Sempringham* (1901), p. 23.

[3] Bradshaw and Wordsworth, *Lincoln Cathedral Statutes*, i. 284, 285.

[4] Le Neve gives 1192. Canon Foster has given me the earlier date. William may, of course, have come to Lincoln before he was promoted to the dignity of chancellor. During Stephen's boyhood the chancellor was Master Hamo, who died 17 August 1182: see the obituary of Lincoln Cathedral in *Giraldi Cambrensis Opera*, vii. 160. Hamo compiled the catalogue of books printed as Appendix C in the same volume, pp. 165–71.

[5] *Opera*, i. 93. For William's writings see Bale, *Index Britanniae Scrip-*

have been a master in Paris many years before this, for the seculars had ceased to teach on the mount by 1180. It is just possible, therefore, that Stephen met the famous scholar, whose biblical and theological interests were in many respect similar to his own. This, however, is pure hypothesis. All that we may safely affirm is that, in order to get through his courses in arts and theology and become qualified to teach both—and he was teaching theology in the last years of the century, he must have gone to Paris about 1180 or soon afterwards.

What influence had moved him we cannot tell. The fame of the teachers of Paris would be spread at this time in every ecclesiastical circle in England, and among the intelligent laity who lived in the neighbourhood of monasteries and cathedrals. A great writer of our own day has described the sensations of a young man in circumstances less happy than Langton's, as he meditated upon the life, the attraction, the prospects of a career in the schools. His feelings have been those of boys in all ages. They are to be found, expressed almost in the same words, in the correspondence of the twelfth century.

'It is a city of light', he said to himself.

'The tree of knowledge grows there,' he added, a few steps further on.

'It is a place that teachers of men spring from and go to.'

'It is what you may call a castle, manned by scholarship and religion.'

After this figure he was silent a long while, till he added: 'It would just suit me'.

Before following Stephen to Paris, we may linger for a little while upon the two aspects of ecclesiastical life, which must have been familiar to him from childhood, and frequent topics of discussion among his friends. I refer to monasticism and the great issues raised by St. Thomas of Canterbury.

torum, ed. Poole, 130–2; *Dict. Nat. Biog.*, s.v. William of Leicester; and cf. Grabmann, op. cit., ii. 490.

Once, when he was teaching in Paris in later years, Stephen, like many others, took as his theme the problems, raised in the Gospel and by St. Paul, of scandal or stumbling-blocks. One of his illustrations was possibly suggested by his own experience. 'My father is scandalized because I am going into a monastery. It would seem that, if I can save my soul in the world I ought not to go to the scandal of my father.' [1] Stephen was intensely interested in the religious life. He frequently, in the course of his lectures, refers to details of monastic life and experience and to the monastic rules. In the bitterest hour of his life, when he saw all his hopes of a peaceful reorganization of England shattered, he hesitated—as we know from a long letter written to him by Gerald of Wales—whether or not to become a hermit or to enter the Carthusian order. He had grown up within easy reach of the Cistercian abbey of Kirksted, the Benedictine abbey of Bardney, the Gilbertine house at Bullington and several other religious houses. [2] It is unlikely that the desire to become a religious had not at some time or other come to him. But his treatment of this problem is very characteristic. He had a deep concern for the well-being and the good administration of secular life in its various social forms, from the home to the body politic. The responsibility of man to his neighbours and the problems of social intercourse always attracted him. Naturally, therefore, he was intensely interested in the life and work of the secular clergy, in the government of the Church. The choice between the religious and secular life would not appeal to him, as it did to St. Bernard and so many more, as a choice between the only way to fullness of life and a second best. It would appeal rather as a con-

[1] 'Item si pater meus scandalizetur de hoc quod transeam ad religionem, uidetur quod, si possim me saluare in seculo, non debeam transire cum scandalo patris.' St. John's College, Cambridge, MS. 57, f. 221ᵛ. For this manuscript, hereafter cited as 'Cambridge MS.', see Chapter III and Appendix III.

[2] See the list of monastic houses in Lincolnshire comprised in the Mappa Mundi of Gervase of Canterbury, edited by Stubbs, *Historical Works of Gervase of Canterbury*, ii. 429, 430.

flict between two possible vocations.[1] In after years, when he was archbishop, the growing tendency to appoint regulars to high office in the Church alarmed him. Gerald of Wales, in one of his books, recalls how, during a conversation which he had heard in Stephen's household, the archbishop deplored the fact that, when left to themselves, monastic chapters would always elect a monk as bishop. Only a monk of real eminence in life and learning could ever be expected to make a successful bishop.[2] His was not the kind of function for which the religious were fitted. Stephen's sympathy with monasticism was genuine. He spent the greater part of his exile in the Cistercian abbey of Pontigny, following the example of St. Thomas and adding a new example to St. Edmund Rich, and there is not a hint in his writings, so far as I am aware, of the critical spirit which inspired the treatment of the subject by Gerald of Wales and other secular contemporaries. At the same time, his references generally imply an appreciation of the regular life as a distinct system with peculiar aims and problems. I will take a few examples from his *questiones*.

Stephen, as we would expect, had no sympathy with the practice by which parents solemnly gave their children to the monastic life before they could choose for themselves (*oblatio*). He met the argument that a father or mother can pledge a boy to enter a monastery, just as his

---

[1] Ravaisson, in his *Rapport sur les bibliothèques des départements de l'Ouest* (1841), pp. 407 f., printed from the Avranches MS. 230 an interesting *questio* 'si contemplatiua melior sit actiua', in which Langton compares the contemplative life of prayer, meditation, and study with the active life, whose works are alms, preaching, and testifying by suffering (*martyrium*). On the whole he decides that the former is the better. Compare a very similar treatment in one of the Paris manuscripts (Bibliothèque Nationale, MS. lat. 14556, f. 260^v). In these passages the contemplative life is not, of course, identical with the religious or monastic life, but that which Langton was living at Paris. But he sees clearly that the active life has its advantages.

[2] Speculum ecclesiae, Dist. ii, c. 25, in *Opera*, ed. Brewer (Rolls Series), iv. 75. It is significant that the most strenuous opponents of the confirmation of the monk, Walter of Eynsham, as Stephen's successor, were the archbishop's old friends and helpers. See Appendix VI.

godfather gives an undertaking for him at baptism, by the distinction that, whereas belief is compulsory—*quilibet tenetur ad credendum*—monastic vows are voluntary. The cases of Samuel and Samson do not prove the contrary. Exceptional privileges cannot establish a general rule—*dicimus quod privilegia paucorum non faciunt legem communem.*[1] Here Langton was expressing the policy of the Church at this time. The form of oblation, expounded in the rule of St. Benedict (c. 59) was not unlawful, but Alexander III and other popes decreed that the practice was undesirable and that the oblate must decide for himself at the age of fourteen. St. Bernard, who would have passionately resisted Langton's view that before taking monastic vows a man should consider the effect on his parents,[2] would have agreed with him in this matter.[3]

The monastic life inspired obligations which might complicate, or at least add emphasis to simple problems of morals. Langton was anything but a pedant; he took the view that in the interpretation of the Rule monks must be supposed to know its meaning in doubtful matters better than others. Thus in a *questio* on venial sin, he cites St. Benedict's rule (c. 39) that two separate dishes should be prepared for the daily meal—*propter diversorum infirmitates*—so that those who did not care for one might eat of the other. This appears to imply that monks should not eat of both and the question was raised whether those sinned who did eat of both. No, he says, we must not draw this conclusion, 'for monks know by word and example how they should understand the rule of St. Benedict'.[4] Yet Langton is emphatic about the major implications of the Rule. Monks should not eat rich delicious fish like salmon or pike (*lucius*), for they, like John the Baptist, are denizens of solitude, and John ate austere food, locusts

---

[1] Cambridge MS., f. 310ʳ, de exorcismo et catechismo.

[2] Epistle CXI, in *Opera S. Bernardi*, ed. Mabillon, i. 109.

[3] Epistle II, ibid. i. 4. On the whole subject see the Decretals of Gregory IX, lib. iii, tit. xxxi, cc. 8, 14, and Coulton, *Five Centuries of Religion*, i. 224, 327.   [4] Cambridge MS., f. 201ʳ.

and wild honey. This passage comes in a lecture on fasting, and the very pertinent objection is raised, why rich
fish of this kind, which is so much nicer than meat, is not
universally prohibited (i.e. during fasts) as mutton is.
Langton replies that, when Adam sinned, the earth, but
not the water, was put under a curse, and, remembering
perhaps a passage of St. Ambrose, says that fish is born of
water the purifier.[1] Again, the rule of silence and the
great rule of obedience admit of no compromise. In the
discussion to which I have already referred on venial sin,
Langton takes the case of a monk who, though silent, by
signs induces another to tell a lie. He lies himself (*inter-
pretatione iuris*), whereas, if he reduced the other to a state
of intoxication, he would not commit himself to the same
degree, for he would not be drunk himself.[2] Or take the
case, mentioned in the discussion on scandal, of the monk
who meets a man dying of hunger. The monk has with
him the means to feed the starving man. 'But he knows
that his abbot will not endorse his action if he gives anything away' (he is, of course, carrying monastic property).
'Is he obliged to give? No, for although the goods of the
Church belong to the poor, they cannot be demanded by
any casual person.'[3] This problem brings us to the chief
characteristic of the monastic life. It was a corporate life,
it was strengthened and intensified by its corporate
quality, and in the consideration of monastic problems,
the corporate aims are more important than personal
issues. Some duties were, in Innocent III's phrase, so
essential to the monastic life, that the pope himself can
grant no exception from them. Innocent was referring to
the abdication of private property—*adeo annexa regulae
monachali, ut contra eam nec summus Pontifex possit licentiam
indulgere.*[4] Langton had used this duty to illustrate the

---

[1] f. 260ʳ. Cf. Hexaemeron, lib. v, c. 3 in *Sancti Ambrosii Opera* (Paris,
1686), i, col. 82.

[2] Cambridge MS., f. 201ʳ.   [3] f. 221ᵛ.

[4] This letter was included in the Decretals of Gregory IX, lib. iii, tit. xxxv,
c. 6.

nature of property at the disposal of secular clergy. Was it held *iure proprietatis* or *iure dispensationis*? If in the latter way, then it was held as in a monastery:

'A monk who has the disposal of any goods cannot turn anything to his own use without the licence of the abbot or chapter. If, before he enters the cloister, he is in debt he cannot pay his debts from goods committed to him *in dispensatione*, save with the licence of the chapter.' [1]

In spite of authority to the contrary Langton argues that the secular clergy have at least a right of possession in ecclesiastical property—it is not simply given to them, as it might be to a monk, to dispose of in a particular way, although they are much more in a position of trust, more limited by moral undertakings, than a layman is.[2] In another place, Langton speaks of the value of prayer in a monastery:

'Suppose that a man, possessing the necessary qualification of charity (*habens caritatem*), is received into a monastery. Do his prayers as a monk prevail more than they did before he became a monk? When prayer is made for the brethren a livelier devotion is stirred, and so his prayers avail more than before, in this respect. But is it not possible that (his) devotion and charity may not grow as a result of this? Granted. In what respect then would he prevail more in prayer? I answer—in the frequent example, in the devotional act of prayer, and perhaps in other ways.' [3]

We must not look too curiously, he seems to say, into the interior working of the soul. In a well-ordered monastery a monk gives and takes from the very fact of the common life. Here, as indeed generally, Langton shows a reverent sobriety. His touch is certain, as though he had lived, both at home and in the schools, among sensible people who were accustomed to discuss serious problems in an independent, practical way. And it is characteristic of him that his sagacity is best displayed when he is dealing with problems, especially problems of everyday life, which would naturally occur to the ordinary

[1] Cambridge MS., f. 195ʳ.   [2] f. 195ʳ.   [3] f. 264ʳ.

man. If he cannot solve a question, he says so and passes on. He is not frightened by a dilemma. Thus he draws a logical conclusion from the duty of restitution:

'Is a man who sells something for more than its just price bound to restitution? Yes, to the church, not to the buyer; for he sins and is freed from his sin if he gives to the church, and he has sinned none the less, even though the contract is not rescinded. In the same way, I hold that an advocate or lawyer is bound to restore what he has received above his due, to him from whom he received it or to the church. Again, if a monastery has been built with the aid of money made by usury, the abbot ought to give it all back, even though he has nothing left to live upon; but let him do it through the bishop. Even though the bishop or the pope should forbid him to make restitution, he would not be bound to obey, for a matter of this kind is contrary to the Decalogue.' [1]

Here the point is, I think, that while restitution is always due, it *need* not involve the re-opening of a contract which is over and done with; but, if an error which involves a fundamental inconsistency, a breach of the supreme law of God, has been committed, then careful restitution is due, and not even the pope can excuse it. Langton takes the case of a monastery—and he could not have chosen a better, for a monastic house dependent on usury would, so to speak, have a lie in its very being. His contemporary Robert Curzon regarded this evil, indeed, as one of the chief evils of the time.[2] One would like to have their views on the different and frequent case of the monastery built with money which was *borrowed* from Jews and usurers. But, although Langton takes the case of a monastery, it is quite likely that he was thinking of an incident which is said to have occurred while he was living in Paris, during the building of Notre Dame. The story is told by Caesarius of Heisterbach. A rich usurer

---

[1] f. 314ᵛ. The text is not very good. 'Item si aliquod monasterium constructum est de usura, abbas totum debet restituere, licet non habeat unde uiuat, sed hoc faciat per episcopum; licet episcopus vel papa prohiberet ne restituat ne (*sic*) teneretur obedire quia hoc est contra decalogum.'

[2] See below, p. 88.

of Paris, named Theobald, went to Maurice of Sully, the bishop, in a state of compunction. The bishop, intent upon his great work, advised him to give his wealth to the building fund of the cathedral. Theobald was somewhat doubtful of the soundness of this advice, and went to a famous theologian, Peter the Chanter, who sternly ordered him to restore every penny to those whom he had robbed.[1] As we shall see, Peter the Chanter was almost certainly Stephen Langton's master.

At the risk of some irrelevance, I have tried to illustrate the attitude of an able, well read and sensible young Englishman of the twelfth century to the nature and claims of the secular and of the monastic life of the Church to which he was dedicated. In the course of this exposition we have already met the problem of fundamental law—Langton seems to call it indifferently the law of nature and Scriptural law—which was to perplex him throughout his public life. Langton, like Pope Innocent and everybody else, regarded this law as binding upon the pope and, still more clearly, upon princes. More clearly upon princes, for in their case the issue of the plenitude of power residing in the pope did not arise. As we shall see, Langton had no difficulty as a rule in accepting papal authority. His tragedy began when, after striving to maintain it, he found himself faced with a papal command which affronted his conscience. He could not obey, but he acquiesced in his punishment. He could not do less than submit, for in the eyes of the world, and no doubt in his own eyes, he stood out as the true successor of St. Thomas of Canterbury.

The years of Stephen's childhood were the last years of the great archbishop. Thomas, in his circuitous flight from Northampton to the Continent, at the end of 1164, came to Lincolnshire, finding guidance and hospitality from the friendly canons of the Gilbertine order. They helped him

---

[1] Caesarius of Heisterbach, *Dialogus miraculorum*, ii. 34. The passage is quoted in Migne, *Patrologia Latina*, cv. 15; also by Marcel Aubert, *Notre-Dame de Paris* (Paris, 1920), p. 28 note.

to escape and sent money to him in his distress.[1] The story
of the conflict with King Henry, of the flight, of the
anxiety of the archbishop's friends, would be well known
to Stephen's family, and he himself would be able to remember the horror caused by Thomas's death, the news
of Henry's expiation, the remarkable growth of the cult
of the new saint. At Paris he would find that, in all ranks
of society, St. Thomas was reverenced as much as he was
in England. One of his companions, the future Pope Innocent III, visited the shrine at Canterbury before he returned to Italy. The first thing which King Richard did,
when, after his captivity, he landed in England, was to
offer thanks before the shrine, and it is curious to find the
names of King Richard and of Stephen Langton inter-
twined in the memories of pious men who lived in the
tradition of St. Thomas. Henry of Sandford, bishop of
Rochester, announced publicly in 1232 that on three
occasions it had been revealed to him or another, that on
one and the same day the souls of Richard, king of the
English, and Stephen, archbishop of Canterbury, had issued
from purgatory to enjoy the beatific vision.[2] The story
became common property. The Dominican, Nicholas
Trivet, ascribes the vision to St. Edmund Rich.[3] Henry
of Sandford, who had been archdeacon of Canterbury
before his appointment at Rochester in 1227 had been
closely associated with Stephen; St. Edmund followed
Stephen's example, both by his support of the Charter
and his exile at Pontigny. To them, Stephen would be, in
the succession of St. Thomas, the first archbishop after
him, as Gerald of Wales explains in a well-known passage,[4]

[1] The itinerary of Thomas between Northampton and his port of departure Sandwich is confusing. But it is definitely stated that he came to Lincoln
and hid in the house of a citizen called James; Grim in *Materials for the
History of Thomas Becket*, ed. Robertson (Rolls Series), ii. 399; cf. Herbert
of Bosham, ibid., iii. 324. Miss Graham, *S. Gilbert of Sempringham*, pp. 17–18,
attempts a reconstruction of the archbishop's journey in the Fens and South
Lincolnshire.

[2] Roger of Wendover (ed. Coxe), iv. 234.

[3] *Annales* (ed. Hog), p. 229.   [4] *Opera*, iv. 77; cf. iii. 125–7.

to maintain the liberties of the Church; while King Richard—his sins and violence all forgotten—had become a legendary figure, the great crusader, an ecclesiastical hero.[1]

This strange partnership suggests certain qualities in medieval life which it is well to bear in mind while we are considering the career of a man like Stephen Langton. So far as the issues raised by St. Thomas of Canterbury were issues of law, of political and ecclesiastical principle, we shall have to deal with them later. But they were more than this. In the eyes of succeeding generations, St. Thomas stood for a way of life, an outlook on life, opposed to that of the world. And just as Thomas, with all his impatience and frailties, could be its exponent, so King Richard, with all his vices, could be the champion of this way of life. It was the way of the Cross, the sight of which calmed the saint in his wildest outbursts of passion, the call of which stirred the soldier to a holy war while he was fighting for his inheritance. It was a recognition that the visible is controlled by the invisible, the tangible by mysterious forces and constant divine interventions, the expedient by a law which moves the whole of nature and is the breath of God. In the weak and superstitious it intensified excitement, credulity, and suspicion; to the strong and sane it brought confidence in adversity and quietness in prosperity—while mixed natures, like St. Thomas and King Richard, each in his own way, were now uplifted and now merely excited, now subdued and now merely indifferent or depressed, in the presence of a power beyond their understanding.

It is perhaps unfair to speak of the legend of King Richard; for in his own lifetime he roused an enthusiasm by no means confined to his barons and mercenaries. The man who trounced papal legates and wished that he could let his mercenaries loose upon St. Hugh of Lincoln, was popular with the clergy. He found favour with the papacy

[1] Cf. the stories which Wendover inserts in his chronicle after relating the bishop's vision (iv. 234 ff.).

and excited an interest which was rarely, if ever, untouched by admiration. His 'kingliness could not be hid', and although he was accused of avarice, he had many of the virtues associated with the Scriptural and medieval idea of a king—generosity, courage, loyalty, a sense of fair play, and a capacity to respond to high appeals. Now Stephen Langton, it is interesting to learn, wrote the life of Richard. The book is lost, but its contents have come down to us indirectly through Ranulf Higden, the fourteenth-century chronicler, who professes to have 'taken the flowers' of Stephen's excellent work.[1] If Higden followed Stephen's book at all faithfully, we conclude that the latter was specially concerned, not with the king's military career, but with the attacks upon the Jews, the general history of the crusade, the course of events in England during Richard's absence, the riots in London (he gives a long account of William fitz Osbert) and with moral questions. Unfortunately it is not possible to distinguish Higden's comments from Langton's, nor without a tedious investigation, which could only give us tentative results, to analyse the probable relations between Langton's work and other contemporary accounts of Richard's reign. Higden, for example, is unsympathetic with the attempt made by Archbishop Baldwin to establish a great secular college at Canterbury.[2] One would like to know if here he reflected Langton's view, or, as is more likely, was expressing the opinion of a monk of Chester, jealous for the rights of monks of Canterbury. Again, Higden tells the story of Stephen of Marçai, seneschal of Anjou—how he consulted a necromancer on the prospects of Richard's return, and

---

[1] *Polychronicon*, lib. vii, cc. 25–31, ed. Lumby (Rolls Series), viii. 82–168. Chapter 25 begins: 'Mortuo Henrico rege apud Fontem Ebrardi et sepulto, successit filius suus Ricardus, per decem annos regnaturus. Cuius mores et actus Stephanus Cantuariensis luculenter descripsit. At ne praesens historia careat insigniis tanti ducis, libellum Stephani cursim studui deflorare.'

[2] viii. 126. Innocent III was believed to have desired to substitute canons for monks at Christ Church, Canterbury. See a letter from Ralph of Arden to Ralph, bishop of Chichester (ascribed by Shirley to December 1228) in *Royal Letters*, i. 340.

was fooled by him. The story suggested others of a similar nature, which are duly narrated.[1] These stories, I suspect, would have appealed to Langton, who may well have inserted them in his book. In any case, it is clear from Higden's work that Stephen was a genuine man of his time. As we look back upon the past, in the light of constitutional history, he seems to take a place beside the great common lawyers, or Somers, and Burke; and the quality of his mind justifies the comparison. But this quality of mind asserted itself through a medium very strange to us. Minds of this type and training were steeped in Scripture and the Fathers. We can best understand them, if we read the psalms along with the allegorical interpretation handed down from the great expositors of the past. They looked at the political and ecclesiastical problems of their time in this light:

Quam magnificata sunt opera tua, Domine; nimis profundae factae sunt cogitationes tuae.
Vir insipiens non cognoscet, et stultus non intelliget haec.

One passage in Higden, whether written by Langton or not, might well have come from him. The chronicler is commenting upon the failure of the Third Crusade. God, he says, seems to take small account of the welfare and safety of his servants, but in his wisdom he takes toll of men in their miseries and sorrows, for the building up of the city of heaven. Those who passed away fared more graciously than those who went home again to their evil ways. And so Christ our king, even while he gave Jerusalem into the hands of enemies on account of the sins of those who lived therein, cunningly enriched therefrom the Jerusalem which is on high. But, beyond a doubt, the time will come when evil men shall be cast out of the Holy Land, perhaps by a much weaker force, so that God's own strength may be better known. Among the Maccabees one said, 'It is easy for Almighty God to overcome many men with the might of few men', and this was shown when one

[1] c. 29 (viii. 132 ff.).

pursued a thousand, and twelve chased ten thousand. And Gideon destroyed a great multitude with three hundred men that lapped water into their mouths.

But, he concludes, 'Christian men should not tempt God and start out, headlong and proudly, few against many, because they have a good Lord and a mighty. For God wishes his servants so to trust in Him that they be not reckless and negligent to work wisely.' [1]

[1] viii. 118, 120. I have adopted some phrases from Trevisa's translation.

II

LANGTON AT PARIS: HIS BIBLICAL STUDIES

THE Paris to which the young Stephen Langton came early in the reign of King Philip—a lad of very much the same age as he was—was at the beginning of a period of much splendour. The lovely land in which it lay—France in the strictest sense of the term—as it had long won the conscious affection of its inhabitants, was regarded by men in the west of Europe with peculiar respect. It had a quality of distinction: it was fine, with the fineness of a man who has nourished his soul in self-confidence during days of poverty. In its gentle undulations, its forests and rivers, castles and cities, it seemed to hold in suspense the nobler and more gracious traits of the proud and ambitious kings, the turbulent lords, the striving merchants who had clung to it with a fierce devotion—so that, in regarding it, in remembering it in their travels, they could find in it an incentive to fresh efforts, a belief in themselves, a justification for a more refined, a better directed egotism. Such, at any rate, is the part which 'sweet France' seems to play in the lives of heroes in the *chansons de geste*.[1] And in the last quarter of the twelfth century, Paris, drawing ahead of its companions, Orleans, Etampes, Senlis, Corbeil, reflected, in a special degree, these qualities of distinction and progressive activity.

At this time the island was still the city proper. The Seine, flowing here from east to west, and turning in a southerly direction before it pursues its devious course to the sea, divided the growing town on either bank into two outlying districts, which in the days of Philip Augustus, acquired distinct characteristics. The northern area, con-

[1] Marcel Poëte, *Une vie de cité: Paris de sa naissance à nos jours*, i (Paris, 1924), Chapter XI and *passim*. For the meaning of *Francia* see Olivier Martin, *Histoire de la coutume de la prévôté et vicomté de Paris*, i (Paris, 1922), 25–42. On the early history and topography, Halphen, *Paris sous les premiers Capétiens*.

nected with the island by the Grand Pont, was the main centre of trade and shipping. The port of Paris was near the Grand Pont on this northern bank. There the vessels, laden with corn or salt, wine or wood, were moored; and planks were laid from quay to deck. This was the centre of the activities of a community of merchants, which was rapidly becoming a corporation and would in due course take a leading part in the administration of Paris. While Langton was in Paris, the Halles were built, and about them their walled enclosure occupied by covered stalls. The great fortress of the Louvre—the Tower, as it was called, just as Englishmen spoke of the Tower of London— was being built, and in 1190 the citizens enclosed with strong ramparts the wide area—then mainly open ground —which for centuries was to be sufficient for the needs of northern Paris. The southern area, connected with the island by the Petit Pont, was still more open. There were quays there also, and shops on and about the bridge, but life was as yet less concentrated and the king did not build the southern ramparts and order the exploitation of building sites until 1209, three years after Langton left Paris. The busy settlement depending on the great abbey of St. Germain des Prés lay near the river to the west, the monastery of St. Geneviève, now reconstituted as a strict house of canons regular, crowned the wooded hill, the beautiful Romanesque church of St. Julien le Pauvre, but recently built, lay almost opposite the bridge. This was to be the students' quarter. Just as in other parts of Paris, the craftsmen—jewellers, harness and armour-makers and the like—and the dealers in luxuries were finding room, so here, among the vineyards and enclosures of nobles and monasteries, countrymen were coming in from their lord's estates; they were settled in new streets, many of them let lodgings. By the end of Philip's reign the area between St. Germain and the Petit Pont was an urban rather than a rural district. The King, glad to gaze from the windows of his island palace upon these scenes of growing activity, had his full share in the development of Paris. He built its markets, ordered its enclosure, and the paving of its streets, encouraged and employed its merchants, built strongholds to protect it. For travellers the scene had a peculiar charm. Taking the noise and clamour, the filth and stench for granted, they sometimes break into rhapsodies on the great river, the encircling woods, the monasteries and churches—ever increasing in number—and the vivacity of the place.

And in the midst of it all was the island, the seat of the royal palace and the Cathedral. Here also this was a period of incessant change. Philip Augustus, for example, ejected the Jewry and when he restored the Jews to favour, saw that they settled down in new quarters in the northern part of the city. The island was becoming less a centre of town life and more a political, ecclesiastical, and intellectual centre, as though Westminster had grown up in the heart of London. The first stone of the new cathedral had been laid by Pope Alexander III in 1163, at the beginning of the long episcopate of Maurice of Sully (1160–96).[1] The choir built, perhaps consciously, in Cistercian fashion, with an ambulatory whose symmetry was undisturbed by chapels, was nearly finished in 1177, when it was seen by the Norman chronicler, Robert of Torigny. A papal legate consecrated the high altar in 1182, the patriarch of Jerusalem officiated there in 1185. In 1186 Geoffrey Plantagenet, in 1190 Isabella of Hainault, the young wife of King Philip, were buried before it. The nave was rising when Langton was teaching near by, the transepts were roofed by 1198, and by 1206, when Langton left, the church was completed except for the façade, upon which the masons were already at work, and upon which, and the towers, they were to work for nearly forty years more. Even in the early days of its building, the size of Notre Dame and the care and wealth so lavishly expended upon it, had stirred the indignation of the more austere, like Langton's master, Peter the Chanter.[2] We may regard it as a symbol,

[1] Marcel Aubert, *Notre-Dame de Paris* (Paris, 1920), pp. 30–5.
[2] Aubert (p. 63) thinks that the attack on the craze for building, &c., in

a counterpart in stone, of the intellectual activity with which its erection synchronized; for this was the period in which Paris became the most famous seat of learning in Europe, and the teachers of the island formed themselves into a corporation of masters, and became the governing body of the University.

If we are to understand the academic life of Paris in Langton's time, and his share in it, we must clear our minds of preconceptions. In the first place, we must not suppose that the schools of Paris sheltered an enormous crowd of students—an idea which is easily conveyed by the enthusiastic allusions of contemporaries to the rapid growth in fame and numbers of the schools on the island or to the attraction which they exerted over men from all parts of the world. Mr. Salter has estimated the whole academic population of Oxford in the later fourteenth century as less than seven hundred,[1] and although Oxford had seen better days and greater numbers in the past, it would be absurd to suppose that the numbers in Paris, before the University was formed, were as high as the numbers at Oxford in Wyclif's day. It would be surprising, indeed, to find that they reached much more than a couple of hundred. In 1207, when the theological interests of the schools were already supreme, Pope Innocent III restricted the number of masters in theology to eight, in order to prevent confusion.[2] If we think of eight theologians teaching in eight small rooms, we cannot imagine an immense theological faculty. For, in the second place,

Peter's *Verbum abbreviatum* (Migne, *Patrologia latina*, ccv, cols. 255 ff., cf. 106–7), was mainly directed against Notre-Dame. See also the article, referred to by Aubert, on twelfth-century critics of architectural extravagance by Victor Mortet, *Mélanges Bémont* (1913), pp. 105–37.

[1] H. E. Salter, *Medieval Archives of the University of Oxford*, ii. 275–6. Mr. Salter, referring to a rather later period (*c.* 1425) in another work, estimates the number of residents in halls at Oxford at 700; *Essays in History presented to Reginald Lane Poole*, p. 432.

[2] Denifle and Châtelain, *Chartularium Universitatis Parisiensis*, i. 65, no. 5. (Letter to the bishop, 14 Nov. 1207). I refer to this work henceforward as *C.U.P.*

we should not give a dignified meaning to the word
'school'. *Scola* in the singular was the master's room, hired
by him for use and instruction. In the plural the schools
meant the practice of and facilities for teaching. At first
there seem to have been schools in more than one part of
Paris or its immediate neighbourhood, notably at St.
Geneviève, where Abelard taught publicly; but in Langton's time the only schools open to seculars, i.e. to clerks
who were not members of a monastic house, were in the
Island or on the Petit Pont, and possibly in his last years
as a teacher on the southern bank of the river, in the
newly opened district known as *Garland*, about the rue
de Fouarre. The famous monastery of St. Victor had lost
its reputation as a centre of learning, the abbey of St.
Geneviève held only claustral schools for its canons regular, and as the letters of its head, Stephan of Tournai,
show very clearly, regarded the disputations on the island
with a suspicion amounting to hatred. The schools in the
city had at one time been claustral schools in the sense that
they were held within the precincts of Notre-Dame, but
by this time they were outside. Bishop Maurice of Sully
forbade his canons to let their houses to masters,[1] and the
latter probably taught in the district to the west of the
church and on the Petit Pont, in hired rooms among the
butchers' shops and the stalls of street vendors. The
schools were still under the direct jurisdiction of the chancellor of Notre-Dame. They were cathedral schools, like
those of 'Reims and other neighbouring cities', which are
coupled with them by Pope Alexander III as late as 1177.[2]
Only the chancellor, acting for the bishop, could grant the
licence to teach. Thirdly, we know almost nothing about
the organization of studies in Paris before the statutes
issued by the legate, Robert Curzon, in 1215. A few

[1] *C.U.P.*, i, Introduction, p. 56, no. 55. Cf. no. 54, letter of Gui de
Bazoches for logical disputations on the Petit Pont.

[2] Ibid., p. 9, no. 9. Compare Langton's phrase, in one of his lectures,
'quicunque *ad fabricam huius ecclesie* obtulerit relaxetur ei tertia pars peni-
tentie sibi iniuncte'; Cambridge MS., f. 259ʳ.

points are clear. For example, it was usual to study arts before turning to theology. Peter of Blois upbraids a young friend of his who, after some arduous years as an artist, had decided to work quietly by himself—to take his ease—instead of devoting himself rigorously to theology.[1] I am inclined to think that, in Langton's time, theology normally followed arts[2] in the *scolaris militia*, and that Curzon's statutes, fixing the periods of study and the ages which masters in arts (20) and theology (35) must have reached, defined the tendencies of general practice. Again, it appears from a letter of Innocent III (*c.* 1210), that during Langton's later years at Paris, there was a recognized or 'accustomed order in lectures and disputations'.[3] This, presumably, would include some accepted method of proving the fitness of candidates presented by their masters for the licence to teach. On the other hand, we hear nothing of faculties[4] or curricula. A master opened his school. He might teach anything provided that by his apprenticeship in the school of another, he had qualified himself to teach, and did not, as Abelard did at Laon, set himself up to teach *sine magistro*.[5] His best pupils would successively become his assistants on their

[1] *C.U.P.*, i, Introd., p. 30, no. 26.

[2] In May 1207 Innocent III wrote to King John that Langton 'Parisius diu uacans, litteralibus studiis in tantum profecit, ut meruerit esse doctor non solum in liberalibus facultatibus, uerum etiam in theologicis disciplinis' (*Gervase of Canterbury*, ed. Stubbs, ii, p. lxxii).

[3] Rashdall, *The Universities of Europe in the Middle Ages*, i. 301.

[4] Except in the general sense in which the word is used by Innocent III in the letter quoted above (note 2). In his latest work, *The Renaissance of the Twelfth Century* (Harvard University Press, 1927), p. 382, Professor Haskins goes rather farther than I have done in the text. He describes the organization of the schools as more definite than I have felt able to do.

[5] The account given by Gerald of Wales, in the 'De rebus a se gestis', of his life at Paris is illuminating (*Opera*, i. 45, 46). 'Tantum in causis decretalibus, quae dominicis diebus tractari consueuerant, gratiam optinuit, quod die quo ipsum causari uelle notum in urbe fuerat, tantus ad uocem eius iocundam doctorum omnium fere cum scolaribus suis concursus extiterat, quod uix domus amplissima capere poterat auditores.' Note the references to Sunday as the day for lectures on canon law, and to the large room. The date is *c.* 1180.

way to the mastership. Thus Adam of Bangor, the teacher who was called Adam of the Petit Pont, because he was one of the first to open a school on the bridge, had been 'clericus et prepositus scolarium' to Peter the Lombard. Odo of Ourscamp, whose *summa* throws much light upon methods of disputation in the middle of the twelfth century, refers to a pupil 'qui prepositus meus in scolis fuerat, mihique successit in scolis'.[1] Now, in later times, the master lectured in one faculty only. His philosophical teaching would be foreshadowed while he was exercising for his mastership, and developed when he was 'magister regens'; if he went on to theology or law or medicine, he would pass through the same stages in another faculty. In the later years of the twelfth century, academic organization had not reached this stage. Alexander Neckam studied and taught in Paris on the Petit Pont during a great part of the period 1175–95, and he included in his range of interests the liberal arts, theology, medicine, and civil and canon law. Other famous teachers—greater teachers than Alexander—had, it is true, less discursive interests. Peter of Poitiers (*d.* 1205) studied and taught theology in Paris for thirty-eight years. Peter the Chanter (*d.* 1197) was concerned as a teacher with biblical and theological questions for over twenty-five years. Yet a brief examination of their writings and of the writings of their contemporaries suffices to show that the conception of theology, as a systematic and specialized field of thought, was only emerging very gradually. They felt at liberty to discuss a wide range of problems, to which unity was given by a moral purpose rather than by any inner coherence.

Stephen Langton, then, during the twenty or more years of his studies and teaching in Paris, lived on the island. He went to school and opened his school in houses on or about the Petit Pont. The swirl of the grey waters would always be before his eyes, the tap of the masons at work on the great church behind him would always be sounding in his ears. Around him, day by day, were scenes

[1] *C.U.P.*, i, p. xxviii.

of high life and of low from which he drew examples for his teaching, and, in his later days, for his sermons.

It is probable that his master—the teacher to whom he owed most—was Peter the Chanter, for in one version of his *questiones* he seems to refer to him as *magister*, and not to use the word as he and his contemporaries generally use it, as a synonym for Peter the Lombard, the Master of the Sentences.[1] If this is so, he perhaps became a *prepositus* in Peter's school, before he opened his own schools. In due course he became a well-known and honoured scholar. Of his pupils, unhappily, we know nothing, except of one, who, sad to say, became a heretic. Among the scholars condemned in the decree of 1210 was a certain Master Guerin, priest, of Corbeil, of whom Caesarius of Heisterbach, in his comments upon the decree, says that he had learned theology from Master Stephen, archbishop of Canterbury.[2] This might have happened to any man; it certainly did not tarnish Stephen's reputation. He was marked out for preferment by Pope Innocent,[3] whom Stephen, in his early days, must have found as a student at Paris, a young man a few years older than himself. Like other theological teachers of the day, Stephen was closely connected with the church of Our Lady. I can find no

---

[1] Quoted by N. Paulus, *Geschichte des Ablasses im Mittelalter*, i. 219, from Gillmann's text, taken from the Bamberg MS. of one of Langton's *questiones* (*Katholik*, i (1913), 375). The deduction is not conclusive, and the general similarity of Langton's teaching and method to those of the Chanter is the best argument for their relationship. See Grabmann, *Die Geschichte der Scholastischen Methode*, ii. 498, and Ghellinck, *Le mouvement théologique du XII*e *siècle*, p. 165.

[2] *Dialogus Miraculorum*, v. 22, ed. Strange, i. 307, apud *C.U.P.*, i, part i, p. 71 note: 'magister Garinus, qui conuentauerat Parisius de artibus, et hic sacerdos audierat theologiam a magistro Stephano, archiepiscopo Cantuariensi.'

[3] Cf. Robert of Auxerre, in *Historiens de la France*, xviii. 275*a*: 'nunc nuper in cardinalem dominus Papa promoverat, virum quidem vita honestum, praeclarumque inter Parisienses magistros tam fecundia quam scientia scripturarum'; and Alberic of Trois Fontaines, ibid., 771*b*: 'nominatissimus Doctor theologus, cuius habentur libri super Prophetas, super Psalterium, et postillae super beati Pauli Epistolas, et multa alia dicitur scripsisse.'

evidence for the statement, repeated in nearly all the modern accounts of him, that he was at one time chancellor, the administrative head of the Paris schools. The list of chancellors during his time is sufficiently complete to exclude the probability, if not to make it impossible that he ever filled this high office. The famous Peter le Mangeur (*Comestor*) is found in 1168 and 1178, a certain Hilduin in 1185 and 1191, Peter of Poitiers in 1193, and still in 1204, the year before his death, Bernard Chabert in 1205–6, magister Prepositinus, the theologian from Cremona, in 1206.[1] On the other hand, we have the explicit statement of Pope Innocent that Stephen was a canon of Notre-Dame, and although no cathedral document confirms this and mentions him by name, as his brother Simon Langton is mentioned, as a canon, his obit was celebrated in later years by the canons on 7 July, the day of the translation of St. Thomas of Canterbury.[2] Entitled to a house and stall, endowed by his prebend, Stephen would find more comfortable quarters and live a more spacious life for a few years than he had enjoyed hitherto.

The letter in which Pope Innocent refers to Stephen's connexion with the church of Notre-Dame is the letter addressed to King John, defending the new archbishop's qualifications as a gentleman, a scholar, and a canon of York, a more important church than the church of Paris.[3] In the absence of records, it is impossible to say when Stephen was given his prebend in York. It may have been given before he began to teach. At this time there was considerable discussion about the relative claims of the academic life and the duties of a canon to his church. We should not lay too much stress upon the evidence which suggests that the scholars of Paris were undisciplined boys, just as we should not exaggerate their numbers. That there were turbulent, pretentious, and ignorant elements

---

[1] *C.U.P.*, i. xix note.

[2] See the Obituarium ecclesie Parisiensis in Guérard, *Cartulaire de l'église Notre-Dame de Paris* (1850), iv. 105.

[3] *Gervase of Canterbury*, ed. Stubbs, ii, p. lxxiii.

among them is indisputable; but the tendency of moralists
and gossips to generalize from a few instances seems to be
ineradicable. The absence of other evidence, however,
and the facility in vituperation of the medieval moralist
give additional plausibility to the statements of grave and
earnest men who wrote seven hundred years ago. The
medieval world was a world of young men. There were in
most periods many very remarkable old people, but in
general the time of achievement was the time of youth.
St. Thomas, Duns Scotus, Bartolus were at the height of
their fame at an age when a modern scholar would diffi-
dently be putting out his first book. They were in this not
exceptional; they were young men among young men,
a few seniors to watch them. According to the Paris
statutes of 1215, a boy of 20 could begin to teach in arts
and a young man of 35 be a doctor in theology. Among
the youths who attended a master in the schools in Langton's time, a good proportion would be experienced
people, young in years but established in status. About
1180 Alexander III ordered an unnamed chapter to provide a prebend for two years for a canon who found himself in financial difficulties *in scolis*.[1] In 1205 Bishop Odo
of Sully laid down regulations on this matter in his new
statutes for the canons of Saint Marcel (one of the four
'daughter' churches of Paris). After eight months' residence, canons who wished to go on pilgrimage or to study,
should be permitted to go and a suitable period of absence
should be prescribed by the chapter. If a canon is summoned back from the schools before his term of leave ex-
pires, he must show reasonable grounds (*impedimentum*)
for disobedience, but on the other hand he has the right
of appeal to the bishop if the chapter does not grant
reasonable facilities.[2] These regulations were made in
virtue of the peculiar relations in which the bishop of
Paris stood to the churches of canons in the neighbourhood, but the policy which they expounded dealt with a

[1] *C.U.P.*, i, Introd., pp. 10, 11, no. 13.
[2] Guerard, *Cart. de l'église Notre-Dame de Paris*, ii. 95–7 (*a.* 1205).

general problem. As the scholar advanced to the mastership or became useful, honours would increase. Thus in
1178 a successful teacher, Gerard Pucelle, drew 'rents'
from preferments in Germany and England. Pope Alexander, after referring to the progress *in scientia litterarum*
made by many of Gerard's pupils, allowed him to draw
his revenue from England for four years, provided that he
continued to teach (*si scolas rexeris*). He was not to be
forced to return unless he were presented to some important dignity or benefice.[1] In 1183 he was elected bishop
of Coventry.

Stephen Langton, on more than one occasion, used this
situation as an illustration in his discussion of moral problems. Thus, in dealing with venial sin, he says:

'If the pope should order the bishop of Paris to give one of two
prebends to a clerk (*isti clerico*) and the bishop is free to give which-
ever of the two he prefers, the bishop would understand that he
was empowered to give only one, he would not give the other to
the same clerk.' [2]

A much more interesting case is discussed in a *questio* on
obedience, in connexion with the limits of obedience to
episcopal authority:

'A canon is at the schools. His bishop, without giving a reason,
summons him back. The canon has reason to think that the
bishop's action is done from regard to the canon's temporal well
being, and not *propter utilitatem ecclesie*. Query: is the canon
bound to obey? We reply: if the custom of the church does not
make residence obligatory, and he has reason to think that the
bishop is acting for his good, he is not bound to obey. But suppose
that his colleagues (in the chapter) are bad, and he is a good clerk
and has reason to think that he is able to improve them, and the
bishop orders him, ought he to obey? We reply: if he is in a state
of perfection and knows that he will not be infected by their com-
panionship, it is better for him to go. But if he is conscious of
moral weakness (*expertus sit infirmitatem suam*) and is firmly con-

---

[1] *C.U.P.*, i, Introd., pp. 9, 10, nos. 10, 11. Gerard is quoted by Prepositinus (see Denifle's note to no. 10), and in the Leipzig MS. of the
Summa Decreti Lipsiensis, on which see Ghellinck, op. cit., 224 n., 361 n.

[2] Cambridge MS., f. 201ʳ.

vinced that they would easily corrupt him? We reply that he is not bound to obey in this case. But what if his conscience tells him that he can improve the canons? If indeed his conscience tells him so and also that he would not be corrupted, then he is bound to return.'[1]

This passage, I think, throws light upon Langton no less than upon the problem of obedience which it elucidates and upon the relations between cathedral chapters and the schools.

As a teacher Stephen made his mark in Paris in two closely related fields of learning. His *questiones*, or lectures on theological and moral problems, survive in several manuscripts, in various forms. They will be dealt with in the next chapter. His biblical studies have given him a more enduring fame. Let us begin with a well-known passage in the annals of the Dominican scholar, Nicholas Trivet, written a century or so after Langton's time:

'(In 1228) Stephen, archbishop of Canterbury died. He commented upon the whole Bible and divided it into the chapters which we moderns use. While he was teaching theology at Paris he was made cardinal priest of St. Chrysogonus. Then as archbishop, among other good deeds, he built the beautiful hall in the palace at Canterbury.'[2]

The commentaries or postils on the Scriptures remain, and will require some attention later. But I should observe that there is some evidence for the belief that at least some of them were written while Langton was teaching at Paris. The church of St. Stephen at Troyes preserved a thirteenth-century manuscript (now Troyes MS. 1046) which contains expositions by Langton on eight of the twelve minor prophets. Several manuscripts of the same work survive elsewhere. If the official catalogue gives the *explicit* of this Troyes MS. correctly—*Explicit moralitas super XII prophetas. Amen. Anno gratie MCCIII*—we have proof that the work was complete before the year 1203, three years before Langton became a cardinal.[3]

Probably, about the same time, Langton was at work

---

[1] Cambridge MS., f. 237ᵛ.   [2] Trivet, *Annales*, ed. Hog, p. 216.
[3] *Catalogue général des manuscrits des bibliothèques publiques des départements*, ii (1850), 431, no. 1046.

upon the text of the Bible. Trivet's explicit statement
that the division into chapters used in his day—that is to
say in the accepted text of the Vulgate known as the Paris
Bible—is confirmed by several manuscripts in which the
lists of chapters are given and are ascribed to Langton. In
1887 Paulin Martin—to whom the confirmation was first
due—discovered a list in a manuscript in the Bibliothèque
Nationale.[1] Another manuscript, now at Lyons (no. 340),
contains an item, beginning 'Incipiunt Parabole Salomonis
distincte per capitula secundum magistrum Stephanum
archiepiscopum.' There is a list in a Bodleian manuscript,
and another is inserted, among sermons preached by Langton and others, in a Magdalen manuscript 'according to
Master Stephen'.[2] Denifle, arguing from a study of the
origin of the Paris Bible, ascribed Stephen's work to the
end of the twelfth century. I am able to add a little
evidence from the *Questiones,* suggesting that the work
was done in the later years of Stephen's residence in Paris,
and after the first version of his *Questiones* had been written. In what I consider to be a rather later and more
formed version of some of his *questiones,* references to the
Bible occasionally quote the text according to the new
division,[3] but in one place at least in what seems to be an
earlier text, Stephen is found at work upon an older
division. He is dealing with the very difficult problem
raised by the text (Matthew xviii. 15): 'Si autem peccauerit in te frater tuus, uade et corripe eum', &c. He says:
'That this precept is intended for everybody seems to follow from

---

[1] MS. Latin 14417, ff. 125-6, a St. Victor manuscript of the thirteenth
century. On Langton's Bible see E. Mangenot's article 'Chapitres de la
Bible', in Vigouroux, *Dictionnaire de la Bible,* ii, col. 564; J. P. P. Martin,
Introduction à la critique générale de l'Ancien Testament, ii. 461-74; also 'Le
texte parisien de la Vulgate latine' in *Muséon,* viii (1889), 444; O. Schmidt,
*Ueber verschiedene Eintheilungen der Heiligen Schrift, insbesondere über die
Capitel-Eintheilung Stephen Langtons* (Graz, 1892); S. Berger, *Histoire de la
Vulgate pendant les premiers siècles du moyen âge* (Paris, 1893).

[2] Bodleian MS. 487, f. 110; Magdalen College MS. 168, ff. 78-86. This
last is a list of the *initia* of the chapters (*capitulatio bibliothece*) according to
Langton. [3] See below, p. 69.

the tendency (*finem*) of the gospel; for this chapter is inserted between a chapter on scandal and a chapter on forgiving injuries; and as the chapters on either side (*extrema*) are addressed to all, this is also. And these same conclusions follow from the gloss', &c.[1]

The reference is to verses 6 ff.: 'whosoever shall offend (*scandalizaverit*) one of these little ones,' &c., and verses 21 ff.: 'Then came Peter unto him and said, Lord, how often shall my brother sin against me, and I forgive him?' All three passages, regarded by Langton as three distinct chapters, now compose Matthew xviii; and Langton's observations on their connexion with each other help us to see why he afterwards grouped them as one. Now, as an incidental reference in another *questio* shows that these lectures belong to the years after the captivity of Richard of England and the collection of his ransom, i.e. after 1194 or 1195,[2] it would seem to follow that Langton's work on the Bible was done at the very end of the century or in the first years of the thirteenth.

In the discussion to which I have referred on the correction of one's brother, Langton shows that he was accustomed to compare different texts of the Scriptures. Speaking on the point whether the command 'corripe eum' was especially addressed to prelates or not, he observes, in favour of this view, that it could be urged 'ex circumstantia scripture', for in old manuscripts the words are found:

'Jesus looking upon his disciples said to Simon Peter "If thy brother sin against thee", &c., and again at the end of the chapter (i.e. Matt. xviii. 18) we have the reference to the keys—"Whatsoever thou shalt bind", &c.; and so it is clear that it was said to the apostles and their successors, since they alone have the keys of the church.'[3]

Here we are on the edge of very deep waters. I refer to the passage simply to show that Langton's work upon the Bible must be regarded as a whole, and in relation to the biblical studies of his age. The condition of the text was causing anxiety. Father Denifle in 1888 called attention to a letter on this subject, written by a certain Nicholas

---

[1] Cambridge MS., f. 261ʳ. [2] Below, p. 93. [3] Cambridge MS., f. 261ʳ.

Maniacoria, a Roman deacon and a protégé of Queen Constance of Sicily (*d.* 1198). Nicholas—a contemporary of Stephen Langton—tells how he laboured on manuscripts of the Bible, and gives striking examples of the variety of readings disclosed by his collation.[1] A century earlier Stephen Harding, the abbot of Citeaux, had done the same, employing learned Jews to help him in the comparison of Latin and Hebrew texts. But efforts of this kind could have no widespread results. The text of the Vulgate demanded co-operative effort, and, on the other hand, the necessity for some kind of revision was urgent after the Bible became the object of widespread systematic study in the theological schools of Paris.

Langton came to the study and exposition of the Bible as a teacher. He found that the traditional divisions of the text were both inconvenient, being of such unequal length, and did not assist understanding. The teacher required chapters of fairly good length, and also, as in the case of Matthew xviii, with some natural inner unity in thought and matter. In the light of modern scholarship we may well doubt whether Stephen succeeded in a task, the two objects of which could not in any event always coincide. In his own day there were some differences of opinion. In the Paris Bible, for example, Isaiah, c. 10 begins more appropriately at verse 5; and in other places the theologians who adopted the Paris Bible tried to standardize, though in vain, a slightly different division. Occasionally Langton's division was permanently modified. Thus, the beginnings of the chapters of the Song of Songs in the list copied into the Magdalen MS. are not in every case exactly the same as those which we accept. But as a whole Langton's work was accepted in his own day and has stood ever since. In the opinion of Samuel Berger he was also responsible for a slight revision in the order of the Books of the Bible, established in the Paris Bible and

[1] Denifle, 'Die Handschriften der Bibel-Correctorien des 13. Jahrhunderts,' in the *Archiv für Literatur- und Kirchengeschichte des Mittelalters*, iv (1888), 270–6.

in the modern Vulgate.[1] St. Jerome, in his arrangement of the Old Testament had adopted the Hebrew division into Law, Prophets and Hagiographers and had naturally added the Apocryphal books, omitted from the Jewish scriptures, as a further section. The Western church adopted a modification of this division in accordance with the principle of the three *ordines*, the *ordo* of the Old Testament, the *ordo* of the Prophets, and the *ordo* of the Histories. In this arrangement the Octateuch (i.e. the Pentateuch with Joshua, Judges, Ruth) was followed by the four books of Kings (i.e. the two books of Samuel and our two books of Kings), Chronicles, the Psalter and the Books of Wisdom, including the wisdom of the Apocrypha, and the Prophets were followed by Job and the historical books of the Apocrypha. Langton, if it was he, brought the third section, Esdras, Tobias, Judith, with Esther and Job into the first section after Chronicles; that is to say, he put all the historical books together, leaving only the Maccabees as a link between the Old and the New Testaments. As Berger remarks, there was no force in separating the historical books of the Hebrew Bible from those of the Apocrypha, as the Church had already put the rest of the Apocrypha upon the same footing as the rest of the Old Testament. And in any case it was an advantage to teachers and scholars alike to have a definite grouping into historical, doctrinal, and prophetic books. Langton was doubtless influenced also by the similar arrangement used by the Greek fathers. Langton's division of the New Testament was not so completely adopted in the Paris Bible. He seems to have put the Catholic epistles after the epistles of Paul, and Acts just before the Apocalypse. The Paris Bible put the Catholic epistles after the Gospels. In the modern Bible, Catholic and Protestant, Langton's arrangement is adopted, with the exception that the Acts come after the Gospels.

The researches of Denifle have established a close connexion between Langton's work and the adoption of a

[1] Berger, op. cit., p. 304; for the manuscripts, p. 334, no. 92.

definite text by the theologians and booksellers of Paris.[1]
It is true that the first dated Bible in which the new division into chapters is found was written in 1231,[2] but it is
also clear that, in the early decades of the thirteenth century, Langton's work was widely known, and that the
persons responsible for the Paris Bible were influenced by
it. One of the manuscripts in which this method was
followed was taken as a basis. It was doubtless revised and
collated, and became the archetype of a *textus receptus*
which was henceforward used in the schools. No attempt
seems to have been made to subject this text to elaborate
scientific examination. The theologians were dissatisfied,
not so much with the text of the Vulgate in general, as with
the existence of variant readings which embarrassed them
as teachers. In due course, under the guidance of the
Dominicans, a school of *correctores* arose, who prepared
lists of variant readings to be used in class alongside the
Paris text. Roger Bacon, as is well known, entertained a
lively contempt both for the 'shortsighted' policy of the
theologians and booksellers in choosing a text at random,
and for the unsound methods of the Dominican *correctores*. He pleaded for a thorough revision and laid down
canons of criticism with which modern scholars could not
seriously quarrel; and his plea was repeated by others
periodically in medieval and modern times. But the fact
remains that, mainly owing to the initiative of another
great Englishman, the University of Paris, in the greatest
period of its history, had a definite text of the Bible,
divided into convenient sections, and arranged in a logical
order.

In the passage from the *Annals* already quoted Trivet
says that Stephen Langton commented upon the whole
Bible, and I have pointed out that at least one of his commentaries, that on the twelve minor prophets, was written
in his Paris days. Manuscripts of this and other exegetical
works of his are scattered all over Europe, especially in
France, and one or more may be seen in most of the

[1] Denifle, op. cit., especially pp. 285–92.   [2] Mazarin MS. 29.

European libraries. Any adequate consideration of them would demand a long period of preliminary investigation, but it is certain that Langton's work would be found to contain many observations upon social and political problems, and would tell us much about his mind. The commentaries were copied freely in the thirteenth and fourteenth centuries, and that Stephen was regarded as one of the great expositors is shown by the inclusion of extracts from his writings in collections of passages taken from various authors, upon the Old and New Testaments.[1] Later testimony comes in a note of some interest inserted in a Douai manuscript written in the thirteenth and fourteenth centuries, and at one time belonging to the abbey of Marchiennes, near Douai. The manuscript contains the work on the twelve prophets, and on the first page is written in a late hand, 'Stephen archbishop of Canterbury on the Twelve Prophets is unedited and in the opinion of the reverend (*dominus*) George Colveneere, chancellor of the academy of Douai, is well worth editing. Dom. Raphael de Beauchamps, priest and religious of Marchiennes.'[2] Both the writer of this note and his friend the chancellor have a place in literary history. The former worked at the Marchiennes manuscripts and edited chronicles; the latter, chancellor of the University, collected a library of his own, and read and annotated estensively in the manuscripts of neighbouring libraries. He was the editor of Thomas of Cantimpré's curious work 'Bonum universale de Apibus', which he found among the manuscripts of the Dominicans at Douai, and published in 1597. Unhappily he did not act upon the opinion which he gave to Dom Raphael on the desirability of publishing Langton's commentary on the Minor Prophets.

In Dominican circles—as we have learned from Trivet—

---

[1] e.g. a fourteenth-century manuscript, once belonging to St. Vedast, Arras, now Arras MS. 96, contains 'expositiones ueteris et noui testamenti', culled from St. Bernard, Hugh of St. Victor, and others, including Stephen Langton. See *Catalogue général, Départements*, iv. 59.

[2] Douai MS. 29. See *Catalogue général*, vi (1878), 18–19.

Langton was naturally remembered as a student of the Scriptures. On the Church at large he made more impression as a preacher.

'To his credit and undying memory,' says Matthew Paris, 'there remain some admirable treatises on Ecclesiasticus and on the Penitence of the Magdalene; and he wrote, in the true manner of a master, other writings including sermons of a theological kind for special occasions. He could be likened to Augustine, Gregory and Ambrose. By these works the hearts of learned theologians were enlarged, and crowds of the faithful were recalled to a better life.' [1]

The precise meaning of this passage is not clear. The *sermones speciales theologicae*, in this context, may possibly refer to his theological teaching, but the following sentence shows, I think, that Matthew Paris was thinking of his sermons. Langton's fame as a preacher is well attested. Matthew Paris refers elsewhere to his success, when he joined Robert Curzon in a preaching mission, especially in Artois and Flanders. Their efforts were mainly directed against the prevalence of usury, a subject upon which Stephen touches in his *questiones* and to which Curzon devoted very particular attention in his own *Summa*. The chronicle adds that copies of their sermons, and of those of the famous preacher, James of Vitry, could be found in the great commonplace book (*liber Additamentorum*) at St. Albans.[2] James of Vitry himself also refers to the two Englishmen as successful preachers during his time.[3]

Like the commentaries the sermons are unpublished, and, as so often happens in the case of medieval sermons, it is not easy to disentangle them with certainty from those of other prelates. Here again work remains to be done. Two distinguished French scholars, Lecoy de la Marche and Hauréau, have made some preliminary in-

---

[1] Liebermann, *Ungedruckte anglo-normannische Geschichtsquellen*, p. 328.

[2] Ibid. No entries of this kind are to be found in the surviving volume of the Liber Additamentorum (Cott. MS. Nero D. 1). Liebermann (pp. 321–2) discusses the difficulties in accepting Matthew Paris's date—during Langton's return from Rome in 1218—of this mission.

[3] *Hist. hierosolymitana*, l. i, c. 8, together with master Walter of London, Alberic of Laon, and others.

vestigations.[1] In the light of the former's criticism, for
example, it is no longer possible to ascribe to Langton the
best known of all the sermons attributed to him, in which
the preacher takes as his text the opening lines of a French
love poem or *lai*, 'Bel Aliz matin leva'. It is not in the
archbishop's manner, is also ascribed to others, and is not
such an isolated specimen of the kind as is generally supposed.[2] Yet enough remains to show that Langton preached
on all sorts of occasions—to ecclesiastical councils, to
learned audiences, during special periods of the ecclesiastical year, and to the people.[3] His sermons to the people
would be given in French or English,[4] as the case might
be, but sermons in the vernacular rarely, if ever, survive
from this period, and naturally those sermons of Langton
which do remain in manuscript are for the most part
addresses originally given in Latin to audiences which
could follow them in that language. Yet several of his
sermons *ad populum* survive in a Latin translation. One
of them, in a Troyes manuscript, as we know from the
Annals of Waverley, was preached at St. Paul's on a great
occasion (25 August 1213), and caused some disturbance.
The archbishop had recently absolved King John from
excommunication at Winchester. He was now busy with
ecclesiastical affairs at a council of the clergy, and already
in touch with the baronage investigating the problems of
political reform. At the promising opening of this new
epoch, in a spirit of thankfulness, he took as his text, 'My
heart hath trusted in God, and I am helped, thereupon

---

[1] A. Lecoy de la Marche, *La chaire française, spécialement au XIIIe siècle*
(second edition, 1886), 89 ff.; B. Hauréau, *Notices et extraits de quelques
manuscrits latins de la Bibliothèque Nationale*, ii (1891), 114 f.

[2] Lecoy de la Marche, pp. 91–4. For the bibliography see also Miss
Norgate in the *Dictionary of National Biography*, s.v. Langton, Stephen.

[3] See Appendix II.

[4] On preaching in the vernacular see Lecoy de la Marche, and Owst,
Preaching in Medieval England (Cambridge, 1926). Some excellent English
sermons, obviously composed by a scholar who had a gift of simple exposition,
may be read in Mr. A. O. Belfour's edition of the *Twelfth-Century Homilies* in
MS. Bodley 343 (Early English Text Society, original series 137, London, 1909).

my flesh has rejoiced'. A voice from the crowd was raised, 'Thou liest: thy heart never trusted in God and thy flesh never rejoiced'.[1]

There seems in all his work to have been a curious double strain in Langton. At one time he was simple and direct, at others far-fetched and allusive, running after conceits and hair-splitting refinements. His sermons bear witness to both aspects of his thought. As M. Hauréau has said:

'They have the rapidity of movement, the casual style of the extempore discourse, and must have won the success which always comes to literary facility. The man of action is speaking, saying in pithy brusque phrase everything that he wishes to say. Yet at the same time he plays far too much upon words, as men of his age did —and he goes beyond the fashion in exaggeration.'[2]

This mingling of directness and subtlety is not uncommon in great men whose public life is inspired by profound conviction, and is perhaps especially common in Englishmen. Here it is sufficient to say that in his sermons Langton gives ample evidence of his quickness in observation, and of his intimate acquaintance with the life of men in all kinds of society. The sermons scattered among those of others in the Magdalen manuscript to which I have already referred in another connexion may provide a few examples. These sermons were obviously preached in France, and may go back to his Paris days. Here is a passage on safe-conducts [3] or letters of protection:

'If a man wishes to go safely through the Kingdom of France

[1] *Annales Monastici*, ed. Luard (Rolls Series), ii. 277; Troyes MS. 862, originally in the Clairvaux library, contains a sermon by Langton from the text 'in Deo sperauit cor meum' (*Catalogue général*, ii, 1850, p. 356).

[2] Hauréau, loc. cit., p. 114.

[3] On more than one occasion in later life Langton had to be careful about royal letters of protection, which, if not drawn up in proper form and as letters patent, might be disregarded as invalid. See the letters of the bishops of London, Ely and Worcester, and of Stephen to John in 1210 (*Gervase of Canterbury*, ed. Stubbs, ii, pp. cv–cvii) and compare the remark attributed to John in his interview with the papal legate in 1211 (annals of Burton in *Annales Monastici*, i. 210). For a safe conduct issued to Stephen during the crisis of 1215, see *Rotuli litterarum patentium*, p. 142 (27 May 1215)

and carries the King's seal with him, he will be safe anywhere in the kingdom. But if he were to cast the seal away and take the seal of some obscure person, would he not be regarded as a madman? And how much more is he who casts away the seal of the eternal King and takes the seal of the devil.' [1]

And Langton probably had a definite instance in mind, when he says later—'a man would not be safe if he carried through the Kingdom of France the seal of an alien and enemy prince.' [2] He speaks of the circular disk set up before a tavern as a sign that wine was for sale, and of the *hospites* (established as we know by their lords in recent years) in the rue Saint-Jacques who say that they have excellent beds to let, 'but when the travellers go to bed they find them nothing but straw '.[3] Or again, he compares the unsafe castles of the plain with the 'castra religiosorum' set high upon a rock, and says how wise the Templars are who bear the sign of the cross, 'for the Lord has taken their castles, and has set up his standard thereon, as those who capture castles are wont to do '.[4] He takes a simile from the sport of fowling, and says that those who refuse to come to Our Lord's hand, red with the blood of his passion, are like a well-fed hawk, which disdains the hand on which it has fed, even though it sees raw flesh there; and he quotes in French a hawking phrase about the bird (*ostour*) which will not answer the call (*ne vuolt pas venir a reclaim*).[5] And this is how he explains the story of the calling of Matthew:

'Suppose an earthly King should appoint one of his household to hear cases and complaints in his court, and a poor man who had greatly offended the King should bring before this steward some grievance which he had suffered, and should count upon the royal

[1] Magdalen College MS. 168, f. 65ᵛ, in a sermon 'in festo beate Marie Magdalene'. [2] f. 66.

[3] f. 60, 'sicut circulus [MS. circlⁱ] ante tabernam est signum uini'; f. 60ᵛ, 'sic hospites in via beati Iacobi ostendunt lectos pulcherrimos set cum dormitum uadunt peregrini nihil reperiunt nisi paleam.' For the settlement of *hospites* from the country on the left bank of the Seine and the growth of the students' quarter, see Poëte, *Une vie de cité*, i. 165–6.

[4] f. 58. [5] f. 58ᵛ.

pardon and reconciliation because he had suffered; and suppose the steward should say to him that although his sin against the king was still the same, neither greater nor less, yet he was pardoned, and had been appointed also to the office of steward, so, Beloved, on this day the King of kings appointed the blessed Matthew to hear the petitions of his men in his court.' [1]

Matthew Paris refers to Langton's work on the Penitence of the Magdalene—a work sometimes ascribed to his brother, Simon Langton.[2] It survives in a Balliol manuscript of the thirteenth century where it fills nearly one hundred folios. The correct title is 'de poenitentia, sub persona Magdalene', for a contemporary rubric adds the words—'sic voluit dominus Cantuarie ut vocaretur libellus iste'.[3] The theme—or at least the cognate themes of the sacraments of penance and confession—was a favourite with Langton while he was teaching at Paris, but I imagine that this work, of a more devotional character, was more likely to have been written during his exile, perhaps at Pontigny.[4] To the leisure of this period we may, perhaps, also ascribe his lost historical works on the life of King Richard and on Mohammed.[5] It remains to speak of Langton as a poet.

Perhaps he should not be called a poet. Rather he was a cultivated ecclesiastic who knew the hymns of the Church and liked to string verses together. A Bodleian manuscript contains a rhymed exhortation, in seven

[1] Magdalen College MS. 168, f. 54, in festo Mathei.

[2] e.g. Pits, *Catalogus Scriptorum* (1619), p. 320.

[3] Balliol College MS. 152, f. 25. There is another copy in Corpus Christi College, Cambridge, no. 226. The title-page, which is now in MS. no. 222, f. 1a, shows that this book once belonged to Hugh de Gerunde. It then came to Christ Church, Canterbury (James, *Descriptive Catalogue of MSS. in the Library of Corpus Christi College*, i. 520, 526; and the same writer's *Ancient Libraries of Canterbury and Dover*, p. 113, no. 1310). So far as I could judge from a casual examination of the Balliol manuscript this work is of little interest.

[4] Cf. Alberic of Trois-Fontaines in *Historiens de la France*, xviii. 771*c*, 'apud Pontiniacum secum habitavit, *ubi multa scripsit.*'

[5] Higden, *Polychronicon*, ed. Lumby (Rolls Series), vi. 14, used this in his account of Mohammed.

strophes, to his clerks on the way they should go.[1] Here
is the sixth:

Caute dispone domui.
pauca set vera loquere.
Verba confirmes opere,
quia non decet temere
os sacerdotis pollui
mendacio.
Prudencium te consilio
fratrum non displiceat,
nec te sinistre moveat
salubris exhortacio.

Langton also composed a rhymed psalter, that is to
say, a poem of 150 verses, each of them a salutation to the
Virgin, and each of them containing some play on the
words—sometimes many words, sometimes only a phrase
—of the corresponding psalm. In this form of composition
Langton was in line with St. Anselm, St. Edmund of
Canterbury, St. Bonaventura, and many more. In course
of time the original idea was lost sight of, allusions to the
psalms were omitted, and a rhymed psalter became a
religious poem of 150 strophes in honour of Our Lord or
Our Lady, of the Holy Cross or the Passion. Thus, it came
about that the rosary, the third part of a psalter, is a
rhythmical prayer in fifty strophes to Our Lady, the repetition of which was checked by counting a string of beads.
The psalter was sometimes used as a prayer, sometimes
sung, especially by clerks or monks in groups or even in
choir. Langton's composition, which was popular in
South Germany, was printed in 1579 at Tegernsee, 'can-
tandum sub melodia *Patris sapientia*'. It survives in sixteen
manuscripts found in England, France, Bavaria, Switzer-
land, and is variously attributed to St. Augustine, Albert
Magnus, and Archbishop Pecham.[2] Addressed to Our
Lady it faithfully brings in some allusion to the phrasing

[1] MS. Bodley 57, f. 66ᵛ. 'Documenta clericorum Stephani de Lanketon'.
See below, Appendix IV.

[2] G. M. Dreves, 'Psalteria Rhythmica: Gereimte Psalterien des Mittelalters' (*Analecta Hymnica medii aevi*, xxxv, Leipzig, 1900), pp. 153–71. The

of each of the 150 psalms. The result is not always happy. Thus, Psalm 117, v. 22—Lapidem quem reprobauerunt aedificantes, &c. is brought into the 117th strophe, in the simile of a corner-stone encircling a vine:

> Aue uitis gratie,
> Vitis salutaris
> Quam uallauit undique
> Lapis angularis.

Once, at any rate, Langton was inspired. I have said that he was fond of the great hymns of the Church. One of his compositions, widely distributed in manuscripts, was a sermon or commentary (*tractatus*) on the famous poem of Venantius Fortunatus, *Ave maris stella.*[1] And there appears to be no doubt that he, and not King Robert of France or Pope Innocent III, was the author of one of the greatest of all hymns, the *Veni, Sancte Spiritus.* In the year 1855 cardinal Pitra published numerous extracts from a curious work in five books, *Distinctiones monasticae et morales,* one of those alphabetical interpretations of scriptural words, the fashion in which was set by the *Clavis* of St. Melito.[2] The author was an English religious, well acquainted with English writers of the twelfth century and with the scholars of his day in Paris.[3] He was a contemporary of Langton's, and wrote before the archbishop's death. In a chapter on the word 'mother', he speaks of the Holy Spirit as the Mother of the Church, training, guarding, counselling; and he quotes in testi-

---

attribution to Pecham in the Catalogue of manuscripts in the University Library, Cambridge (ii. 519) is due to a misunderstanding (Dreves, p. 171).

[1] e.g. Royal MSS. 8 A x, f. 36, 8 C vii, f. 22, 8 F iv. See also M. R. James, *The Ancient Libraries of Canterbury and Dover,* pp. 275 (no. 760), 280 (no. 798), 282.

[2] Pitra, *Spicilegium Solesmense,* ii, pp. xxvi–xxvii, iii. 452–87, and *passim.* The work is in Mazarin MS. 3475 (formerly 1252); see Auguste Molinier, *Catalogue des MSS. de la Bibliothèque Mazarin,* iii (1890), 97, 98. The manuscript, of the thirteenth century, came from the library of St. Nicholas, Angers.

[3] References to Peter the Chanter (ii. 98, 128), Alexander Neckam (iii. 454), and frequently to the poet Laurence of Durham, &c.

mony what Master Stephen Langton, archbishop of Canterbury, says in the noble sequence which he composed on the Holy Spirit:

> Consolator optime,
> Dulcis hospes anime,
> Dulce refrigerium.[1]

It is probable that Stephen composed his hymn while he was in Paris. It belongs to the musical tradition of Notre Dame.[2] If this be the case the most familiar, perhaps the noblest thing that he ever wrote, may be associated in our minds with the new church of which he was a canon, and the schools in which he taught.

[1] Pitra, iii. 130. Cf. an article by W. H. Grattan Flood in *The Tablet*, 22 May 1926, for the history of the discussions about the authorship of the 'Veni, Sancte Spiritus'. On the evidence in favour of Innocent III's authorship see Raby, *A History of Christian Latin Poetry* (Oxford, 1927), p. 343, and the paper, there cited, by Dom Wilmart.

[2] Amédée Gastoué, *Les Primitifs de la musique française* (Paris, 1922), p. 39, claims Langton as one of the remarkable group of Englishmen interested in music, whose residence at Paris and methods of singing in unison are supposed to have influenced the polyphonic music of the contemporary organist of Notre-Dame, the sub-Chanter, Peter, usually called Perotin the Great (ibid., pp. 16–22).

III

LANGTON AT PARIS: HIS *QUESTIONES*

STEPHEN LANGTON, in the words of Pope Innocent, studied for a long time in Paris and became a doctor in the liberal arts and in theology.[1] His teaching has come down to us in the form of *questiones*, or discussions of theological and moral problems, and collections of these discussions are frequently described in the manuscripts as *summae*. It was the fashion to speak of a master's *summa*. But a *summa*, as systematic teaching and writing developed, was also naturally regarded as a more organic body of thought than a mere collection of *questiones* might be. In one manuscript Langton's *questiones* are preceded by a short theological treatise which, in contrast with what follows, is called his *summa*.

Before we consider these manuscripts and their contents it is advisable to describe the development of theological study at Paris, so that we may know what to expect; and we cannot do better than begin with this tendency to distinguish a *summa* from a number of discussions on all kinds of themes. The tendency may be generalized in the form of an answer to the question 'How far was theological inquiry at Paris systematic at the end of the twelfth century?' With this is connected a further question—'To what extent was inquiry free?'

Several Roman Catholic scholars have busied themselves with these historical problems in recent years, and it is sufficient for our purpose to note their conclusions.[2] The theological movement of the twelfth century was part of a general movement towards orderliness in what may be called co-operative thought. It implied not merely the use of authorities, which might result in haphazard

[1] Above, p. 28 note 2.
[2] A useful introduction, with bibliographies, in Maurice de Wulf's *History of Medieval Philosophy*, second English edition (1926), i. 196–216, 250–9.

repetition on the one hand, or on the other assist the isolated mental achievement of an Anselm; it implied the frank comparison of authorities. Much had already been done before Gratian's *Decretum* to straighten out the law of the Church, but the great work of Gratian was a *tour de force* in comparative study, and had a profound influence upon intellectual development. The sentences of Peter the Lombard, Abelard's disciple, who died in 1160 as bishop of Paris, did for theological studies in Paris what the *Decretum* of Gratian did for legal studies in Bologna; moreover, as they had much in common—common interests, common authorities—the study and teaching of law and theology tended, as they became more self-contained to run into each other and influence each other, just as two partners trust each other the more as they become more sure of themselves.[1] The idea of the *summa* grew from an effort to systematize both abstract thought and the practical problems of life. Martha and Mary grew up together in one house.

Now, as the Lombard, like Abelard before him, worked in the atmosphere of the schools, his Sentences were a handbook, which as it sprung from his teaching, set an example to other teachers. It was the fruit of discussion and it provoked discussion. And the freedom of speculation which ensued soon began to cause alarm, especially in contemplative circles. We must not imagine that there was a clear issue between orthodoxy and heresy. The books and persons, for example, condemned at Paris in 1210, fifty years after the Lombard's death, represented several types of thought, from the extravagances of Joachimite prophecy to the pantheism of David of Dinant. Father Théry has shown that the association of David with the Amauricians was purely fortuitous. David with some probability may be identified with a chaplain of Innocent III (1206) and, in spite of his condemnation, seems to have received some protection from the pope. He was a student of Aristotle, as well as of the Areopagite,

[1] Cf. Paul Fournier in the *Journal des Savants*, April 1915.

so that a study of his work is of value for the study of Aristotelian developments in Paris.[1] Again, we have already seen that another person condemned in 1210 had been a pupil of Stephen Langton.[2] In short, the ferment of thought, in which the danger of heresy was always lurking, was beginning in Paris. At the same time it is clear that much of the general criticism directed against Parisian studies was not concerned with theology at all, but with the hectic discussions of the students in arts. This was no new thing. Earlier in the century 'shallower and more pretentious masters' and 'empty-headed crammers' (to use Dr. Poole's phrases) had 'abandoned the thorough and honest system of the school of Chartres'. They were attacked by William of Conches and later by John of Salisbury.[3] The gradual penetration of still more learning from Spain and the East intensified the tendency at Paris. The range of studies is well illustrated by the long list of textbooks, discovered by Dr. Haskins, who ascribes it to Alexander Neckam.[4] After reading it we can understand the diatribe in the well-known letter of Peter of Blois on how to educate boys—against the foolish youths who, before they have learned the elements, are taught to investigate the point and the line, fate and the bias of nature, chance and free will, method and motive; the meaning of time and space, sameness and difference; the existence of universals, the origin and practice of the virtues, the causes of things, the tides, and the source of the Nile, the secrets of nature and Heaven knows what, all of which require a basis of sound learning and conspicuous ability for their elucidation.[5] In those, as in all times, the search after

[1] G. Théry, *Autour du décret de 1210: I, David de Dinant, étude sur son panthéisme matérialiste* (Bibliothèque Thomiste VI, Kain, 1925), especially pp. 9, 10, 81 ff.   [2] Above, p. 30.

[3] See John of Salisbury's *Metalogicus*, e.g. lib. i, c. 3, and especially Poole, *Illustrations of Medieval Thought*, Chapter VII and Appendix VII. The phrases quoted in the text come from pp. 359, 361 of the first edition (1884).

[4] C. H. Haskins, *Studies in the History of Medieval Science*, pp. 356–76.

[5] I have summarized the text given from the Paris MS., 'qualiter pueri sint erudiendi', in *C.U.P.*, i, Introd., pp. 27–9, no. 25.

system and omniscience could foster shallow pedantry, and pedantry could defeat its own end by encouraging wildness and sophistry.

The theologians were older, saner men; moreover, they were protected by the theological systematization in the Sentences and by tradition; yet they did not escape the charge that they abused their freedom. Stephen of Tournai, writing from that cloister where Abelard had once taught publicly, urged his friend, the archbishop of Lund, not to let 'his Peter'—a young relative of the archbishop's —fall among the 'vendors of words' in the secular schools. If Peter is not to take monastic vows, at least let him study elsewhere than in Paris 'lest he offer up before our eyes, instead of the morning and evening sacrifices which he ought to offer to the Lord with us, the clamour of words and the clash of disputations'.[1] And some years afterwards, when he was bishop of Tournai, the same writer complained to the Pope of the new modes of teaching in the schools. Sacred studies were all in confusion; the disciples applaud only new things; the masters seek fame rather than sound doctrine, and were always writing new, up-to-date *summae* and theological commentaries, seducing and deceiving their hearers, as though the Fathers were not good enough for them. In public disputations the incomprehensible deity was discussed and 'de incarnatione verbi verbosa caro et sanguis irreverenter litigat'. The indivisible Trinity was cut in pieces *in triviis*; there were as many errors as doctors, and so on.[2] This is valuable testimony, not to the reputation of the doctors but to the vitality and nature of their teaching. Yet we may find an echo of the bishop's alarm in the warnings of some of the theologians. A certain Master Martin, whose *summa* is bound up with Langton's *questiones* in a Cambridge and also in a Paris manuscript, and who was Langton's contemporary at Paris, explains in his preface that he dare not depart from Holy Scripture, as those do who pervert

[1] *C.U.P.*, i, Introd., p. 43, no. 42.
[2] Ibid., i, Part I, pp. 47–8, no. 48. Cf. de Wulf, i. 206.

it by their own peculiar comments and imaginings, and who reverence the philosophy of heretics as much as the authors of the Old and New Testaments. If Scripture seems to err, then either the text is corrupt or the interpretation at fault. Antiquity, says Martin, will be his sole exemplar, and although envious detractors may charge him with despising the careful work of others he prefers his method to the adoption of authorities who, if they are subjected to critical comparison, differ from the doctors in both the form and method of their disputations.[1] Martin, I may observe, dealt with the same kinds of problems as Langton did, and Langton, I imagine, would have agreed in general with his conservative attitude to authority.

Martin got nearer than Stephen of Tournai to the real issue. Stephen was in the tradition of St. Bernard, and of Walter of St. Victor, who had abused Peter the Lombard and his influence in his tract on the 'four labyrinths of France'—Abelard, Gilbert de la Porée, the Lombard, and Peter of Poitiers. For a time the reaction had prevailed. In December 1164 Alexander III, at a gathering of scholars in Sens, issued his prohibition of 'omnes tropos et indisciplinatae questiones in theologia'. Later the Christological nihilism of Abelard, of which Alexander himself, when teaching at Bologna, had once felt the influence, was attacked.[2] But the current of theological disputation was too strong to be checked for long. On the other hand, the point of view of Master Martin was to become enlarged and to gain powerful adherents in the future. Martin himself, of course, was an active and orthodox theologian, who preferred the old and the safe to the subtle verbosity of some of his contemporaries, but his criticism touched the point which the scholars and humanists

---

[1] The passage is printed by Grabmann, ii. 525, 526, from MS. Latin 14556, f. 267. It appears also in the Cambridge MS., f. 9.

[2] Ghellinck, *Le mouvement théologique du XIIe siècle*, pp. 152, 153; Denifle, in the *Archiv für Literatur- und Kirchengeschichte des Mittelalters*, i. 407; Grabmann, ii. 398 ff.

were to emphasize. Roger Bacon, when he pleaded for a thoroughgoing study of the Bible and for real textual criticism, and attacked the endless dialectic of the commentators on the Sentences, put the same point more forcibly. And Petrarch expressed it rather differently, when he turned his back upon the teaching of the universities and read St. Augustine and St. Bernard in his own way.

In Langton's time, however, the Sentences of Peter the Lombard exercised a healthy influence upon all phases of theological inquiry. Historians have been able to trace two main tendencies in the schools of Paris at the end of the twelfth century.[1] The one, represented first by Peter of Poitiers, and later by the theologian of Cremona, known as Prepositinus, led straight on to the scholastic method of the thirteenth century. Both these scholars wrote commentaries upon the Sentences and, in the pursuit of its method, helped to develop the dialectic of the future. In their work and in the work of others of their kind there is system, a reliance upon logical technique, a fondness for distinctions and refinements. The other tendency is represented by Petrus Comestor, Peter the Chanter, and Langton himself. It shows increasing reliance upon the Lombard as an authority, he is the Master; but men like Langton used the Lombard, just as they used St. Augustine and St. Ambrose; they did not adopt him. They were moral or pastoral, rather than systematic theologians. They lectured with no particular sense of order upon the nature of God, the virtues and vices, transubstantiation, ecclesiastical property, a difficult text from the Scriptures, simony, usury, the sacraments, the political doctrine of the two swords. At one time they discarded the technical forms of logic, at another they lost themselves in dialectical subtleties. They were at once more artificial and more humane than the Lombard and his followers.[2]

---

[1] See especially Grabmann, *passim*.

[2] Ghellinck, pp. 159, 165. He points out that the disciples of the Chanter had a more practical object than the Lombard had, yet at the same time

Whether or no the criticisms of Master Martin, who on the whole belongs to this second group of theologians, were directed against the first group, I cannot say. As the decree of 1210 revealed, there were other forces at work in Paris, and Martin may have been thinking of people like David of Dinant. It is easy, indeed, to exaggerate in the search for tendencies, the difference between the two groups. They are the artificial creation of modern scholars who are trying, with much skill, to trace the growth of the traditions which produced St. Thomas Aquinas and Duns Scotus; and I cannot but feel that Dr. Grabmann, in his interesting and learned work, has conveyed a mis-leading impression of conscious divergencies which were not apparent to the eminent teachers of Langton's time. In the eyes of their pupils the personal foibles, the tem-perament, the measure of their sympathy, or their powers of exposition were doubtless the traits which distinguished one master from another. Some would be more systematic than others, but they all lectured and disputed on the same things. There was one fashion common to them all.[1]

lacked his method. They 'supposent connu tout ce qu'enseigne le Lombard, et y ajoutent des compléments'. The Lombard appears simple and reserved by contrast with Langton. Father Ghellinck's statement (p. 129) that Langton gave the original manuscript of the Sentences to the library of Notre-Dame appears to be due to a misunderstanding of a document given in Guérard, *Cartulaire de Notre-Dame*, ii. 495–6, and Delisle, *Cabinet des manuscrits*, iii. 2, 3. In 1271 John of Orleans, chancellor of the church of Paris, acknowledged the receipt (from his predecessor) of a number of books, previously left by Stephen, archdeacon of Canterbury, for the use of poor scholars in theology. 'Stephen' is probably a mistake for his brother Simon, archdeacon of Canterbury, and canon of Paris (d. 1248). To this list two items are added, which were not part of the bequest. The first refers to a Biblia postillata, given by bishop Stephen, the second is the 'originale Sententiarum' of the Lombard. Delisle (op. cit., i. 427) supposed that the Lombard left it himself to his church.

[1] John of Salisbury, in his comparison between St. Bernard and Gilbert de la Porée, and his whole treatment of Gilbert's theological views, gives an exceedingly interesting impression of the kind of education which, in an earlier period, was regarded as requisite in a good theologian. See Poole, *Joannis Saresberiensis Historiae Pontificalis quae supersunt* (Oxford, 1927), pp. 27–41, notably p. 28.

Englishmen took a large share in the theological movement in Paris. The *Sentences* were read at Lincoln before 1166,[1] and English scholars taught theology in Paris before 1180. For example, Adam of Bangor—nicknamed Parvipontanus—was the champion of the Lombard and had been *prepositus* in his schools; and Gerard Pucelle, who became bishop of Coventry in 1183, is quoted by Prepositinus.[2] William of Leicester, the later chancellor of Lincoln, we have already met. Alexander Neckam was teaching in Paris during Langton's earlier years there, and with characteristic versatility taught, as we should say, in all faculties. If his theological teaching was like his unpublished *Speculum Speculationum*, now among the Royal manuscripts in the British Museum, his orderly and abstract approach to theological problems must have been in strong contrast to the methods of Peter the Chanter, under whose influence the young Langton seems to have come.[3] Finally, a contemporary of Langton and an even more distinguished theologian, was the Englishman Robert Curzon, like Langton a disciple of the Chanter and a future cardinal.

Moral theology was indeed firmly entrenched at Paris. Peter of Troyes, chancellor of Paris, known as the Manducator or Comestor, was probably dead when Stephen came to the schools. A work on the *Sentences*, now at Madrid, is ascribed to him, but he is better known by his history of Biblical times, the *Historia Scholastica*. This was one of the books most widely read in the Middle Ages, and earned for its author the title 'Master of Histories'. Langton studied it, and doubtless possessed it, for a Paris manuscript contains annotations on it, which are ascribed to him.[4] The other moralist, Peter of Rheims, or the Chanter,

---

[1] See the catalogue of the Lincoln Cathedral library, printed in the *Opera* of Gerald of Wales (vii. 169), 'sententiae magistri Petri Lumbardi', among the books given by bishop Robert (d. 1166).   [2] Above, p. 33 note.

[3] British Museum, Royal MS. 7. F. i, f. 2: 'Speculum speculationum magistri Alexandri canonici Cirecestrie.'

[4] Bibliothèque Nationale, MS. Latin 14417, ff. 125–309. Cf. Grabmann, ii. 498.

was canon of Notre-Dame from 1169, cantor from 1178 until his death in 1197. He was the most impressive among the Paris teachers of his time, and was almost certainly Langton's master. Apart from the fact that in one manuscript of the *questiones*[1] Langton appears to refer to him, and not—as he usually did—to the Lombard, under the simple title *magister*, the similarity between the two men in outlook and method is striking.

Peter's personality so attracted his contemporaries that we know more about him than we do about most of the other masters. An old official of the royal chancery, Stephen of Gallardon, who used the last pages of the register which he made for the cathedral of Bourges to write down some anecdotes, tells of the conversations which King Philip had with the Chanter. One day they talked about the duties of kingship. Philip bore Peter's homily very well, and said, 'If you ever make a king, make him as you have described him.' 'But tell me,' he went on, 'why we had so many bishops who were saints in the old days, and have none now?' Peter answered mysteriously, 'The wise man gives counsel when he is sent for, the fool comes unbidden.' 'By the lance of St. James,' the king exclaimed, 'what has that to do with my question?' The tiresome scholar proceeded methodically to show that the wise man of his parable was the Holy Spirit, the fool the devil. He then came to the point and explained that in old days bishops were chosen with much anxiety, after long fasting and with many tears, so that only men of good life who loved Christ were chosen; while now the devil, the prince of fools, pressed in uninvited.[2] If we recall the illegal elections in Canterbury, which preceded Langton's own election, and Langton's own strong views about the episcopate, this story is seen to throw some light upon the in-

[1] Above, p. 30 and note.
[2] Delisle, *Étienne de Gallardon*, in Bibliothèque de l'École des Chartes, lx (1899), 23, 24. The story is summarized by Cartellieri, *Philipp II August*, iv. 590. On Peter the Chanter generally see F. S. Gutiahr, *Petrus Cantor Parisiensis: sein Leben und seine Schriften* (Graz, 1899).

fluences which shaped the younger man's life. Again the German historian, Caesarius of Heisterbach—to whom we owe the story of Peter and the Parisian usurer[1]—tells us that, when the masters of Paris were discussing the death of archbishop Thomas of Canterbury, Peter declared emphatically that he was a martyr, for he was slain while defending the liberty of the Church.[2] This attitude would confirm Langton in his reverence for St. Thomas. Memories of Peter's phrases and teaching were treasured in distant places. An English writer, the author of the *Distinctiones monasticae*, refers to them more than once. Speaking of the verse in the Psalms (cxxxii. 6): 'Lo, we heard of it at Ephratah; we found it in the fields of the wood', he observes, 'Master Peter the Chanter used to say, of this verse, that Christ is heard in well-lettered clerks, but is found in good-living peasants.'[3]

The Chanter compiled an alphabetical dictionary of biblical theology in the form whose tradition was set by the *Clavis* of St. Melito.[4] A very similar work, now in the library of the school of medicine at Montpellier, is definitely ascribed to Langton.[5] Peter also wrote a treatise on the sacraments, and we find Langton, in his *questiones*, discussing the sacraments very much in his manner, mingling theological with practical and legal matter. But the best

---

[1] Above, p. 17.

[2] Caesarius of Heisterbach, *Dialogus Miraculorum*, viii. 69. The Master Roger who took the opposite view about St. Thomas was probably Roger the Norman, afterwards dean of Rouen, to whom Gerald of Wales refers in his 'de rebus a se gestis', *Opera*, i. 46.

[3] Pitra, *Spicilegium Solesmense*, ii. 128; another quotation from him on ii. 98.

[4] See Grabmann, ii. 483 for this 'Summa Abel'. Much of it is printed by Pitra, op. cit., vol. iii, and in his *Analecta Sacra*, vol. ii.

[5] 'Interpretationes M. Stephani de Langotonia, Cantuariensis archiepiscopi', in MS. 341 of the school of medicine at Montpellier. See *Catalogue Général*, i. (1849), 425. This identification requires further investigation. Cf. a Clairvaux manuscript, now Troyes 1385, which contains, without any ascription, an alphabetical work, interpretations of Hebrew names, followed by a Promptuarium Patrum, also alphabetical, attributed by a later hand to Langton (*Catalogue Général*, ii. 574-5).

illustrations of the master's influence are to be found in his best-known work, the 'Verbum abbreviatum', a very practical exposition of moral theology. The first chapter, 'against superfluous and foolish glosses and useless questions', defines Peter's attitude towards biblical and theological study, and explains very clearly the right use of authorities, expounded some years later, as we have already seen, by Master Martin. If the incarnate word condescended to be confined in the virgin's womb, how much more should the written word—the Bible—the guide to life, be abbreviated. The endless superfluity of words is alien to it. As Seneca says, the multitude of books distracts us. So, as you cannot read all that you have, be content to have as much as you can read. But, you say, I wish to consult now one book, now another. Too great a variety of food is bad for you. Read well-tried books, compare others in their light, remember that the end of knowledge is to improve the mind and regulate life. So far Seneca in his epistles. We must read and study Scriptures in this way.

'The study of Scripture consists in reading, disputation, preaching. In each of these exercises prolixity is the mother of forgetfulness, the step-mother of memory. Reading is the foundation of all, for through it the rest is achieved. Disputation is the wall, the building, for nothing can be properly understood or faithfully preached, if it is not chewed by the tooth of disputation. Preaching, which is held up and served by the other exercises, is the roof, sheltering the faithful from the heat and temptation. It must come after, not before, the reading of holy Scriptures and the investigation of doubtful matters by disputation.' [1]

In this passage the words *lectio* and *disputatio* are obviously used in the sense of the schools; they refer to deliberate teaching and academic exercises.

I take a very different passage, from the 78th chapter, because it shows how practical, how well informed by anecdote, the discussion of moral issues was; also how legislation was prepared by the opinion of the schools. The Chanter, in this chapter, analyses the practice of trial by

---

[1] Migne, *Patrologia Latina*, ccv, col. 1–3.

the ordeal, and critically distinguishes the various methods of ordeal. He tells a story of an English pilgrim who returned from Jerusalem without his companion, who had left him to go on to Compostella. The relatives of the missing man accused the one who returned of having slain him on the journey. He went to the ordeal by water and was hanged. Soon after his companion returned. Peter proceeds:

'In doubtful cases, and especially in a case of homicide (*in causa sanguinis*), great care should be taken not to act on conjectural or probable, but on absolutely clear and certain evidence.'

The ordeal, it will be remembered, was abolished by the Lateran Council in 1215. But Peter does not mean to imply that the church was at fault. Far from it; he desires in such cases to give to the Church full right to protect the accused.

'Persons who are condemned by the ordeal should not be handed over to death, for this form of judgement is in some degree ecclesiastical, for it requires the presence of a priest, and when the accused is handed over to die, the priest hands him over, for he is responsible.'[1]

Another text, which gives this passage rather differently, adds, 'For this reason the blessed Thomas of Canterbury incurred the king's hatred, because he did not allow a clerk, who had been condemned *coram Ecclesia* to be handed over to the court. First he degraded him, and then did not give him to the executioners, for he said that he had punished his offence by degrading him. 'The Lord does not punish twice for the same offence.' *Dominus enim non punit bis in idipsum.*[2]

It is interesting to find the archbishop's famous argument brought into connexion with the ordeal, which his

---

[1] Migne, *Patrologia Latina*, ccv, col. 230, 231. The implication seems to be that condemnation by the ordeal should be followed, not by secular penalties, but by spiritual. Peter continues: 'Sed et B. Thomas Cantuariensis clericum degradatum noluit pro eodem crimine alias puniri, quia *non punit Deus bis* in idipsum.' Here the point is different, for a clerk is concerned. Peter obviously regarded the ordeal as belonging to the *forum ecclesiasticum* just as St. Thomas regarded clerks as subject to it alone.

[2] Ibid., col. 547.

adversary, King Henry II, had treated with a scepticism
equal to Peter the Chanter's, but with a very different
application. The words 'non punit Deus bis in idipsum'
come from the prophet Nahum (i. 9). They are a corrup-
tion of the version in the Septuagint, 'non uindicabit bis
in idipsum in tribulatione,' as given by St. Jerome.[1] More
than this, they are quoted in an intermediate form by
Gratian from the canons of a council held at Mainz in
847.[2] The issue there was whether a criminal who confessed before his execution could be allowed communion
and Christian burial, but the existence of a Biblical text
so explicit, and its use by the canonists, would have much
more weight with St. Thomas and the doctors of Paris
than any of the arguments adduced by his critics from
King Henry down to Maitland. Here, again, we catch a
breath of the air which Langton breathed at Paris.

It must have been a stimulating place, for the discussions there did more than sharpen the wits of a young man.
They revealed to him the implications of practical issues,
whose future history might even be shaped by the opinions
of the doctors of Paris. An archdeacon of Bath once wrote
to Peter of Blois about the mental trouble which a problem, arising from some academic dispute (*conflictus sco-
lastica*), was causing him. You are in the schools, Peter replied with a touch of irony, and Paris is the place for these
inquiries. There the most intricate knots in difficult questions are unravelled. You can find the answer to your
question more easily if you ask the people who are versed
in these matters.[3] As we have seen, these perplexities
could be urgent and practical. The masters discussed together whether St. Thomas was or was not a martyr.
Peter the Chanter dealt freely with the ordeal and with
criminous clerks. Henry II was at one time prepared to

---

[1] *Sancti Hieronymi Opera* (Paris, 1704), iii, col. 1563. The Vulgate reads,
'non consurget duplex tribulatio.'

[2] Decretum, causa xiii, questio ii, c. 30: Scriptum est enim 'non iudicat
Deus bis in idipsum'. (*Corpus Iuris Canonici*, ed. Friedberg, i, col. 731.)

[3] *C.U.P.*, i, Introd., p. 35, no. 29.

submit his dispute with his archbishop to the judgement
of the scholars of Paris.[1] In 1198 we find the masters
called in to decide upon a point of law. A canon of Tournai had died at Rome, and Celestine III—this is rather an
early case of a well-known papal prerogative—appointed
his successor. Bishop Stephen refused to admit him, and
the dean of Paris, to whom the pope had entrusted the
case, instituted the canon 'by the common counsel of the
masters, prudent men and legal experts who had come together at his call to decide the suit'.[2] Paris was a good
training-ground for a future cardinal and archbishop.

And now, after this summary of the theological activities
at Paris, and this glance at Peter the Chanter—'our master
of immortal memory', as Curzon called him—we may
come back to Stephen Langton.

In this study I am primarily concerned with Langton
as a man of affairs, not as a theologian. His significance
in the history of theology has not been overlooked altogether by the historians, although only brief extracts from
his *questiones* have been printed.[3] His work has been consulted by students of the history of indulgences and of
sacramental doctrine, and a more comprehensive study
will some day, I hope, come from Louvain.[4] Yet, if we

[1] See St. Thomas's letter of Nov. 1169; ibid., pp. 21–3, no. 21.

[2] Ibid., pp. 12–14, no. 16.

[3] In addition to the works of Grabmann and Ghellinck, and the notice
in the *Histoire littéraire de la France*, see also, for Langton's *questiones*, a
short article by Ghellinck, 'La somme théologique d'Étienne Langton', in
Recherches de science religieuse, iv (1913). Among the writers who have
printed extracts from one or other of the manuscripts are Ravaisson, who
gave the beginning of the Avranches MS. (*Rapports sur les bibliothèques des
départements de l'Ouest*, pp. 407 ff.), and F. Gillmann, who has printed
from the Bamberg MS. passages on indulgences (*Katholik*, 1913, i. 373–6)
and on the sacraments (*Zur Lehre der Scholastik vom Spender der Firmung
und des Weihesakraments*, Paderborn, 1920, pp. 42, 225). N. Paulus has
quoted from the passages printed in *Katholik* (*Geschichte des Ablasses im
Mittelalter*, i. 218, 219.)

[4] I hope also to arrange for a study of the manuscripts and for a more
exhaustive treatment of the ecclesiastical and political significance of the
questiones.

are to use the *questiones* as material for Langton's attitude to contemporary problems, it is desirable to know something else about them and to satisfy ourselves that what we use is really his.

Manuscripts purporting to contain a *summa* or *questiones* of Langton survive in Paris, Avranches, Arras, Douai, Laon, Rouen, Bamberg, Erlangen, and Cambridge. Three of these, one of the Paris (B.N. lat. 16385) and the Arras and Avranches manuscripts form a distinct group. Those at Laon and Rouen appear to contain only *questiones* on virtues and vices. The rest contain varying recensions.[1] It will be convenient to take the Cambridge manuscript as the basis of investigation, and the more so as there is reason to believe that it contains several groups of lectures in an earlier text.

The Cambridge manuscript, in St. John's College, was written in the first half of the thirteenth century. The first item is the *questiones* of Master Martin, Langton's contemporary. The rest of the manuscript, twenty-five quires of eight folios each, contains works definitely ascribed to Langton.[2] The similarity in writing and the juxtaposition of Martin and Stephen suggest a Paris origin for the manuscript, and a date not very much later than the period when the two masters were teaching. Langton's work is divided into two main sections: (1) a short *summa* of twenty-four folios or three quires, and (2) groups of *questiones* occupying the next twenty-two quires.[3] At the end of the volume an index of Langton's *questiones* is inserted. An examination of this index reveals two facts of interest. In the first place, the manuscript at one time contained another big group of *questiones*, which preceded the others, that is to say, it came between the short *summa* and the existing *questiones*. The short *summa* is not indexed. Secondly, the index was completed before the quires were bound together, for it ends with the contents

---

[1] See Appendix III. [2] ff. 147–346.

[3] ff. 171–346. The text ends on 345ᵛ, top of the second column. The index follows.

of two quires which now come earlier in the book. From these facts we may hypothetically conclude that the short *summa* did not form part, or was not regarded as part of the *questiones*; also that the latter did not comprise a single coherent work, but consisted of distinct groups written as distinct bundles of quires. Further examination confirms these hypotheses.

The *summa* need not detain us. It is a short, and apparently incomplete treatise on the divine essence and attributes, and goes on to some general *questiones* on the virtues. Some of the sections are not unlike some of the *questiones*, and there is no reason, so far as I can see, to doubt that Langton wrote the work. On the other hand it shows more systematic effort than he generally exerted. He displays his argument logically—statement, arguments for and against, solution—and here approaches nearer to the method of his contemporary Curzon than he does in his *questiones*.[1] The distinction drawn in the manuscript between the *summa* and the *questiones* is sound. In the middle of the twelfth century Robert of Melun, a teacher on the Mont St. Geneviève, who afterwards became bishop of Hereford (1163–7), had insisted that a work was not a *summa* if it did not articulate its subject clearly; brevity was necessary, but in trying to be brief the writer must never forget that he should distinguish and expound with precision every particular.[2] By the end of the century, when the word *summa* was used in speaking of collections of theological *sentences* and *questiones* it was very desirable to apply a test of this kind in order to distinguish a systematic treatise from a series of casual discussions. The use of this term to describe Langton's treatise is, therefore, significant; it betrays a consciousness of development in method, such as Robert of Melun, neglected as this penetrating scholar was, had tried to promote.

Although the other and later manuscripts always describe Langton's *questiones* as his *summa*, possibly because

[1] On Curzon's method see Grabmann, ii. 494–5 and the authorities there cited.　　　　　　　　　　　　　　[2] Grabmann, ii. 341 note.

they had been recast into a more orderly whole, I shall act upon the warning of the Cambridge manuscript, and refer to these lectures or discussions as *questiones* and *questiones* alone.

If we follow up the hint given by the index and analyse the contents of the twenty-two quires in the Cambridge manuscript, we find that the *questiones* fall into several groups.

A. The first six quires, written in a beautiful small hand, form one group. The last folio is blank, but on its verso a chapter is inserted in a hand very like that of the *corrector* of the preceding *questiones*. It is entitled 'de hoc nomine *Deus*', and deals with the same theme as the little *Summa* does. It is indexed.

B. The next six quires (7–14) also form one group.[1] Here the last four folios were blank when the index was made, for the three questions, written in three distinct hands, now found on it, are not indexed.

C. Quires 15–17 form a third group. The last folio is blank.

D. Quires 18–19 form a fourth group. The verso of the last folio is blank. This is the section which was omitted from the index, or rather indexed last.

E. Quires 20–2 form a fifth and last group. To these groups (containing about 250 *questiones*) should be added the group or groups of 114 *questiones* which, as the index shows, at one time preceded them. The scribes, therefore, had over 360 *questiones* to transcribe, including, of course, many duplicates and variants. The index, I should add, appears to be written in a contemporary hand, from which it follows that the whole collection must have been formed from various manuscripts at an early date, and was not the result of slow accretion. It looks as though several scribes were at work copying different groups of sentences, and the handwritings of the marginalia suggest that the scribes may have corrected each other's work.

With very great diffidence I venture to think that we

[1] ff. 219–78^v.

have here the actual process of collecting from various reports, the work of a famous master. There is little or no evidence[1] that the master arranged the work himself in the first instance. I will take one example. In the twelfth quire in section B, two *questiones* on fasting follow each other. The first is repeated in the twenty-first quire in section E, and comparison shows that in the twelfth quire it has been made longer by the addition of twenty-two lines from an entirely different question 'de relaxationibus', which is found in the nineteenth quire in section D. The second question on fasting in the twelfth quire stops short in the middle of a sentence, and a space of fifteen lines is left. The same question, with some variations and much abbreviated, also is repeated, but this time before the other, in the twenty-first quire, where it runs on smoothly to the end and does not stop short. It seems to follow that the master had two lectures on fasting, and that his reporters inserted them in two different collections.[2] Gaps, sometimes filled in later, sometimes left blank, frequently occur, especially in the first three groups, and the whole work required and received careful revision from the correctors. Occasionally, both in the margin and in the index, a cross reference is made, when the same question occurs in more than one place.

A recent writer has said, with a good deal of truth, that whereas 'to-day the publication of a work is the beginning

---

[1] It is tempting to suggest that some of the insertions and marginalia, in a more cursive hand, are Langton's own, but there is no evidence; and the fact that some of the later quires are written in this or a very similar hand tends to a contrary conclusion. On the other hand the first part (A) may well have been copied from a later recension prepared by Langton or under his direction. The second part (B) was glossed before the copyist had it. No certain inference can be drawn from the use of phrases such as 'istud tamen plenius explicatur in alia questione' (f. 201^v, section A); 'ut in sequenti questione habetur' (f. 240^v, section B).

[2] Cambridge MS., f. 259^r–259^v is the same as the *second* half of a question on ff. 337^v–338^r, with the addition of twenty-two lines which come on f. 317^r (beginning with the thirteenth line of the second column); f. 260^r (another *questio* on fasting) is the same as the *first* half of 337^v–338^r, but stops short.

as a rule of discussion, in the Middle Ages publication marked the culmination of a long tournament in the lecture rooms and schools'.[1] In the twelfth century the rules of this, as of other kinds of tournaments, were not far advanced, but it is clear that lectures were not uninterrupted and were not intended to be monologues. The *questiones* of Odo of Ourscamp, printed by Pitra in 1888, show how in the time of the Lombard, the scholars raised issues in the course of a discussion begun by the master. At times it seems as though another master was taking part in the debate. The report was made by a scholar, presumably the *clericus* or *prepositus*, and the treatment of a *questio*, though more informal, must have been rather like the debate on a *quodlibet* in the thirteenth century.[2] If this was so, it is easy to understand why we have variant versions of the same question, why some subject was sometimes treated more than once in different ways, how different titles could be attached to the same question, and how the master's teaching could survive in various collections, some long, some short, some arranged in one way, some in another. The Cambridge manuscript of Langton's questions abounds in examples of all these results.[3] That the Paris manuscripts do not, and that the *questiones* of other masters do not, is due to the fact that at some date the material was revised, duplicates omitted, and some sort of system introduced. Any one who has studied the history of the work of Duns Scotus or of Wyclif can recall parallels from later times.[4] In Lang-

---

[1] H. B. Workman, *John Wyclif* (1926), i. 258.

[2] Grabmann, ii. 25–6; P. Glorieux, *La littérature quodlibétique de 1260 à 1320* (Bibliothèque Thomiste, v, Kain, 1925).   [3] See Appendix III.

[4] That Duns Scotus gave two sets of lectures on the *Sentences* at Paris is suggested by recent examination of the manuscripts; see C. Balic in *Revue d'histoire ecclésiastique*, xxii. 563–6 (July 1926), and F. Pelster, in *Zeitschrift für Kathol. Theologie*, li. 79 (1927). Again, Wyclif's *De Ecclesia* (1377–8) seems to have comprised various elements of different dates (see Loserth's edition for the Wyclif Society, 1885, p. xxv) and all his writings were later arranged in a more or less systematic Corpus. See the Vienna Catalogues printed by Buddensieg in the *Polemical Works*, i, pp. lix ff. (Wyclif Society, 1883).

ton's own day, Robert Curzon obviously revised his own
work. He perhaps lectured more systematically. He arranged his *questiones* on a deliberate plan; for example, he
makes the sections on penitence precede those on the
sacraments, for John the Baptist with his call to repentance was a forerunner of Christ.[1] Each of his questions is
long, subdivided into chapters, and each argument is pursued in scholastic fashion. He was altogether more 'academic' than Langton. Langton frequently tried to observe
the rules—which were taking shape in his time—of statement, argument, counter argument, discussion, solution;
and he tried in his *summa* to write a systematic little
treatise on divinity, but he rarely succeeded in keeping to
a scheme. When he puts a question and then curtly replies 'I do not know', or when he lets himself go on a long
series of queries which have a practical rather than a
logical bearing on his theme, we can almost see him sitting
among his pupils. No wonder the titles and rubrics sometimes get mixed, or that one question sometimes runs into
another in the Cambridge manuscript.

If I am right in this analysis, the happy survival of the
Cambridge manuscript helps us to vindicate Langton's
claim to the *questiones* as a whole, although they appear in
the other manuscript in such different sequences, with
striking textual variations and variations in content. It
would require a long and arduous examination to discover
on what plan, if any, the other manuscripts are arranged.
One of the Paris manuscripts, which was left to the Sorbonne by the well-known master Gerard of Abbeville (d.
1271), begins with the question 'Utrum homo possit resurgere in tanta caritate a quanta cecidit'. This manuscript or its original established a text, for the Arras and
Avranches manuscripts begin in the same way. But in the
other Paris manuscript, which belonged to the priory of

---

[1] Bibliothèque Nationale, MS. Lat. 3203, f. 1, cited by G. Lefèvre, *Le
traité 'de usura' de Robert de Courçon* (Lille, 1902), p. ii. For an account of
Robert's *Summa* see Hauréau, *Notices et extraits*, i. 168–85, and cf. above,
p. 56

St. Victor, this question appears as the 106th, and in the Cambridge manuscript it comes in the last section. Again the last *questio* in the Bamberg manuscript 'on extreme unction' comes in the first section (the sixth quire) of the Cambridge manuscript. Yet, so far as I have been able to compare them, the questions in the various manuscripts generally come somewhere, in some form or other, in one or other of the Cambridge groups, and the text is identical in a number of cases, sufficient to justify us in regarding the whole *corpus* of material as substantially Langton's work—a more or less accurate presentation of his teaching.

The later English bibliographers knew of works by Langton on penitence and penance, a theme which has a large share in the second and fifth sections of the Cambridge text, and apparently in the Douai manuscript. Is it possible that these were versions of some of the *questiones*? Similarly the Rouen text (102 chapters) and the Laon text are described as *summae* on the virtues and vices; and it would be interesting to discover if they correspond to the numerous questions in the Cambridge and Paris texts on ethical problems. I have not examined these manuscripts and cannot express any opinion.

Returning to the Cambridge text, I am inclined to think that the first section is a more mature and deliberate collection of questions than the rest. It does not repeat itself. Some of the quotations from the Scriptures have references to the new division into chapters.[1] Moreover, in this section, Langton quotes his contemporaries, Prepositinus and Peter of Corbeil,[2] who, so far as I have noted, are not quoted in the later sections. Peter of Corbeil was

---

[1] f. 175ᵛ: ' Item xlv Isa. Ve qui contradicit factori suo [Isaiah xlv. 9]. xxiii numeri Non est Deus quasi homo ut mentiatur, nec ut filius hominis ut mutetur [Numbers xxiii. 19].

Item Samuel xv primi regum. Triumphator in Isrel non parcet et penitudine non flectetur [1 Kings (Samuel) xv. 25].

[2] f. 192ᵛ. This passage is inserted in a gap by a later hand and flows over into the margin and on to the schedule; but it appears to be copied from the original. The handwriting occurs frequently in marginal notes throughout the manuscript.

a very distinguished man, canon of Notre-Dame, and an old teacher who had at one time had the future Pope Innocent III among his pupils. He became bishop of Cambrai in 1199 and archbishop of Sens in the succeeding year. He was in his earlier days a chaplain of Philip Augustus.[1] Langton refers to him in a discussion on the first death of Lazarus. Prepositinus, to whom Langton was more indebted, became chancellor of Paris in 1206, but had been teaching for some years in the schools. His commentary on the *Sentences* was one of the few books of this period which had permanent influence on the later scholasticism. It was read and quoted long after the work of Peter of Poitiers and Langton and Curzon was forgotten.[2] Yet in view of the preference of Peter the Chanter and his followers for ancient authorities, it may be doubted if Langton would use his contemporaries until the later years of his teaching, when their authority was fully established. It is always possible of course that he revised some of his questions during the period of his exile (1207–13). All this, however, is pure surmise. It would be foolish to go farther in an attempt to establish the priority in time of the various versions of the *questiones*. The copyist of the second section evidently did not work upon an untouched text. In a few places he finds room for a gloss within the space of the columns, a fact which proves that he had a glossed text before him. Some one with more pretensions to methodical analysis than Langton made, had possessed this batch of questions and commented upon them.

Langton, as one would expect, was very conventional in his use of authorities. The Bible, the gloss, St. Augustine, St. Ambrose, St. Gregory, are his chief guides. He quotes Bede and Rabanus Maurus and knew his Boethius and the 'old logic' of Aristotle. His references to St. John

---

[1] See *Histoire littéraire de la France*, xvii. 223–8, and Chevalier, *Bio-bibliographie*, s.v.; Peter of Corbeil, as archbishop, presided over the council of bishops who issued the decrees of 1210. For his political career, Cartellieri, *Philipp II August*, iv. 55, 66, 501.

[2] Grabmann, ii. 552 ff. and works there mentioned.

Damascenus and St. Chrysostom probably came not directly from the translations of Burgundio of Pisa, but from the *Sentences*.[1] Indeed, he did not hesitate to borrow from the *Sentences* quotations from the well-known fathers, even Augustine, and he frequently acknowledges his debt.[2] Peter the Lombard, the author of the *Sentences*, is *the* master, or occasionally 'the philosopher'. Now and then he refers to the life of a saint, e.g. the famous story of St. Giles and Charles the Great,[3] or to the Decretum and papal letters and church councils. In a discussion of transubstantiation he quotes Peter Comestor or Manducator.

'The Manducator used to say that when all has been said, all has been done, and would go no further (*nec aliud ibi dicere volebat*), but his followers used to say that the transubstantiation of the bread is not prior to that of the wine.'[4]

In previous lectures Langton's questions have given us examples of his thought, and they will give other examples later. Before I close the story of his life and teaching in Paris, I will briefly illustrate some of his more intimate and personal traits.

In his discussion of transubstantiation he had occasion to touch on several of those problems of which Pope Innocent said 'subtiliter magis quam utiliter possent inquiri'.[5] To the question whether transubstantiation takes place if the wine is not mixed with water, he replies:

'I dare not commit myself (*hic non audeo sententiam precipitare*). The master says in the Sentences that it does, so long as the celebrant intends no heresy. In that case he must be punished.

---

[1] Cf. Ghellinck, op. cit., p. 271; and, for the knowledge of these Fathers, the same writer in *Miscellanea Francesco Ehrle*, v. 345–7.

[2] f. 181r: 'Item augustinus dicit in quarto libro de trinitate et auctoritas illa est in sententiis'; f. 211r: 'Utrum quatuor cardinales uirtutes sint in patria. Hic asserit Augustinus. Unde sicut habes in tercio sententiarum'; f. 228r: Langton, after saying 'Augustinus dicit deus predestinat iustos', points out later that, according to the *Sentences*, St. Augustine included this among his retractations; f. 292v: 'Sicut legitur in sententiis phylosophus ita describit liberum arbitrium'.

[3] f. 312r.   [4] f. 206v.

[5] Migne, *Patrologia Latina*, ccxvii, col. 870.

Cyprian the martyr says on the contrary that it does not, because it was revealed to him that the Lord used mixed wine; perhaps the wine of Palestine is such that only mixed wine is drunk and the Lord gave this to his disciples at supper.' [1]

This is not the only occasion on which Langton suspended or gave only a hesitating judgement. He was rather more bold in following Prepositinus on the text 'If thy brother sin against thee, correct him.' This command seemed to be opposed to the view, enforced so strongly by the authority of the canon law, that a man cannot be both witness and judge, and that one witness is not sufficient for a condemnation. Prepositinus argued that Christ was speaking to the apostles and that in this respect they are typified by the inhabitants of a cloister. For it is the custom in monasteries that if one monk knows anything against a brother he is to report it to others who will admonish the erring brother. If the latter is recalcitrant, he is treated as a heathen, for he is not allowed to eat with his fellows, or is imprisoned and even deprived of his habit. The pope endorses this practice when in monastic visitations he forces every monk to reveal on oath what he knows; nevertheless, the visiting prelates are ordered to add one witness. In other words, in such cases witness and accuser are the same, as in the case of Naboth and Susanna, whose condemnation would have been judicial if the witnesses (and the accusers are called witnesses) had spoken the truth. The situation, says Prepositinus, is not confined to the choister; 'a sin against God is peculiarly an offence against God's worship, and if a crime is such as to tend to the damage of the whole Church or is heresy, I am bound to do what I can to stop it, even though I alone know about it.' [2] I quote this passage because its doctrine may have helped to shape parts of the later procedure against heretics.

Cambridge MS., f. 207ʳ: 'tamen Cyprianus martir dicit quod non, quia reuelatum fuit ei quod mixtum uinum transubstantiauit dominus, cum uinum terre palestine ita forte est quod non nisi mixtum bibitur et tale dedit dominus discipulis in cena.'　　　[2] f. 171ᵛ.

In his discussion on prayer Langton argues that, while prayers for definite persons are more generally effective by reason of the greater devotion inspired, such prayers are also as effective for all as they are for the persons prayed for, 'just as a lamp or candle is as useful to those who did not have it made as for those who did. But, he adds, this should not be preached to the laity.'[1] The reference to the laity is very significant. Langton did not wish to hurt the popular belief in the peculiar efficacy of special prayer.

He employs another simple illustration—as simple as that of the candle—to explain how in Gehenna every one is equally deserving of his punishment. A boy carrying a small stone is in a better case than a strong peasant carrying a heavy millstone on his shoulders. We must regard not the strength only, but the ratio between strength and burden. All the damned equally deserve their punishment, and this is secured by adjusting the penalty to the gravity of the sin.[2] Here strength corresponds to sin, the burden to punishment.

Langton's common sense was sometimes revealed with a lighter touch. He brushes aside some frivolous instances of 'scandals'. 'Some people may find scandal in my lectures, but they have their remedy, and therefore, I am not bound to stop.'[3] 'A parishioner is scandalized by having to pay tithes. It is his duty to pay. Make him.'[4] In another question, the problem is put whether the devil sins with all his might.[5] The argument follows:

'The devil wishes to be either good or bad. If the former, when

[1] f. 264[r]: 'hoc autem non est laicis predicandum'. Cf. f. 317[r] in a questio de relaxationibus: 'Dicimus quod non oportet quod omnia uera dicantur, sicut omnia opera facta ex eadem caritate sunt eque meritoria uite eterne; et non est dicendum quia, si hoc, forte minus essent homines proni ad magna opera facienda', &c. [2] f. 194[r].

[3] f. 221[v]: 'Item licet quidam scandalizentur de lectione mea, quia ibi potest esse recompensatio, non teneor cessare.'

[4] f. 221[v]: 'Item parrochianus scandalizatur de solutione decimarum, tamen quia tenetur ad hoc compelle eum.'

[5] In a questio de accionibus: 'queritur utrum dyabolus omni suo motu peccat.'

he does evil he must feel the sting of a biting conscience, that is to say, *synderesis*; and authority says that *synderesis* is extinct in the devil. If he wishes to be bad, he wishes to deserve punishment and so to be punished.'

The solution of this last dilemma follows :

'It may well be that the devil is so obstinate that he wishes to be bad and yet does not wish to be punished.' [1]

The theological and moral teaching of Langton was effective in its time. When Pope Innocent made him a cardinal in 1206, he was presumably the most outstanding figure in the schools of Paris—'nominatissimus doctor theologus' as Alberic of Trois-Fontaines terms him.[2] His *questiones* were occasionally copied in the thirteenth and fourteenth centuries; a well-known Paris master had them and left them to the Sorbonne. Yet as a theologian he was soon forgotten. As a preacher and commentator Langton had a wider reputation [3]—the kind of reputation which in the end obscures identity. His name was twisted into 'Linguatonans'. His sermons sometimes appear under the name of Stephen with the Tongue of Thunder. The name of a little Lincolnshire village achieved this unreal, fleeting, apocalyptic fame.

[1] f. 229ᵛ. Eckhart gives a good definition of synderesis: 'The spark of the soul, which is sent there by God and is his light striking down from above . . . ever opposed to anything ungodly; not a power of the soul, as some theologians make it, but a permanent tendency to good. According to the masters, this light is of the nature of unceasing effort; it is called synderesis, that is to say, a joining to and turning from. It has two works. One is remorse for imperfection. The other work consists in ever more invoking good, and bringing it direct into the soul, even though she be in hell.' Pfeiffer's *Meister Eckhart*, translated C. de B. Evans (London, 1924), p. 88.

[2] Above, p. 30, note 3. Cf. the letter of Honorius III on behalf of Michael Scot, 16 Jan. 1224 (*C.U.P.*, i, part 1, p. 105, no. 48): addressing Langton 'qui inter ceteros per orbem scientia preditos eminenti litteratura et profundioris prorogatiua doctrine coruscas.'

[3] 'Étienne Langton, l'ami des Cisterciens, est à Villers en Brabant, en 1309, et fréquemment cité dans les relevés d'Angleterre, de Normandie, de France, etc., jusqu'en Autriche; mais il manque à Avignon en 1375.' J. de Ghellinck: 'En marge des catalogues des bibliothèques médiévales', in *Miscellanea Francesco Ehrle*, v. 357.

IV

CUSTOM AND OPINION IN ENGLAND
I. THE DISPUTE WITH ROME

THE story of King John's quarrel with the pope has frequently been told. I do not intend to tell it here. In this chapter I shall try to illustrate English opinion— the views of the king and his barons, and of Stephen Langton as the representative of the Church. Before we turn to Langton's share in the preparation of the Great Charter, we must know something about these views, and examine the measure of their dependence upon custom and authority.

In any case there is little to be said about Langton's life before his return to England. He became cardinal priest with the title of S. Chrysogonus in 1206; he attested a papal letter on 22 June of this year.[1] He was influential in the curia and is said by one English chronicler to have continued his theological teaching at Rome.[2] In December he was elected archbishop of Canterbury by the monks of Christ Church in the pope's presence, and he was consecrated at Viterbo on 17 June 1207. He was not able to live in England until July 1213, six years after his consecration. During these years he was either busy with negotiations with pope, king, and clergy, or living in retirement at Pontigny, the great Cistercian monastery in the diocese of Auxerre. St. Thomas of Canterbury had found refuge there. Another very distinguished visitor, the queen mother, Adela of Champagne, had recently been to Pontigny. In 1205 the Cistercian general chapter rebuked the abbot John because he had received the queen with

[1] Potthast, *Regesta pontificum Romanorum*, i. 463. He attested again on 27 March 1207.

[2] *Memoriale Walteri de Coventria*, ed. Stubbs (Rolls Series), ii. 198: 'a domino Papa ad ecclesiam Romanam, ubi prebendatus erat et theologiam docebat, accitus.'

too many ladies, and had decorated the church with too
elegant a pavement. She died in June 1206, and was
buried in the abbey.¹ It now became the archbishop's
head-quarters for six years. He was joined by some of his
suffragans, one of whom, Mauger of Worcester died and
was buried there in 1212. In a charter of 1222, granting
to the abbey an annual revenue of fifty marks from the
church at Romney, Stephen refers to the hospitality so
cheerfully and generously given to him during his exile;²
and a tract written at Pontigny on St. Thomas's promise
that one of his successors would reward the abbey refers
to Stephen's distress that he was so long unable to acquit
his obligation to his hosts.³ Yet Stephen was not in Pontigny all the time.⁴ We find him dealing with the monks
of Canterbury, who had been received, seventy in number,
by the monks of St. Bertin. The prior with sixteen monks
had lived at St. Bertin for over a year; the archbishop then
arranged for the distribution of most of them in other
French abbeys.⁵ At intervals during 1209 and 1210 the
archbishop was engaged in attempts to heal the breach

¹ *Gallia Christiana*, xii (1770), cols. 440, 445; the 'Historia Pontiniacensis
monasterii' in Martène and Durand, *Thesaurus novus anecdotorum*, iii
(1717), cols. 1243, 1245; see for Adela's death Cartellieri, *Philipp II
August*, iv. 252.

² In the *Historia Pont.* (Martène and Durand, iii, c. 1246) with charters
of St. Edmund Rich and archbishop Boniface. The rector of Romney 'sub
pena beneficii sui' was to pay an annual rent to the monks of Pontigny,
who later had an alien priory at New Romney, founded by John Mansel,
provost of Beverley (1257). This afterwards came to All Souls College,
Oxford, in the reign of Henry VI.

³ Martène and Durand, iii, c. 1875. Cf. Prior Bertrand's Life of St.
Edmund Rich, ibid., c. 1813.

⁴ About 1175 Guichard, archbishop of Lyons, conceded to Richard,
archbishop of Canterbury, and his successors 'terram de Quiniaco cum
omnibus pertinenciis suis et domum in claustro nostro' (deed A 25 in
muniments of dean and chapter of Canterbury, Hist. MSS. Commission,
5th Report, Appendix, pp. 448–9). I cannot discover whether this refuge
was still open to Langton, nor any evidence that he used it.

⁵ John of Ypres, Chronicon sancti Bertini, in Martène and Durand, op.
cit., iii, cols. 688, 689. (Cf. Pope Innocent's letter to the abbot and convent
of St. Bertin, 15 Sep. 1207; Potthast, no. 3177.)

with England. The pope on 12 January 1209 authorized
him to visit England with the executors of the interdict,
the bishops of London, Ely, and Worcester. Mass could
be celebrated in a low voice wherever they went.[1] Promising negotiations had been opened on King John's behalf
by the abbot of Beaulieu. The pope had been hopeful,
and had sent to the abbot of the Cistercian abbey of
Clairmarais, near Saint Omer, a *privilegium* with strict injunctions that it was not to be opened or forwarded without instructions.[2] He was now beginning to realize that
the king was not prepared to endorse the terms arranged
by his envoy. A conference of bishops, barons, and others
was at last held at Dover in September, and a form of
peace was sealed. The king thereupon sent for Langton,
who arrived at Dover on 2 October. John, however,
would not come nearer than Chilham, the negotiations
were suspended, the archbishop returned, and soon afterwards the king was excommunicated.[3] On 20 December
Langton was at Melun, where he consecrated Hugh of
Wells as bishop of Lincoln.[4] In the following year Langton
was again summoned, but on this occasion got no farther
than Wissant, where he was warned by his friends in
England not to proceed. He had an interview, as fruitless

[1] Canterbury chronicle in *Gervase of Canterbury*, ed. Stubbs, ii, pp.
xcvii, xcviii.

[2] Ibid., pp. cx, cxii. St. Thomas came to Clairmarais after his flight
from England. It was conveniently near to Gravelines (for Sandwich) and
Wissant (for Dover). The abbey had some disputes with the count of
Boulogne, Renaud of Dammartin, in this period: see Malo, *Renaud de
Dammartin* (1908), pp. 94, 101.

[3] *Gervase of Canterbury*, ii. 104; and Langton's memorandum, in the
same volume, p. cxi. The bishop of Arras and the abbot of St. Védast
declared John excommunicated at Arras in the presence of the bishops of
London and Ely, 'adstante cleri et populi multitudine'; *Chronicon sancti
Bertini*, loc. cit.

[4] For the circumstances of Hugh's election and consecration and his
desertion of King John, see Armitage Robinson, *Somerset Historical Essays*
(1921), pp. 153, 154. Gerald of Wales makes interesting reference to Hugh
and his consecration in the dedication to Langton of his Vita S. Remigii
and Vita Hugonis (*Opera*, vii. 5).

as the last, with two ecclesiastical envoys from the king (October 1210).[1] This seems to have been his last attempt at a personal settlement. In September 1211 he was in Paris, for we are told by the Margan annalist that he buried there the great baron, William of Briouze, who died in exile at Corbeil (4 September).[2] If he had been in contact with William during his last days, he would probably have become aware, not only of the persecution to which the house of Briouze had been subjected by King John, but also of the circumstances of the murder of Arthur of Brittany.[3] Other news from England would strengthen his belief that nothing but force would avail. In the latter months of 1212 he made a journey to Rome with the bishops of London and Ely, the two survivors of the papal commission. When the three bishops returned in January 1213 they brought with them a papal sentence of deposition. At a great council in Paris the papal legate Pandulf authorized King Philip to attack England by a holy war on behalf of the suffering Church.[4] But, as we know, Pandulf had his private instructions. John was brought to reason and the archbishop at length reached Canterbury, not under the protection of a French army, but as the adviser of a penitent king.

The trouble had arisen over the question of election to bishoprics. This was a wider issue than that of freedom of election; it involved also the demand of ecclesiastical reformers for canonical and valid elections. Now this question was not a matter of occasional significance, it was present everywhere in Christendom and all the time. When Peter the Chanter lectured King Philip of France

---

[1] *Gervase of Canterbury*, ii. 105–6, and Langton's memorandum, pp. cx–cxii.

[2] *Annales Monastici*, i. 31; cf. v. 40 and the index; *Roger of Wendover* (ed. Coxe), iii. 237.

[3] Powicke, *Loss of Normandy* (1913), pp. 468–71, for the view that William of Briouze was cognisant of the circumstances of Arthur's death.

[4] *Roger of Wendover*, iii. 241–3; Cartellieri, iv. 342; Gütschow, *Innocenz III und England* (1904), p. 164.

about the contrast between old and new elections, when Langton deplored the tendency of monastic chapters to elect monks as bishops, or in his *questiones* emphasized the necessity of perfect charity in prelates,[1] they were speaking of things of vital importance in the mind of every canonist and every serious ecclesiastic. A busy pope like Innocent III was advising the Church on such points very frequently; his quarrel with King John would appear to him a very serious case among hundreds of cases relating to elections in all parts of Europe.[2] I doubt if the insularity of English historical inquiry from the days of William Prynne onwards has had as misleading consequences in any matter as in its treatment of this quarrel.

We must, to start with, rid our minds of any idea that the pope was only concerned to exert his authority. He was concerned to see that the law of the Church was carried out. And we have only to turn over the pages of the *Decretum* or of the letters of Pope Alexander III or Innocent III to see how complicated the traditions were and how carefully the law was being straightened out. Early in his pontificate, for example, Innocent dealt with the difficult case of Mauger, bishop of Worcester, the bishop who was afterwards one of his commissioners in the time of the interdict and who died at Pontigny in 1212. Mauger was of illegitimate birth, yet he had the qualities which make a good bishop. The pope's treatment of the problem was masterly and definite; it was afterwards incorporated in the Decretals of Gregory IX.[3] The fundamental object was the election of men of the best character, and if possible, of learning and experience. As Langton had quoted in his Paris lectures, 'quod tales eligendi sunt qui in conspectu populi optimi judicentur'.[4]

---

[1] Cambridge MS., f. 196ʳ.

[2] For disputed elections, &c., in England and Normandy see Gütschow, pp. 85–126; Packard, 'King John and the Norman Church', in the *Harvard Theological Review*, xv. 15–40 (January 1922).

[3] Decretals of Gregory IX, lib. i, tit. vi, c. 20; Potthast, *Regesta pontificum Romanorum*, i. 91, no. 953 (February 1200).

[4] Cambridge MS., f. 196ʳ.

In early times bishops had been elected by the clergy and people of their city. In general they were expected to be men familiar with the city, grave and mature. The people had an advisory rather than a controlling part in the election.[1] As time went on, the growing unity of the Church involved changes. The local significance of the bishop was merged in his more general or, at the least, his national importance. The complicated issues raised by his double capacity as a political adviser with temporal estates and as a prelate made it necessary to safeguard elections against interference, to eliminate everything of the nature of simony, to lay down definite rules of procedure. The development which followed sometimes had curious results; it might prevent its own object of securing the best available men for the episcopate; then a fresh set of complexities arose, bringing new decisions, new developments in the law. The main change was the gradual substitution of the chapter for the clergy and people as the electorate. Both methods can be traced, for example, in the letters of Ivo of Chartres, in the early twelfth century, but the later method, election by the chapter, was fully accepted by canonists by the time of Gregory IX a century later. It involved the elimination of outsiders, even of bishops. One of the results of the controversy over the successor of Hubert Walter in Canterbury was a definite ruling by the pope that the provincial bishops had no claim to share in the election of an archbishop of Canterbury.[2] Election by chapter, moreover, involved a definite procedure, and this was laid down in the canon 'quia propter' of the Lateran Council of 1179. The election was to be made by 'major et sanior pars' of the chapter—votes, in other words, must be given individually so that they could be weighed. The canonists found great difficulty, as they well might, in explaining the meaning

---

[1] Esmein, 'L'unanimité et la majorité dans les élections canoniques' in *Mélanges Fitting* (Montpellier, 1907), i. 371–9, and the texts there cited, for what follows.

[2] Potthast, no. 2939 (20 Dec. 1706). The text is in *Wendover*, iii. 188–90.

of this procedure. The traditional view, in electoral matters—the texts were in the *Decretum*—was that *sanioritas*, even in a minority, should prevail; the general view in Langton's time and afterwards was that number, zeal or motive, and merit—merit both in the elected person and of the better nourished (*pinguiores*) votes of the wiser electors—should all be considered, or at least two out of the three, if an election was to be regarded as valid. In practice both the *major* and the *sanior pars* was generally required. It is obvious that the new procedure depended for its smooth working upon the supervision of the Church. It could not have been admitted unless the recognition of unity under papal authority and the practice of appeal or reference to Rome had become general. In this sense it helped to establish papal influence and to emphasize the non-local character of the episcopate.

As an illustration I take the disputed election to the archbishopric of Tours, decided by the pope himself in 1207, that is, during the quarrel with John of England. The papal letters state that one section of the chapter had elected the chanter of Paris, John of Vitry, but this section was in a minority, it was inferior in authority and it had not feared to act 'extra capitulum' (like the monks of Canterbury who elected their sub-prior Reginald at midnight in 1205). He accordingly quashes this election. Another section, which had elected the dean, John de Faye, was both wiser and more numerous (*auctoritate longe maior erat et numero*), and, as he hears nothing but good of him, the pope, acting on the common counsel of the cardinals, confirms the election.[1]

The development of this procedure, and of the canonical system in general, raised the issue between the lay and ecclesiastical powers to a new level, from the region of custom to the realm of law. When King John granted free elections in 1214, he surrendered the practice which he had observed, in accordance with the Constitutions of

[1] *Gallia Christiana*, xiv (1856), cols. 100 ff.

Clarendon, as late as the summer of 1213.[1] Delegates of the chapter were no longer to appear before the king and elect their superiors. English custom gave way before the law of the Church. And, as law must in the long run be met by law, the attitude of the State to the hierarchy was, in due course, expressed in legal terms which in their turn implied a restatement of political theory. But this lay a long way ahead in John's reign. Centuries of compromise separated the grant of free elections from the legislation of Henry VIII. The delay was due in part to the fact that the Church, in its work of definition, had no intention of depriving itself of the co-operation of the lay power. Nobody who knew the *Decretum* could adopt that attitude. It would have been inconsistent with the nature of society. Although the texts are inconsistent and caused Gratian some difficulty, the general outcome is clear; elections must be free and lawfully conducted, but the acquiescence, and even the advice, of the lay ruler is of the greatest importance; it safeguards the harmony which should pervade society, and, like the undertaking between the Emperor and a new pope, is a symbol of the unity of the body of Christ.[2] In 1211 the legate explained to King John that one of the reasons why the election of Reginald, the subprior, had been declared invalid by Pope Innocent was that he was regarded by king and kingdom as an unsuitable candidate for the archbishopric. The 'licence to elect', the necessity of action with royal acquiescence, is com-

---

[1] To what extent elections took place in the royal presence after 1164 requires careful examination. It is clear that the practice was not always followed. Alexander III trounced Archbishop Richard (1174–84) for *confirming* elections 'in ipsa camera regis' (Decretals, lib. ii, tit xxviii, c. 25). Gerald of Wales gives a caustic description of the election of the prior of Wenlock in 1176 to St. David's 'in camera regis, coram lecto suo ipso praesente, cum stipatoribus suis' (*Opera*, i. 44). John in 1211 spoke of this procedure as traditional and normal (below, p. 86). In July 1213 he ordered elections to several sees and abbeys to be made in this way (*Rotuli litt. clausarum*, i. 146–50 *passim*, and see Norgate, *John Lackland*, p. 192).

[2] See the texts in the Decretum, prima pars, distinctiones 61–3 (ed. Friedberg, *Corpus iuris canonici*, i. 227–47.

prised in John's charter to the Church, and, as is well known, the active co-operation of the Crown with cathedral and monastic chapters was maintained after it ceased to form an integral part of the process of election.

Co-operation under such conditions was always uneasy, and in John's reign, before any settlement was reached, it broke down entirely. Quite apart from the immediate causes of conflict, there were influences and tendencies at work during the half century after the Constitutions of Clarendon (1164–1214) which made mutual understanding between lay and ecclesiastical interests very difficult. They were closely connected with each other, and I distinguish them only for the sake of convenience.

In the first place the Church during this period had acquired an administrative unity greater than it had ever had, under the guidance of the pope with his council of cardinals and his curia. Papal writs and decisions and papal legates expounded and confirmed the papal will throughout western Europe. The system was elaborate and expensive. Gerald of Wales in his *Speculum Ecclesiae* tells a story that the Emperor Henry VI had played with a plan for the endowment of pope and cardinals with fixed incomes, to be drawn from prebends in cathedral and lesser churches.[1] A suggestion of this kind, as well as seeking to meet the expenditure of the curia, emphasized the unity of the Church. Unity implied law, and a revision of old ideas about local custom. Of course, it was impossible to eradicate custom. In 1208, for example, Pope Innocent settled a dispute which had arisen owing to the appointment of a precentor in St. Paul's by the bishop of London a few years earlier. The bishop had ordained that the new office should be endowed, saving existing rights, as similar dignities were endowed in other English cathedrals, but this was discovered to be impracticable, and the chapter pointed out that custom varied in the various

---

[1] *Opera*, iv. 302. Cf. E. Jordan in *Mélanges d'histoire du moyen âge offerts à M. Ferdinand Lot* (1925), p. 287. For the similar plan proposed by Pope Honorius III in 1225 see below, p. 158.

churches of England. In some places the precentor was a minor, in others a greater dignitary. The pope decided, thereupon, that the precentor of St. Paul's must be content with as much as he could get. His decision was regarded as important enough to justify its insertion in the later Decretals of Pope Gregory IX, where it appears in a special section (*titulus*) on custom.[1] But the general drift of this section is very different. From one point of view, certainly, custom is the best interpreter of law (*optima est legum interpres*[2]). Custom, however, must never stand in the way of natural, positive, divine law. Pope Innocent discovered that in the diocese of Poitiers ecclesiastical cases were decided by the opinion of all present, learned and unlearned, wise and foolish. He forbade the practice.[3] On another occasion he declared that no local custom or privilege could be permitted to interfere with the full operation of an interdict, for a custom of this kind would destroy the very nerve of ecclesiastical discipline.[4] Langton argued at Paris, it may be recalled, that the cases of Samson and Samuel should not be used to support the undesirable practice of dedicating small children as oblates to the monastic life—'Dicimus quod privilegia paucorum non faciunt legem communem.'[5]

As part of the divine economy, the lay power also could appeal to authority, the authority of the Scriptures, of positive law, of reason, and, as we shall see, English kings were not averse to this method of argument. But they, in comparison with the Church, were at a serious disadvantage. They were not Biblical experts, their relations with their subjects were not based upon any body of positive law (appeal, for example, to the civil law was almost closed to them), their power rested upon tradition, custom, his-

[1] Liber i, tit iv, c. 6. King John had endowed the precentorship of St. Paul's earlier (26 March 1204), but it would seem inadequately (*Rotuli Chartarum*, p. 124*b*). In 1215 Langton appointed the first precentor, Master Benedict of Sansetum, to the see of Rochester (Wharton, *Anglia Sacra*, i. 347; *Gervase of Canterbury*, ii. 109).

[2] Liber i, tit iv, c. 8.   [3] c. 3.

[4] c. 5.   [5] Cambridge MS., f. 310[r], above, p. 13.

tory. If they emancipated themselves from it, or improved upon it, then, by a kind of political alchemy, the new regulations in their turn were invested with the authority, not of the royal will, but of custom. Hence Henry II issued the Constitutions of Clarendon as an expression of custom, and John, in his fight with Rome, turned to history. He said in effect that the canon law, by overriding English custom, threatened his rights, and when he was required to prove that his rights were more important than the welfare of the Church, he had either to submit or to become a schismatic and force his people to become schismatic and deny their dependence upon the Church, in which alone they could save their souls.

He took his stand on the precedent set by a famous English bishop, Wulfstan of Worcester. Wulfstan was canonized by Pope Innocent in May 1203. The monks of Worcester had sought and obtained from the pope a careful investigation into the bishop's miracles, and the final success was doubtless assisted by the representations of Bishop Mauger, who had visited Rome in order to defend the interests of his church at Worcester in a prolonged suit with the abbey of Evesham.[1] Mauger was the bishop, to whom I have already referred, whose defect of birth had been set aside by the pope on account of his saintly life. He was a scholar and had been King Richard's physician. The canonization of his famous predecessor redounded to the fame of his church and doubtless revived interest in the stories of Wulfstan's life and miracles. Probably the best known incident in his career appeared in the life of Edward the Confessor. First told by Osbert of Clare in the reign of Henry I,[2] it was popularized by Ailred, abbot of Rievaulx, in the life of the Confessor, especially written for the occasion of the translation of the relics of the king on 13 October 1163. This had indeed

[1] Annals of Worcester in *Annales Monastici*, iv. 391, 392; Potthast, no. 1910 (14 May 1203), cf. Gütschow, op. cit., pp. 86, 87.
[2] The text is printed by Marc Bloch, 'La vie de S. Édouard le Confesseur par Osbert de Clare', in *Analecta Bollandiana*, xli (1923), pp. 116–20.

been a great occasion. King Henry II had acknowledged Alexander III as the true pope; Alexander had canonized St. Edward; and now, in the presence of the king and the leading ecclesiastics and barons of his kingdom, the new archbishop, Thomas Becket, presided over the solemn ceremony of the translation. It was an English occasion, and Ailred, probably the greatest English religious of his day, wrote as an Englishman, of King Edward. He gloried in the fact that England now had an English king, surrounded by so many English bishops and abbots. And, following Osbert of Clare, he told how, when archbishop Lanfranc tried to depose Wulfstan of Worcester because he was illiterate, the bishop had repudiated Lanfranc's right and had appealed to the dead king from whose hands he had received his staff; how Wulfstan had gone to Edward's tomb and appealed to him, and how the king had confirmed him, for when he struck the tomb with his staff, it entered the stone as though it had been pressed into liquid wax, and no man could pull it out.[1] This story, I say, must have become current again after Wulfstan's canonization. It contained a moral which King John's advisers were quick to see. When, in a last effort to bring John to reason, the pope sent his legates, Pandulf and Durand, a Templar, to England in the summer of 1211, the king was ready with his answer. At a conference at Northampton at the end of August, he rejected the papal terms and quoted an earlier letter which he had written to Innocent:

'All my predecessors conferred archbishoprics, bishoprics and abbeys in their chamber. As you may read in holy writings, the blessed and glorious king St. Edward conferred the bishopric of Worcester in his time on St. Wulfstan. When William the Bastard,

---

[1] Ailred, 'Vita Edwardi regis et confessoris', in Twysden, *Historiae Anglicanae scriptores X* (1652), cols. 405 ff. Ailred's narrative is summarized in *Wendover*, ii. 52–5. For the translation of St. Edward in 1163 see Powicke, 'Ailred of Rievaulx and his biographer Walter Daniel' (Manchester, 1922), p. 40 (reprinted from the *Bulletin of the John Rylands Library*, vi).

the conqueror of England, wished to deprive him of the bishopric, because he did not know French, St. Wulfstan replied, "You did not give me my staff, and I will not give it to you": and he went to the tomb of St. Edward and said in his mother tongue (*in lingua sua*): "Edward, you gave me my staff, and now on account of the King I cannot hold it: so I give it into your keeping: and if you can defend, defend." He fixed the staff in the tomb of worked stone, and the staff miraculously adhered to the tomb, so that only St. Wulfstan was able to pluck it out again. Moreover in our days my father conferred the archbishopric of Canterbury on St. Thomas.' [1]

The point that Wulfstan was attacked because he did not know French was a gloss by Ailred on Osbert of Clare's statement that he was illiterate. John seized on it and by implication posed as the successor, not of the bastard Conqueror, but of St. Edward the Englishman. He preferred to uphold not merely local custom, but English custom. But the Church does not allow its saints to be treated in this way. The legate took the point boldly.

'You are not Edward's successor: you are not fit to be compared with him. He protected the Church; you persecute it. We gladly allow you to be the successor of William the Bastard, for he attacked the Church by this very attempt to deprive St. Wulfstan of the bishopric of Worcester. . . . Moreover you love to observe the evil laws of William, but you despise the excellent laws of St. Edward.'

He then brushed aside with contempt the argument from the royal appointment of St. Thomas—which St.

---

[1] Annals of Burton in *Annales Monastici*, i. 211; cf. annals of Waverley, ibid., ii. 268–71. For recent discussion see Tout in the *Dictionary of National Biography*, s.v. Pandulf, and Norgate, *John Lackland*, p. 161. The dialogue between king and legate was regarded by Pauli as apocryphal, and may have been touched up. It comes from a later source. On the other hand, the Burton annalist had a large number of documents at his disposal, and I see no reason to dismiss his 'suspiciously minute and circumstantial account', as Professor Tout describes it, altogether. The king's devotion to St. Wulfstan goes to confirm it. According to Wharton, *Anglia Sacra*, ii. 524 note, the chancellor of the university of Oxford, in an oration given in 1313, referred to the passage. The chancellor at that time (1313) was Henry de Harkele; see *Snappe's Formulary*, ed. Salter (Oxford Historical Society, lxxx, 1924), p. 325.

Thomas had repudiated and King Henry had deprived of any validity as a precedent by his later surrender.

Historically—if a legend can be described as history—John had the better argument. Morally, the legate was right. The king stuck to his strange allegiance to St. Wulfstan. He committed his body to the saint's keeping, and lies to this day before the high altar in the choir of Worcester. And his little son was brought up to call St. Edward his patron saint. But we must remember that John died and Henry III was educated under the protection of a forgiving Church.

Morally, I repeat, the legate was right. He said in effect that an appeal to custom implied a respect for custom. It was impertinent in a man who had sworn to observe the law of St. Edward and who had foresworn himself ever since, to appeal to St. Edward. This brings us to a second point in our consideration of the relations between the lay and ecclesiastical powers in John's reign—the place of moral and natural law.

There is a very interesting passage in the *summa* of the Englishman, Robert Curzon, the later cardinal, who was teaching in Paris when Stephen Langton was. The passage occurs in the section on usury, which has been edited by M. Lefèvre. Curzon deals at much length with a matter, also touched upon by Langton, which their master Peter the Chanter had much at heart—the building of churches, and especially of monasteries, with money given by usurers. Usury was bad enough, but to spend the profits of usury on churches and abbeys, windows and dormitories, hermitages, hospitals and lazar houses, was a sin against the Holy Ghost. 'It is a fundamentally Christian and indissoluble rule that nobody is in a state of salvation who knowingly lives on the profits of usury, or in any way has intercourse with a thief.'[1] But suppose a bishop had the power, as he has the duty, to destroy all such buildings? They have been consecrated and their inmates may

[1] Georges Lefèvre, *Le traité 'De usura' de Robert de Courçon* (Lille, 1902), p. 37.

have nowhere to go. Curzon answers that the drastic and necessary course must be adopted as part of a definite scheme for the organization of the Christian society, clerical and lay:

'This pest can only be destroyed if a general council is called of all bishops and princes under the presidency of the Pope, where the Church and princes together shall decree under penalty of excommunication and condemnation that *everybody* must work either with soul or with body, that everyone may eat, as the Apostle commanded, the bread of his own labour and that there may be no parasitic (*curiosi*) or idle folk among us. And so all usurers and mischief makers and idlers would be done away, alms could be given, churches built and all things restored to their old state.' [1]

If the orthodox and austere theologian had been forced to elaborate his suggestion, he would, I think, have modified considerably its apparent communism. He had a chance at the great council of the Lateran a few years later, but he probably knew as well as any one how impracticable his scheme was; at any rate the Council (in its 67th decree) confined itself to a regulation designed to limit the activities of the Jews. The future was to lie with men like that notorious capitalist, William Cade.[2] I am concerned with the implications of this remarkable paragraph. The Christian world is one; the moral law is binding upon princes and bishops alike, and nothing must stand in the way of it. The moral law is natural law; it expresses the nature as well as the will of God; it is to be found in the Scriptures, and, as Langton and others pointed out in their teaching, as pope and cardinals also asserted, there is no escape from it. It is beyond the reach of the pope himself; the pope may deal with problems, but he cannot dis-

[1] Ibid., p. 35.
[2] Named by Robert Curzon (p. 71), in a passage previously printed by Hauréau and copied by Haskins in the *English Historical Review*, xxviii. 730 (October 1913). On this notorious usurer of Henry II's reign see Jenkinson and Stead, in the same volume of the *Review* (pp. 209–25), the notes by Round, Haskins, and Jenkinson, ibid., pp. 522–7, 730–2; and especially Jenkinson's paper in *Essays in History presented to Reginald Lane Poole*, pp. 190–210.

pense from it, so far as the fabric of any form of society is bound up with it. One of its cardinal injunctions is the duty of restitution—a duty emphasized (*non obstante civilis iuris rigore*) in a decree of the Lateran Council (no. 39). All wrongly gotten gains must be restored. Hence, for example, the insistence which the Church made upon the restoration of the goods of the clergy (the *ablata*) as a condition of the removal of the Interdict in England. Any idea of state right, any tampering with the issue on grounds of public convenience or policy, was incredible. King John had defied the law of nature and must make restitution. The law was not imposed by the Church on the world—rather the law was the condition of life. It might be forgotten by the churchmen who preached it and practised by the laymen who heard it. That was why St. Louis of France, with his strong sense of justice and the duty of restitution, wielded moral supremacy in the Europe of his day.

Curzon did not wish to reconstitute society, but to bring it back to its first principles. The bold thinking of popes and theologians was conservative, and was entirely different from the social ideas of the Manichaeans or the utilitarian designs of the legists and publicists who surrounded Philip the Fair, or even the Emperor Lewis of Bavaria. On the other hand it was much more precise than the vague speculations—supported though they were by almost incredible learning—of John of Salisbury and his like. The change may be attributed very largely to the development of dialectic in the schools of Paris and Bologna. By the year 1200 the ablest men in Europe, men often destined for high office, had been trained to discuss practical questions in the light of first principles. Their minds had been fed on problems and disputations. We are inclined to misinterpret the contrast between the twelfth and the thirteenth century, between John of Salisbury and St. Thomas Aquinas, because, in attributing so much to the influence of Aristotle's *Politics* and *Ethics*, we neglect the long development of dialectic methods in the schools. Thus a study of Curzon's work on usury shows that St. Thomas was as dependent upon the traditions of the schools of Paris as he was upon the *Ethics*;[1] and a similar study of Langton and his contemporaries would show, I think, that the contrast between John of Salisbury's insistence upon the duty of slaying tyrants and also upon the duty of obedience, with its unreconciled problems and inconclusiveness, and the incisive work of St. Thomas Aquinas, was not entirely due to the *Politics*.[2] Let us look at the way in which Langton dealt with some of the pressing problems of his time.

I will first take the question of taxation of the clergy. As is well known, the taxation of ecclesiastical property, other than lands held by military service, for lay purposes was not recognized until the fourteenth century. It became a burning issue after the publication of the bull *clericis laicos* by Pope Boniface VIII. Princes, however, had frequently attempted to extort aid from the clergy, and the matter was dealt with in the Council of the Lateran of 1179 (c. 19). All demands were to be resisted, unless the bishops and clergy recognize a real necessity and convenience such that, without ecclesiastical aid, the common weal would suffer; but there is to be no coercion. The Lateran Council of 1215–16 (c. 46) repeated this decision with additions. It made papal approval necessary 'propter imprudentiam quorundam', and pointed out that ecclesiastical penalties and disabilities, arising out of excommunication and other action, endured beyond the lifetime of the offending princes, unless their successors repudiated their action within a month of succession. Much had happened in the interval between the two councils. In 1188 the Saladin tithe was levied under lay control, and Philip

---

[1] Lefèvre, op. cit., pp. iii–viii.

[2] The contrast between John of Salisbury and St. Thomas is brought out in a forcible page in Poole, *Illustrations of Medieval Thought* (first edition), p. 239. In a recent paper on 'The Medieval conception of Kingship as developed in the *Polycraticus* of John of Salisbury' (*Speculum*, i. 308–37, July 1926), J. Dickinson has analysed the inconsistencies in John's treatment of kingship.

Augustus had aroused strong feeling in France by other exactions. In England the ransom of King Richard had fallen heavily on the clergy, who had also had to meet frequent demands for free gifts (*dona*).[1] Langton, teaching in Paris in the last years of the century, had dealt with the question:

A clerk is immune from liberties, but as Christ paid to avoid scandal (Matt. xvii. 26) so clerks ought to pay if there is no scandal. 'But,' adds Langton, 'I do not determine whether in such a case it is lawfully possible to abstain from giving or to refuse to give.' In what cases scandal is to be avoided or not is a bigger question (*altioris negotii*). A case is put, perhaps from contemporary French history. Suppose that a bishop has no regalia, but only tithes and offerings, and the king asks him to give him money for what he knows to be an unjust invasion of a neighbour. Ought the bishop to give? The argument in favour of giving may be found in the words of St. Ambrose 'If the emperor asks gold and silver, I give: if he asks for my church, I do not.' Or again, the bishop knows that if he fails to give he will cause the king to be scandalized and so to fall into mortal sin; ought he not to give to avoid this? On the other hand he knows that through his giving the king would sin because he has a bad cause. Ought he to give? Or he knows that, whereas the king has no *right* to the goods of his church, there are many poor people dependent on it, and that they would suffer. Ought he to give? Then comes the answer. However just the cause may be, the bishop ought *not* to give if he suspects that the Church would be burdened in consequence, that is to say, if the exaction would become the ground of a custom (*talis exactio in consuetudinem vertatur*). But if there is no such fear, and if no scandal will be caused to others, and if the king has a just cause, then assistance may be

---

[1] S. K. Mitchell, *Studies in Taxation under John and Henry III* (1914); Lunt, *The Valuation of Norwich* (1926). For France, see also Luchaire, in the *Histoire de France*, edited by Lavisse, iii, part i, pp. 241–3; Cartellieri, *Philipp II August*, passim.

given from the goods of the Church, as when the English Church ransomed Richard, king of the English. If the cause is unjust, then nothing should be given, for the land of the Church should not be involved (*inconcussa*). In the time of famine, when the lands of the Egyptians were taken by the king, the land of the priests was untouched. Christ found that the children of kings do not pay tribute (Matt. xvii. 24–5), and, as the gloss says, the children of the heavenly kingdom are much more to be absolved than those of an earthly kingdom. But are not the children of the Kingdom of Heaven all the righteous, and so if a man has a revelation that he is just, could he not refuse to pay? This is quite false. Tribute to whom tribute is due, says the apostle, and Peter says, 'Servants, be subject to your masters with all fear; not only to the good and gentle, but also to the froward' (1 Peter ii. 18). The children of the Kingdom of Heaven in the passage of Matthew are not all the righteous, but privileged persons (*persone*), apostles and their vicars, bishops and other ecclesiastics, and these undoubtedly are, or ought to be, free from taxes in every kingdom.[1]

Granted the authority, it is hard to imagine a better statement of the case. The problems are analysed simply and soundly. The warnings against obstinate refusal in all cases and against the antinomianism of the righteous are very characteristic; and we can understand from this passage on what grounds and in which way debates upon taxation were conducted in the councils of kings. Langton's discussion comes in the questio *utrum bona ecclesie a prelatis ecclesiasticis iure proprietatis an ex dispensatione possideantur*. Against much authority he concludes that the secular, as distinct from the regular, clergy have a proprietary right in the goods of the Church and are not merely *dispensatores*. A priest should not pay debts incurred before he receives a church from the revenues of that church, just as Christ did not pay tribute from the bag carried by Judas, for that was for the use of the poor.[2]

[1] Cambridge MS., f. 195ᵛ. [2] f. 195ʳ.

This means, I suppose, that goods held *nomine ecclesie*
should not be diverted from their normal uses. On the
other hand, in spite of the arguments from gospel precepts,
goods are not to be regarded as common property. 'If it
came to argument on the matter I will not agree that my
cloak belongs to any other righteous man.'[1] Yet, though
the clergy have free use of their goods, they are properly
held more responsible than laymen are. Everybody has
duties in regard to property, but a sharper reckoning will
be exacted from ecclesiastics. For one thing, in contrast
to temporal rulers, they have inalienable property, in the
name of the Church—a principle which underlies the
treatment of the goods of the Church in the decretals.[2]
And here we come to a very interesting and realistic distinction. The special responsibility of ecclesiastics follows
from the fact that they are not supposed to seek ecclesiastical promotion for the sake of lordship, but for the sake
of the duty or functions, whereas a layman, so long as he
does not fall into sin, can be ambitious for the lordship
without consideration of the functions, provided that he
submits his lordship to the divine lordship.[3]

This is the voice of the practical man. We can see why
Langton made such a good archbishop of Canterbury and
was an unsatisfactory agent of the pope. In the application of principles he saw things as they actually were. We
might search John of Salisbury's *Polycraticus* in vain for
a sentence like this. Langton did not mean, it is needless
to say, that a ruler need not consider his duties. He adds
at once—he must subject his lordship to the divine lordship, a phrase to which we shall recur. But he saw in what

[1] 'similiter dicit auctoritas quod omnia sunt iustorum et tamen si
uentum sit ad disputationem non concedam quod capa mea sit illius uel
illius iusti.'

[2] Decretals, lib. iii, tit. xiii.

[3] 'non licet eis appetere honores ecclesiasticos causa dominii sed causa
officii siue administrationis, sed laico licet, ita quod non peccabit mortaliter,
appetere aliquam dignitatem tantum causa dominii ita quod non habeat
respectum ad administrationem, dummodo dominium supponat dominio
diuino.' (f. 195ʳ.)

respect temporal lordship actually differed, without sin, from true ecclesiastical lordship. A bishop was dedicated to an office, a king could not be expected to be averse to the pleasures of power, or unresponsive to the pride of race. In another *questio*, on obedience, he makes his view clearer. He deals with a number of problems of political obedience—such as arose every day. A man is unjustly treated by a king. Ought a subject to help this man to escape? The answer depends on the nature of the community. A kingdom ruled by one man (where *omnes sunt sub uno principe*) is different from a commonwealth (*respublica*) in which all are subject to the common counsel of all. In such a kingdom it is not sinful to abstain from help, although one should help sufferers from injustice if one can. Again, a king attacks a castle unjustly. Are his people obliged to go with him? Not if the king acts *proprio motu*, for there is no disobedience then; but if there has been a formal judgement, even an unjust one, then they should go to storm the castle, for the people are not concerned with the judgement.[1] Feudal monarchy, in other words, is not like a republic. Langton does not regard the lay power with which he was familiar as an organized body, in the sense in which John of Salisbury describes all bodies politic. Obedience was due to it provided that the king acted with the counsel of his proper counsellors. Peter the Chanter also had pointed out that a greater lord could not displace a man from his subjection to the jurisdiction and lordship of a lesser lord without cause shown, that is, by a judgement in his court.[2] The king himself was subject to the higher lordship of God. He must observe custom, but he was bound by natural law. There was no absolute right as against the rights of the clergy, who ought not to pay any tax which involved them

[1] f. 237ᵛ: 'si iudicatum esset per sententiam licet iniusta esset sententia, quod castrum debeat expugnare, cum populus non habeat discutere de sententia.' See below, p. 155, for the practical importance of this point about castles.

[2] Verbum abbreuiatum, c. 44, in Migne, *Patrologia Latina*, ccv, col. 137.

in injustice or which might become a harmful precedent. What we call feudalism was not, as it is often termed, a principle of society, running through all society. It is the name which we give to a body of customary relations between rulers and vassals in a society which was also bound together by other kinds of tie, and which was subject to a higher law. The Church recognized these customs and, as Innocent III said, did not seek to interfere with them as such, but it was organized on different principles.

In this spirit Langton wrote his letter to the English people at the beginning of the struggle, in 1207. The king had rejected him as obnoxious, for he had lived in Paris in an enemy country.[1] In 1208 John said that he could never bring himself to invest him personally with the regalia, and the pope agreed that investiture might be made, without prejudice, by his own commissioners.[2] In 1211 John told the legates that, while willing to accept any other archbishop, he would never allow Stephen a safe conduct which would prevent him from hanging him if he dared to enter England.[3] Langton in 1207 wrote as an Englishman, who had always been faithful to the king, devoted to England since his earliest years with natural piety, feeling all the changes in his country's fortunes as his own. His one fear was that now he might be too partial, too considerate in this time of rebellion against the authority and doctrine of the Church. But the cause for which his predecessor St. Thomas had died was at stake, and in a way more flagrant than in the days of King Henry, who had repented of his sin and found strength and prosperity in his repentance. All should combine to retrieve this disaster. Those who cannot meet the king

[1] Pope Innocent's letter to the king, 20 May 1207 (*Gervase of Canterbury*, ii, p. lxxii): 'quia videlicet inter tuos conversatus est inimicos'.

[2] Letter of 27 May 1208 (ibid., p. xc.).

[3] Annales of Burton in *Annales Monastici*, i. 210. This, however, may be a literary allusion to the disputes about Langton's safe conduct in 1210. See above, p. 43 note 3.

face to face can do much by talks with friends and neighbours. The knightly class should remember that they had received their insignia from the Church, that 'by your swords as by ours the same church is protected'.[1] If fighting involves too much danger, they can at least use persuasion. The most dignified passage comes earlier in the letter:

'We exhort you earnestly that no one of you be accomplices of evil, as administrator or counsellor or servant. By human law a slave is not bound to serve his lord in vile deeds (*in atrocioribus*), much less you who are free. This can be shown very clearly. Those among you who have authority over others, saving your loyalty to the king, have received their homage, and if they break their oath at the will or command of lesser lords, they are regarded as traitors and perjurers. Fealty is promised or sworn to kings in precisely the same way, saving loyalty to the superior lord, the eternal king who is king of kings and lord of lords. Hence whatever service is rendered to the temporal king to the prejudice of the eternal king is undoubtedly an act of treachery. And so, my beloved children, holy church has decreed that, if a rebel persists in schism, his men are absolved from the fealty which they owe him as a most just retribution, in that, as the schismatic seeks to draw them from their fealty to the eternal king, so their fealty is withdrawn from them.'[2]

The archbishop was here addressing the barons, the king's natural counsellors. He gives in his letter the gist of his old teaching at Paris, as he applied it later when he came to examine the implications of the coronation oath. He wrote as an Englishman, just as later he deplored, as an Englishman and as an advocate of lawful custom, the king's surrender of his kingdom to the pope. Apart from a historical reference to Alexander III, there is not a single reference to the pope in this letter. The king had rebelled against the *mandata* and the *doctrina* of the Church. He had betrayed his lord, the eternal king. In some of his

[1] *Gervase of Canterbury*, ii, p. lxxxii: 'Filii karissimi, qui praediti estis officio militari, recolite quod ipsius insignia ab ecclesia recepistis, ut videlicet per vestros gladios et per nostros eadem ecclesia tutaretur.' Cf. John of Salisbury, *Polycraticus*, vi. 10 (ed. Webb, ii. 24, 25).

[2] pp. lxxxi, lxxxii.

questiones, Langton had dealt carefully with the supreme authority of the Pope, but I have noticed no discussion of his political power—a confirmation of the point made by Dr. Carlyle that until the thirteeenth century papal claims in temporal affairs were treated with great caution.[1] Indeed, it is hard to see how in Paris, in the days of Philip Augustus, any other attitude was possible, for the French bishops, while opposed to the king on moral issues, his treatment of Queen Ingeborg and his financial exactions, rallied to him when the pope tried to impose a policy in secular affairs. Langton was satisfied to teach that the head of the Church is Christ.

King John, however, was at this time face to face, not with his archbishop, but with Innocent, and Innocent, although he shared Langton's views on the supremacy of natural law and the independent operation of the feudal system, felt no hesitation in using his power as the exponent of the moral law to the full. He was an Italian, not an Englishman, and in his eyes national traditions were merely a form of local custom, patriotic allegiance a form of obligation, of comparatively small significance if the canon law was disregarded, the moral law broken. He felt no particular tenderness for John, just as he felt no sympathy with his subjects after the rebellious king had become a penitent vassal. John met his logical austerity with unscrupulous audacity. If appeal to custom was of no avail, then he would rely on principle, and authority. He had no particular interest in the matter one way or the other, and being a very clever, if short-sighted, person, his impartiality quickened his understanding. In an age of free discussion and ruthless criticism, such as his was, he was one of those people who could emancipate himself from the trammels of prejudice or reverence or loyalty. Even in the Middle Ages there were many people like him, though few quite so unscrupulous or so mean. They were like those irresponsible enlightened people who, in Elizabeth's

[1] Carlyle, *A History of Mediaeval Political Theory in the West*, iv (1922), 389–95.

day, discussed the advisability of turning England into a
republic on an Italian model.[1] John could act like a buf-
foon, but when he turned his mind to anything, he went
into it thoroughly. He got together or borrowed a select
theological library, though unfortunately we do not
know what use he and his advisers made of it.[2] One of his
clerks, Master Alexander of St. Albans, took the lead in
expounding the royal view. John Bale, the Tudor an-
tiquary, whose statement I am unable to verify, says that
Master Alexander had already argued before the pope
himself that the Church in England was free from all external allegiance, as he proved from the letters of Pope
Gregory the Great.[3] The argument, if he did use it, was,
to say the least, a bold one. The tradition current in St.
Albans, Alexander's native place, on Alexander's views,
was more conventional. The disaster which had come
upon England was due, not to the king, but to the sins of
the people. The king was the rod of God's wrath. He had
been made their prince to rule them with a rod of iron, to
break them in pieces like a potter's vessel. Alexander
proved also from Scripture that the pope had no authority
over the lay possessions of kings and princes, nor in the rule
of their subjects. God had granted to Peter the churches
alone and power in ecclesiastical affairs.[4] Taken literally

[1] Edward P. Cheyney, *A History of England from the defeat of the
Armada to the death of Elizabeth*, i. 64.

[2] *Rotuli litt. clausarum*, i. 108, 29 March 1208. The king acknowledges
the receipt from the abbey of Reading, of six volumes of the Bible, including all the Old Testament, Hugh of St. Victor on the sacraments, the
Sentences of Peter the Lombard, Augustine on the city of God and on the
third part of the Psalter, Valerianus *de moribus*, Origen on the Old Testament, and Candidus Arianus ad Marium. On 3 April John acknowledged
the receipt of his copy of Pliny (*librum nostrum*). Valerianus is presumably
the fifth-century bishop of Cemele, whose homilies are printed in Migne,
Pat. Latina, lii. 691 ff. The letter of Candidus the Arian to Marius
Victorinus is printed in Migne, viii. 1035.

[3] Bale, *Scriptorum illustrium summarium* (Basel, 1557), p. 249. I have
dealt with Master Alexander in my paper 'Alexander of St. Albans: a
literary muddle', in *Essays in History presented to R. L. Poole* (Oxford,
1927), pp. 246–60.   [4] *Roger of Wendover*, iii. 229, 230.

this doctrine does not go much farther than Langton's, or even Innocent's. The sting of it is in the implications. Alexander apparently denied any disciplinary rights in the pope over princes, any right of interference with their subjects. The clergy must suffer meekly, the Church endure as best it could any invasion of its canonical system. If the king was subject to the eternal king, he was also his instrument, his weapon for the chastisement of his people. A hundred years earlier the anonymous writer of York had gone even farther in his exaltation of the temporal over the spiritual power;[1] and the author of the *Leges Eadwardi* had described the king as 'the vicar of the Supreme King, appointed to rule and defend from harm his Kingdom and the people of God and above all Holy Church, and to destroy and pluck out evil doers.'[2] Master Alexander's view was not so logical; it approaches more nearly the views of Wyclif.

Up to a point the barons had supported John. They were unanimous in 1209 in insisting that he should not accept the pope's terms unless he received a guarantee that his dignity should be respected (*salva regia dignitate*).[3] The sentence of excommunication made a difference. It would be interesting to hear the language with which the king discussed the situation with his boon companions and his mercenaries from Touraine. He certainly liked breaking people in pieces like a potter's vessel. He hanged prisoners, starved to death a noble lady and her son in Windsor castle, encased in metal an exchequer clerk who had conscientious scruples about serving an excommunicated king, and who, it is said, had dared to read the papal letters before the barons of the exchequer.[4] Then, just

[1] See the analysis of his views in Böhmer, *Kirche und Staat in England und in der Normandie im XI. und XII. Jahrhundert* (Leipzig, 1899), pp. 225–40.

[2] Liebermann, *Gesetze*, i. 642. See H. W. C. Davis, in the *English Historical Review*, xxi. 365–6 (April 1906).

[3] See Langton's memorandum in *Gervase of Canterbury*, ii, pp. cxi, cxii.

[4] Taxster in Thorpe, *Florence of Worcester* (English Historical Society), ii. 170; *Roger of Wendover*, iii. 229.

as he had betrayed his father and his brother, he betrayed his people, by surrendering his kingdom to the pope. In this he went beyond his barons, only a remnant of whom attested the deed of surrender.[1] He disgusted Langton and he was false to Master Alexander. Matthew Paris believed that Master Alexander incurred the papal anger, because he tried to dissuade John from the fatal step.[2] Although John made a feeble effort to save him, he in his turn was broken like a potter's vessel, and died in misery. John was very mean, very astute, very reckless and irresponsible, and also very thorough in his ways.

[1] I refer to the first act of surrender, 15 May 1213. See the list of witnesses in *Roger of Wendover*, iii. 254. Later, both king and barons tried to make capital out of the relations with Rome, and there was general acquiescence for a time. Cf. Norgate, *John Lackland*, p. 182. But an analysis of the eleven witnesses to the unprecedented act of May 1213 shows that John only had with him his relations and personal friends. Saer de Quinci, earl of Winchester, was the least attached among them.

[2] See *Essays in History presented to R. L. Poole*, p. 259.

V

CUSTOM AND OPINION IN ENGLAND
II. MAGNA CHARTA

FOR Langton's activities in England after his arrival
in the summer of 1213, we have to depend in the
main upon the St. Albans chronicler, Roger of Wendover.
Wendover put his materials together twenty years later
and was doubtless influenced by subsequent events. While
capable of strange inaccuracy and not so consistent and
clear in his views as his famous continuator, Matthew
Paris, he felt that the archbishop was the central figure in
the fight for the charter, and, in following him, we cannot
entirely escape the danger of adopting his possible pre-
judices. On the other hand St. Albans was in the centre
of events, its archives contained copies of many official
documents, of which Wendover makes much use, and
Wendover probably had access to authorities now lost to
us. One possible authority was the scholar, poet, and
mathematician, Gervase of Melkley (*de Saltu Lacteo*), for
parts of Matthew Paris's fragmentary life of Langton are
explicitly based upon the authority of Gervase, *optimus
astrologus*, as Matthew describes him elsewhere.[1] Now
Gervase belonged to a Hertford family, which lived at
Melkley or Mentley, in the neighbourhood of Standon,
one of the manors of the great house of Clare.[2] He and
his family would be brought into contact with the abbey
of St. Albans, and from the nature of the information
which Matthew Paris drew from him, we may conclude
that he was on intimate terms with the archbishop. He

[1] *Historia Anglorum* (ed. Madden), ii. 232. On Gervase see Madden (iii,
p. xliii), the *Chronica Maiora*, iii. 43, iv. 493; Liebermann, *Ungedruckte
Anglo-Normannische Geschichtsquellen*, p. 322; Pits, *Scriptores*, p. 293.

[2] For the identification see *Coram Rege Rolls* (Record Commission), ii
(1925), 381, Index, s.v. Melkele; for Standon, *Book of Fees*, i. 123; cf.
Stapleton's preface to the *Liber de antiquis Legibus* (Camden Society), pp.
lxxxv, cvii, cxiv.

wrote a book of epitaphs, one of which, on William the Marshal, has survived, and he wrote treatises on the *ars dictandi* and on versification, manuscripts of which are in Balliol College.[1] A man would not write on the art of composition in those days unless he was accustomed to the various types of public and private correspondence. Gervase was presumably a man of affairs, and very likely one of the archbishop's clerks.[2] In any case he was a contemporary authority on the life of Langton and he was well known to the monks of St. Albans—facts which, so far as they go, encourage us to use Roger of Wendover's chronicle with confidence.

Immediately after Pandulf's arrival, John published in the form of a charter his agreement to a *forma pacis*, by which Langton and his suffragans were free to return to take up their duties in England. His good faith was guaranteed by the oaths and letters patent of three prelates and twelve barons. The king stated that he harboured no rancour and undertook to forgo the rights of custody in vacant churches if the terms of settlement were not observed.[3] Up to this point the archbishop had wholeheartedly accepted the support and guidance of the pope. After his arrival he had a more independent position, and differences of opinion soon began to reveal themselves. In the eyes of Innocent and his legates, England was a vassal state, whose king was under papal protection. They regarded ecclesiastical affairs especially as subject to their control. Early in July 1213 Innocent informed the king, the clergy, and the barons that he was sending as legate with supreme powers—as an angel of safety and peace—

---

[1] Balliol College MSS. 263, f. 153ᵛ, 276, f. 108. The *ars dictandi* does not help us to elucidate the relations between Gervase and Langton.

[2] In 1214 the archbishop sent two clerks, A. and G., to Rome (*Wendover*, iii. 282).

[3] 24 May 1213. *Rotuli litt. pat.*, p. 98*b*; cf. *Rotuli Chartarum*, p. 193*b* (18 July); *Wendover*, iii. 248–52. Early negotiations, in April, with Langton are proved by the expenses of the messengers, Misae Roll, 14 John, in Cole, *Documents illustrative of English history in the thirteenth and fourteenth centuries* (1844), pp. 260, 261.

Nicholas, cardinal bishop of Tusculum,[1] a counsellor who since 1205 had been high in the papal confidence.[2] The archbishop was instructed to give heed to him in all things. Nicholas arrived at the end of September, and took command.[3] He is said to have interfered with clerical appointments and inaugurated that policy which was to divide the English clergy for over fifty years, and to draw many of them, some from good motives, some from bad, into the ultramontane ranks. In years to come Simon, the archbishop's brother, was to earn the hatred of Stephen's admirers by his co-operation with this party. Stephen's attitude was different. He had three immediate objects, the full restitution of ecclesiastical property, the observance of canonical elections, and the establishment of sound government. The king had posed as the loyal son of the Church, and had welcomed injunctions to consider the needs of Christendom and the urgency of general peace in the interests of the Crusade.[4] Langton saw urgency nearer home. He considered the surrender of the kingdom to have been a great and unnecessary blunder.[5] He thought that the papal legates were too lenient to the king in the arrangements for restitution. He protested against the interference of the legate with the rights of chapters and patrons. While putting into practice his old convictions as a teacher at Paris, and his interpretation of his duty as the successor of St. Thomas, Stephen acted from the outset as an English primate. He compromised on the point of restitution, he got his way by forcing the king and

---

[1] Potthast, *Regesta pontificum Romanorum*, i. 416, nos. 4774–8.

[2] Ibid., i. 462.

[3] The archbishop sent ships for his use, met him at Dover and accompanied him to London, where negotiations about the removal of the interdict at once began. The legate's first report, an exceedingly interesting document dated Westminster, 21 October, has recently been discovered by Mgr. Angelo Mercati, and edited by him in *Essays in History presented to R. L. Poole*, pp. 277–89.

[4] *Rotuli litt. clausarum*, i. 165 (September 1213): letters in reply to Cardinal Curzon who had sent envoys to John. The letter shows that Curzon and Langton were co-operating at this time.   [5] Below, pp. 130, 134.

clergy to concentrate on the substitution of free and canonical elections for election 'in accordance with the customs of the realm.'[1] When the legate left England, his work accomplished, in the autumn of 1214, Stephen assumed full leadership of the Church. But the archbishop's prestige in Rome was sadly diminished. The position of affairs is summarized very lucidly by Wendover. In the middle of January 1214, the bishops, assembled at Dunstable under Langton's presidency, complained of the legate's appointment of unworthy persons, recommended by the king, to vacant churches—*intrusione magis quam canonica electione*. The archbishop sent two clerks to the legate, who was at Burton-on-Trent, where in his name they instituted an appeal against this practice, as an infringement of his legal right to order the affairs of his province (*diocesis*). The legate, in order to forestall Langton, ordered Pandulf, whom he was sending, or had just sent to Rome with the royal charter of subjection, to take action.[2] Pandulf, says Wendover, blackened the reputation of Langton and exalted the merits of the king:

'Master Simon Langton, the archbishop's brother, withstood Pandulf, but since the latter had brought with him the royal charter, sealed with a golden seal, subjecting England and Ireland to the Pope and promising tribute, Master Simon could not find a hearing. Moreover Pandulf would say in the Pope's presence that the archbishop and bishops were too stiff and greedy in exacting restitution of the goods taken in the time of interdict, and that they bore inequitably upon the king and the liberties of the kingdom.'[3]

Master Simon could not find a hearing because the king had become the pope's vassal. We should remember this in our consideration of the efforts made by the archbishop to secure domestic stability in England. The pope, it must be remembered, did not know John personally and was quite unfamiliar with English traditions. He had re-

[1] *Rotuli litt. clausarum*, i. 160 (12 Jan. 1214). Cf. Norgate, p. 193. The formal charter was issued on 21 November.

[2] *Roger of Wendover*, iii. 278–9. On Pandulf's departure see Norgate, p. 208 note. [3] *Wendover*, iii. 279.

ceived a submission more far-reaching than he could have
expected, and in response to the king's gesture of humility,
he was glad, as a big man always is, to show generosity and
confidence in the very matter for which he had been con-
tending. When the cardinal legate Nicholas used his
authority, he may have acted hastily or indiscreetly, but
he was acting under Innocent's formal instructions to see
that suitable persons, suitable not only in character and
learning, but also 'as faithful men, likely to be of service
to the realm and weighty in counsel', were appointed to
the vacant sees and churches. And Innocent had added,
'the King's consent should be sought' (*assensu regis re-
quisito*).[1] Reconciliation, in short, involved the renewal of
co-operation between the secular and ecclesiastical powers
in the government of the Church.

The archbishop was as eager for co-operation as Innocent was, but he felt that this was not the right way to
ensure it. The canon law must be formally recognized,
and by the fact of recognition be incorporated, to all
intents and purposes, among the customs of England; and
the King, in receiving him and his colleagues as advisers,
must eschew evil and, in the spirit of his coronation oath,
observe the rest of English custom as one who submitted
his conscience to the leading of the law of God. Stephen
came back to England as the chief adviser of the Crown.

It is advisible to linger at this point for a short time,
especially in view of the fact that John had shown a tendency, during the quarrel, to pose as the champion of
English liberties, and to rely upon pre-Conquest history.
The duty of the archbishop[2] and his suffragans to advise
the king, and of the king to seek their counsel, had its
roots in very early English history. It was not of feudal or
Norman origin. Liebermann pointed out that

'as soon as Canterbury became subject to the supreme power of
England, the primate is scarcely ever absent from her *witenage-
mots*. He is the king's chief counsellor. He alone shares with the

---

[1] 1 Nov. 1213. Potthast, no. 4840; *Wendover*, iii. 277.
[2] I omit any consideration of the position of the archbishop of York.

king the honour of being personally named in some laws . . . it is the witan itself in whose name he makes the king swear the coronation oath.' [1]

This tradition survived the Conquest. It gave to the archbishop of Canterbury a position which, though, of course, not unique, was more definite and authoritative than that of any other primate in any other feudal state. Lanfranc, as archbishop, without whose consent, said Eadmer,[2] no man could by any means be granted the kingdom, used this authority to insist upon guarantees from William Rufus, when he was seeking to succeed his father. Henry I urged St. Anselm to come quickly so that he might have the counsel of his father in God.[3] Moreover, the promises to maintain ecclesiastical liberties and to observe good customs were contained in the coronation oath and charters of liberties. Historically, though he did not know it, King John was quite right to appeal to Anglo-Saxon precedents, when he defended his cause against the Church. Anglo-Saxon kings had appointed and dismissed bishops very much as they pleased;[4] but in the minds of Englishmen after the Conquest, of men like Eadmer and Ailred of Rievaulx, a true English king was one who not only had the blood of the royal house of Wessex in his veins, and observed the traditions of St. Edward, but who also respected the canonical system of the Church. By a curious change of ideas they associated the Hildebrandine and later reforming movements with the memory of the holy English king, whose canonization marked the triumphant close of a long struggle for the right and the just. In a wider sense they were right, for the Church had given meaning to old traditions. It had put them to the test of the *utilitas regni*. It had, in the words of a German historian, given life to the spirit working for peace, given an

[1] F. Liebermann, *The national assembly in the Anglo-Saxon period* (Halle, 1913), p. 31.

[2] Eadmer, *Historia novorum*, lib. i, c. 13 (ed. Rule, Rolls Series, p. 25).

[3] Stubbs, *Constitutional History* (5th edition), i. 330.

[4] Liebermann, op. cit., pp. 77–9.

edge to the ruler's sense of responsibility, and put before him the commanding and fundamental duty to treat his subjects with humanity.[1]

The movement in the Church towards canonical and theological precision reacted in its turn upon this view. It submitted the conception of English kingship to wider influences. It laid stress on the idea of election and suitability in the ruler. There is a strong sympathy with the idea of legitimacy in the thoughts of a man like Ailred of Rievaulx, and loyalty to the royal house as such was everywhere real and deep.[2] John of Salisbury, for example, warns his readers to be long-suffering with a royal line and not to discard it lightly.[3] Feudal prejudice in favour of customary rights of succession moved in the same direction. The powerful influence of these ideas may be seen in the careful efforts of Louis of France to commend his claims to the English, and in the reaction which his invasion of England caused in favour of the royal house. At the same time, the chief tests of kingship in the mind of the Church were not legitimacy, but suitability and power,[4] and at bottom the criterion of suitability was the submission of the royal will to the law of God. In the past there had been a tendency to regard the election and coronation of a king as investing him, in the sight of God and man, with a *character* similar to or greater than that of the clergy. The anonymous writer of York (*c.* 1100) argued in this sense.[5] But by the year 1200 all ideas of this kind were repudiated. A good king was strengthened by this mystical union with the Church, but a bad king could claim in virtue of it no sacramental *character* which could

[1] G. von Below, *Der deutsche Staat des Mittelalters*, i (1914), p. 195. The whole section (Der Staatszweck) is illuminating.

[2] Powicke, *Ailred of Rievaulx*, pp. 35, 36. Cf. Fritz Kern, *Gottesgnadentum und Widerstandsrecht im früheren Mittelalter* (Leipzig, 1915), pp. 14–53 *passim*, 297.

[3] Polycraticus, v. 6.

[4] Kern, op. cit., p. 55 and *passim*.

[5] Böhmer, *Kirche und Staat in England und in der Normandie im XI. und XII. Jahrhundert*, pp. 227, 235; cf. Kern, p. 82.

give an authority destroyed by his natural character. Many years ago William of Malmesbury had denounced the view that the king's curative powers had an hereditary origin, and did not flow from his sanctity (*ex sanctitate*).[1] Pope Innocent III, in 1204, insisted on the difference, shown in the formalities of the anointing, between the authority of a pope and the power of a prince.[2] The Church had developed its own theory of *lèse-majesté*. 'It is a much more serious thing', said Innocent, 'to offend the divine than to offend temporal majesty.'[3] Resistance to excommunication, for example, savoured of heresy, for it implied contempt of the power entrusted by Christ to the Church, the power of the keys.[4] Finally, Langton himself, in one of his lectures raised the question whether the anointing of a king imparted a sacramental *character*. He contented himself with a reference to authority. 'The Master says no; for he is not anointed to the ministry, but to the service of the Church.'[5]

This view of kingship lent authority to the process of election and gave significance to the coronation oath. And it emphasized the position of the archbishop. The constitutional and moral influence of the archbishop in England had declined during the fifty years before the death of Hubert Walter in 1205. Theobald, in the later years of King Stephen and the early years of Henry II, had been the last archbishop to wield unquestioned influence as the first adviser of the crown, in virtue of his ecclesiastical position. His household was the centre of English thought

---

[1] *Historia Regum* (Rolls Series), i. 273.

[2] Letter of 25 February 1204 to Basil, archbishop of Ternovo in Bulgaria, Potthast, no. 2138, inserted in the Decretals of Gregory IX, lib. i, tit. xv, de sacra unctione.

[3] Potthast, no. 643, 25 March 1199; in the Decretals, lib. v, tit. vii, c. 10.

[4] Many passages could be cited. On the general question, cf. E. Jordan, *La responsabilité de l'Église dans la répression de l'hérésie au moyen âge* (Paris, 1907), p. 116.

[5] Cambridge MS., f. 318ᵛ. Cf. the famous letter of Grosseteste, *Epistolae*, ed. Luard (Rolls Series), p. 358, no. 124. See Kern, p. 114 and Marc Bloch, *Les rois thaumaturges* (Strasbourg, 1924), pp. 115 and onwards.

and learning. With John of Salisbury's aid he had firmly established canonical jurisprudence in England. He had worked cordially with King Henry for the recognition of Pope Alexander III and the rejection of his rival, and he had advised the king with kindness and candour. St. Thomas, it is true, set a standard of independence before all his successors, but both through his misfortunes and by temperament, to say nothing of his past, he had become useless as a counsellor. His two immediate successors were overshadowed by the prestige of Henry II and his capable ministers, and also, I think, by King Richard's prestige as a Crusader. The great position attained by Hubert Walter was due very largely to his work as justiciar, and after that to his influence as chancellor. Yet there is sufficient evidence that in course of time the succession to Canterbury modified the direction of Hubert's policy and outlook. He resigned the justiciarship at the instance of the new pope, Innocent, and when King Richard died, he faced the problem of the succession with the mind of a churchman. He had a talk with William the Marshal and doubtless with others about John's fitness for the throne. Both men, it should be noted, discussed the issue on this ground. The Marshal dismissed Arthur as proud and passionate, surrounded by evil counsellors, and as no friend of the English. Under the circumstances feudal custom should be observed—'the son is nearer to the land of his father than the nephew is'. The archbishop prophesied disaster but acquiesced.[1] According to Matthew Paris he spoke with special force at the coronation in order that by insisting upon John's *election*, he might safeguard the realm so far as words could from the evil days which he expected.[2] Again, at the end of his life, he intervened effectually to prevent what he regarded as a foolish piece of foreign policy, and he seems to have done so on the ground that the king was acting without proper

[1] *Histoire de Guillaume le Maréchal*, ll. 11861–908 (ed. Meyer, ii. 62–4; iii. 159, 160). See Powicke, *The Loss of Normandy* (1913), pp. 193–5.
[2] *Chronica Majora*, ii. 454, 455. See Norgate, *John Lackland*, p. 66 note.

consultation and without due observance of the formalities, which helped to secure adequate counsel.[1] The seal
was not at the time in his care, although he was chancellor,[2] and I think that he protested both as archbishop
and as chancellor. How irksome the king found his
attempts at guidance is shown by John's exultation at his
death. John, Roger of Wendover tells us, put forward the
bishop of Norwich as next archbishop because he was a
man after his own heart, a close personal adherent, in
sympathy with his inner thoughts, *magna sibi familiaritate
coniunctum . . . secretorum suorum conscium.*[3]

Langton set to work to redress the balance immediately
after his arrival in England in July 1213. He worked hard
for two years. And he very nearly succeeded in the task
which he set himself—the maintenance of the royal confidence, the observation of the coronation oath, the restoration of union and order, the restatement of English custom
in the light of new necessities. I cannot see that the king
was unfriendly to him—at any rate before the beginning
of 1215—or did not come to respect and value his advice.
The bitterness of the eastern barons and John's violent
and characteristic reaction after his concessions, ruined
Langton's hopes and deprived him of usefulness. But he
had done a great deal, and had nearly succeeded.

The suggestions which I propose to make are not new,[4]

---

[1] *Histoire de G. le M.*, ll. 12921–13038 (ed. Meyer, ii. 101–5; iii. 178,
179 and notes). The archbishop felt

> desdeing e ire
> Que li reis out *sanz son conseil*
> Apareillié tel aparail' (ll. 13000–2).

[2] Hugh of Wells, one of the king's envoys to Philip on what the archbishop regarded as an ill-advised mission (1205) kept the seal at this date
(ll. 12941–3). For Hugh at this time see also Armitage Robinson, *Somerset
Historical Essays*, p. 145.

[3] *Wendover*, iii. 184. One of the objections raised against Walter of
Eynsham, the Canterbury monk elected after Stephen's death in 1228, was
that the monks of Christ Church had chosen a man 'qui sibi inutilis erat *et
regno*', ibid., iv. 170.

[4] C. H. Pearson, *History of England during the Early and Middle Ages*
(1867), ii. 67: 'in forcing John to swear at Winchester that he would observe

but they have been overshadowed by recent discussions, and they have never been set out deliberately in the light of contemporary thought upon political matters and of contemporary documents. They are, briefly, that Magna Charta was regarded by Langton as an elaboration of the coronation oath and that the history of the charter begins in the summer of 1213 and not later.

Unrest was general in England when John made his peace with the Church. The impressive gathering of troops to meet the threatened invasion of Philip Augustus of France concealed much weakness. If we could know more of the mind of the justiciar Geoffrey fitz Peter, of Peter, bishop of Winchester, of William the Marshal, we should probably find that they were very uneasy, in spite of their loyal support of the king. John had good reason to make peace—the fear of desertion by his own barons, the danger from Philip, the general anxiety caused by the excommunication, the irksome interdict, the flights to France, the prophesies of the enthusiast, Peter of Wakefield.[1] His promises to the Church comprised an amnesty for rebels as well as restitution to the clergy; indeed, the terms of restitution comprised the persons and liberties of the laity 'involved in this business'.[2] Langton, therefore, was justified in considering that a settlement must comprise the affairs of the whole community. On St. Margaret's Day, a few days after landing in England he and the other prelates met the King at Winchester (20 July 1213). Amidst scenes of much emotion, he absolved him from excommunication at the door of the church, where the fiftieth psalm was sung:

Averte faciem tuam a peccatis meis, et omnes iniquitates meas dele, Cor mundum crea in me, Deus.

the laws of King Edward, Stephen Langton had in fact indicated a programme of political action which he never afterwards lost sight of.' Cf. Stubbs, i. 565; Norgate, p. 212.   [1] *Wendover*, iii. 248.

[2] *Wendover*, iii. 250, 251. This must refer to a larger number than the few who had fled, of whom Robertz fitzWalter and Eustace de Vesci were the chief. In his letters of July the pope referred to rebels in England; Potthast, no 4777.

John had previously sworn upon the Gospels that he would love, defend, and maintain the Church, recall the good laws of his ancestors, especially those of St. Edward the Confessor, and do away with bad laws, judge all men in accordance with the just judgements of his court, and render his rights to every man. This was obviously an expansion of the coronation oath. After mass, the whole company dined together 'in joy and merriment'.[1]

John was anxious to sail to Poitou, where he wished to strike at Philip, who was engaged with war against the allies in Flanders. He made the bishop of Winchester guardian of the peace of the realm (presumably as his deputy in settling ecclesiastical disputes), entrusted his administration to the justiciar and bishop, and, according to Wendover, ordered them to act with the counsel of the archbishop.[2] The three magnates moved on to St. Albans where the king's undertaking was put into force. Peace was enjoined upon all, and in the king's name order was issued that the laws of Henry I should be observed and that servants of the Crown should desist from exactions and unlawful practices.[3] Here we get the first reference to the laws of Henry I, which would include the charter of liberties. Within a month of his arrival the archbishop had fastened upon these as his guide in the interpretation of the royal promises. It is not surprising that he should in his practical way substitute a law book and a royal charter

[1] *Wendover*, iii. 260, 261. It should be remembered also, in view of later events, that, during the preparations against a French invasion in the spring of 1205, the king 'iurare compulsus est quod iura regni Angliae de eorum (magnatum) consilio pro posse suo conservaret illaesa'; *Gervase of Canterbury*, ii. 97, 98. The Stanley annalist, as copied at Furness, appears definitely to associate Magna Charta with this oath, which he describes as made at 'Rin' on the coast (Howlett, *Chronicles of the reigns of Stephen, Henry II and Richard I*, vol. ii, p. 518). The discrepancies do not matter. The point to notice is that the attitude of the barons was regarded as continuous. Miss Norgate seems to me to misunderstand the action of the barons in 1213, when they insisted that John should be absolved before he took an expedition to Poitou (*John Lackland*, p. 186, on *Wendover*, iii. 259).

[2] *Wendover*, iii. 261.

[3] Ibid., 262.

of the twelfth century for the vague ideals associated with
the memory of St. Edward; but how did he know them?
His general acquaintance may be presumed. Since boyhood the peculiar prestige of St. Edward must have been
familiar to him; and the significance of the reign of Henry
I would not have escaped him. Henry's charter was not
inaccessible; it existed in more than one version, and had
recently been copied from what is known to scholars as the
Winchester text [1] in the collection of English law and law
books, written by a Londoner for the use of the London
officials, or, as Liebermann put it, 'for the London Gild-
hall.'[2] Liebermann has seen in this collection, as a source
of perversion and false additions, the influence of a hypo-
thetical political programme. It is, perhaps, safer to say that
in the opinion of many Londoners at that time the king
ought to rely upon his council and to raise no aids or other
taxes without its consent, that the government of London
should be an example to the rest of the community, and
that the early laws, with their references to *folkmoots*,
seemed to justify and were read in the light of this view.
In other words, reflection upon political issues in the light
of early history had really begun, and in English history
the names of Edward the Confessor and of Henry I stood
out before all others. Now if the Winchester text of
Henry's charter was within the reach of a London citizen,
it was within the reach of an archbishop. A copy may have
been sent to him, or he may have seen one at Winchester,
or may we not presume that his library, with other books

---

[1] Ludwig Riess, 'The Re-issue of Henry I's Coronation Charter', in
English Historical Review, xli. 321 ff. (July 1926).

[2] Liebermann in *English Historical Review*, xxviii. 743 (October 1913).
The collection survives in the first volume (now MS. 155 in the John
Rylands Library, Manchester) of a London compilation made in John's
reign. The second volume is in the British Museum, Add. MS. 14252.
Liebermann had conjectured the existence of this work from his study of
later manuscripts, before his attention was called to the Rylands MS. See
his *Ueber die Leges Anglorum saeculo XIII ineunte Londoniis collectae*
(Halle, 1894). On its relation to the 'Winchester' text of Henry I's charter
see Riess, loc. cit.

on law, included a collection of English law?[1] It was not only justiciars who were *peritissimi* in the law of England. Indeed, we need go no farther, for one of the most learned of justiciars was at Langton's side. Geoffrey fitz Peter had only two more months to live.[2] He was weary after his long labours, dejected by domestic troubles, and on their account at enmity with the king. He was not a particularly good or scrupulous man, but he had been a good justiciar, a real public servant rather than a courtier, and he was very able and very well read in English custom. I can see no reason why he and Stephen Langton should not have discussed English history together, why he should not have pointed out Henry's charter to his new colleague. It was no new thing for Englishmen to talk about history. King John did so, and his father before him. The great Ranulf Glanvill was fond of speculating about it, Walter Map liked to gossip about it, John of Salisbury and Gerald of Wales were steeped in it.

A dramatic story told by Roger of Wendover suggests that in fact Langton had not previously known the charter. From St. Albans the archbishop had come to London, where a great assembly of clergy and barons gathered at St. Paul's on 25 August. It was on this occasion that he preached the sermon, still extant, which was so boldly and rudely interrupted by an indignant hearer.[3] The interdict was not yet raised—that was the legate's business after the Church had been indemnified—and the legate had not yet arrived. The Church was idle in England until the middle of 1214. But Langton granted

---

[1] For Stephen's interest in English affairs see his own manifesto of 1207 (*Gervase of Canterbury*, ii, p. lxxxi). Unhappily, we know little of his library. The library of Christ Church, Canterbury, possessed, under the title *Annales de Durobernensibus Archiepiscopis*, a book which Dr. James has identified with a manuscript in Corpus Christi College, Cambridge, no. 76, a text of Radulfus de Diceto (James, *Ancient Libraries of Canterbury and Dover*, pp. 122, 511, no. 1438). This doubtless accounts for the statement made by the early biographers that Langton wrote the lives of the archbishops of Canterbury (cf. Norgate in *D.N.B.*, s.v. Langton, Stephen).

[2] He died 14 October 1213.   [3] Above, p. 42.

a relaxation, so that the canonical hours might be sung in a low voice.[1] After noting this, Wendover proceeds to say that during the conference the archbishop is said to have called aside some of the leading barons for a private talk. He reminded them of the recent events at Winchester, and went on : 'A charter of Henry I has been found, by means of which, if you desire, you may regain your lost liberty'. Then he read Henry's coronation charter to them. The barons rejoiced greatly when they heard it and took an oath that, when the time was ripe, they would fight for their liberties. The archbishop promised to aid them to the best of his power.[2] There is no suggestion, it should be noted, that these barons were rebels. They were important and they were few. But I suspect Robert fitz Walter to have been one of them.

What were these liberties which the company at St. Paul's swore to recover ? If we accept the story, we must accept it in its literal sense, and answer that the liberties were those comprised in Henry I's charter, the precise definition of the law on such matters as reliefs, wardship, marriage, dower. We must not jump to the conclusion that a few selfish barons were prepared to take advantage of the king's difficulties to extort concessions. On the contrary, the kingdom was in an easier condition than it had been for years. It was a period of rejoicing and hope. The king had sworn to observe good customs and to give just judgements. He had in Langton a new and strong adviser, a man whose courage and moderation were respected by all, yet a man who consciously regarded himself as the successor of St. Thomas and the champion of law and order. It was a time when prudent, anxious, suffering and —we may freely admit—mischievous men would welcome guidance in the endeavour to give reality to John's sworn intentions. Moreover, the need for a restatement of customary law was no new thing. It is indeed more than probable that during the past few years the need had been especially felt. Many great barons had died, and in conse-

---

[1] *Wendover*, iii. 263.   [2] Ibid., pp. 263–6.

quence, many exorbitant reliefs had been paid, much
profit made by fines for wardships and marriages; and, if
some contemporary stories were true, men and women of
the greatest families, the houses of Braose, fitz Walter, the
justiciar himself, had suffered gross personal dishonour at
the king's hands.[1] Yet the need was not new. It had been
felt for many years. As Dr. Round is fond of pointing out,
'the feudal extortions remedied by the Charter were not,
as is so often implied, introduced by John, but are found
in full existence under Henry II.'[2] The movement, I repeat, was not a rebellion, it was the natural and inevitable
response to the solemn scene at Winchester. To speak of
it as selfish or reactionary is entirely to miss its significance,
and to forget, in our absorption in what we wrongly call
feudal law the awakened interest in the nature and responsibilities of kingship.

Now there is a document which exactly reflects the
position which the movement of opinion had reached in
the autumn of 1213, and the following months. It is
known to students as the Unknown Charter—unknown
because it did not attract the attention of scholars until
1893.[3] It begins with the charter of Henry I, based upon
the 'Winchester' text current in John's reign,[4] and is followed by a list of concessions based upon the charter. Also

[1] See especially Norgate, pp. 289–93.

[2] *Magna Carta Commemoration Essays* (Royal Historical Society, 1917),
p. 62, and his introductions to the Pipe Rolls of Henry II.

[3] For the literature on this subject see Petit-Dutaillis, *Studies supple-
mentary to Stubbs's Constitutional History*, vol. i, trans. W. E. Rhodes (Manchester, 1908), pp. 116–26; and Ludwig Riess, 'Zur Vorgeschichte der
Magna Carta' in the *Historische Vierteljahrschrift*, xiii (1910), 449–58.
Riess seems to me to have seen the bearing of this document better than
his predecessors, except Dr. Round, but his hypothesis on the way in which
it has survived in a French copy is fanciful. In the absence of definite
evidence any number of likely suggestions might be made, for English
affairs were clearly watched across the Channel. In 1164 John of Salisbury
was astonished by the minute knowledge of recent debates and private discussions in England, displayed by the Count of Soissons ('ac si interfuisset
omnibus presens'). See the letter in *Chart. Univ. Paris*, i, Introd., p. 17,
no. 19.   [4] Riess, in *English Historical Review*, xli. 325.

it includes a clause, to the effect that the king will not seize a man without judgement, nor take anything from him for doing justice, nor do him injustice. This is a rather more precise statement of the king's oath at Winchester that he would judge men according to the just judgement of his court. There is nothing new in this promise—it is as old as the coronation oath—and it had been definitely recognized in the case of humbler folk by Queen Eleanor in a decree of amnesty issued on King Richard's accession in 1189.[1] John repeated it during the negotiations with the barons early in 1215, and it was embodied in the thirty-ninth clause and other clauses of the Great Charter. But at the very time when Langton was meeting clergy and barons in London, John was flagrantly disregarding it. He was in a towering passion. From the solemnities and rejoicings at Winchester he had gone to the coast expecting to sail with an army to Poitou. He had found everything in disorder, and finally postponed the expedition until the spring of 1214. His main difficulty was the refusal of his northern vassals to regard this distant adventure as an obligation upon them. There was a great deal to be said in favour of their objections. They could hardly regard a previous expedition in 1206 as a precedent, for then the loss of the Norman lands was recent. They had no lands or interests in Poitou, and affairs at home were not settled. Also, the legal obligations to give foreign service obviously required definition. But the king, not unnaturally, was furious. He marched northwards to have vengeance. At Northampton he was caught up by the archbishop, who came straight from London. Langton pointed out that this was precisely an occasion for just judgement in the king's court. A legal issue was involved, a custom had to be defined. He would excommunicate every one who assisted the king in his attack upon the delinquents.[2] And John had to promise

---

[1] *Benedict of Peterborough* (ed. Stubbs), ii. 74.

[2] *Wendover*, iii. 262, 263: 'nisi ab inceptis celerius desisteret, omnes, qui versus quempiam ante relaxationem interdicti hostiliter arma gestarent,

to offer judgement in his court. In the 'unknown charter' we find, among the additional clauses already mentioned, the clause about judgements and a clause limiting foreign service to Normandy and Brittany. The charter in the form in which it has come down to us is obviously a descriptive draft. We have no evidence that it was ever formally issued, but as a provisional settlement it fits this occasion, and I would assign it to the period between the autumn of 1213 and the summer of 1214, as the first legal commentary since Langton's arrival on the oath at Winchester and the charter of Henry I.

This conclusion, originally suggested by Mr. Round, has been rejected by other scholars. Mr. Round perhaps weakened his case by regarding the terms as a concession to a group of northern barons. They were rather the first attempt at a general settlement.[1] There is no force in the objection that an expedition to Poitou did sail in 1214. Obviously there was nothing in the 'Unknown Charter' to prevent service overseas. The chronicler of Coggeshall, in Essex, states explicitly that the earls did not go and that the host was composed mainly of lesser folk.[2] The official records show that this was not altogether the case; but it seems to be clear that the army consisted of mercenaries

praeter ipsum solum [i.e. regem] anathematis vinculo innodaret.' The exception of the royal person is interesting; for on 4 November the pope wrote that he had acceded to the request of John's envoys that his person should not be excommunicated nor his chapel put under an interdict save by the pope himself. Potthast, no. 4842. John obviously began his complaints at once, and intended to make sure on the point.

[1] A settlement of which the grant of free ecclesiastical elections was another part. For Dr. Round's view see *English Historical Review*, viii (1893), 288 ff. An alternative suggestion, made by Riess (*Hist. Vierteljahrschrift*, xiii. 457), is that the document was presented to John, after preliminary negotiations, in January 1215, when the barons came to the king at the New Temple (*Wendover*, iii. 295, 296). This is possible. The document corresponds in several respects with the petitions described by Wendover. On the other hand, whereas Wendover says that the king postponed his reply, the so-called 'Unknown Charter' implies a draft agreement, such as John is more likely to have made before he sailed for Poitou.

[2] *Coggeshall*, ed. Stevenson (Rolls Series), p. 168.

and volunteers (who would be paid after a time).[1] The Marshal, for example, did not go, but gladly allowed John to take as many of his knights as he wished.[2] When the king tried to collect the customary scutage he met with widespread resistance on the ground that this particular scutage was illegal. Service had not been owed. As a matter of fact the archbishop's firmness and John's concessions had probably made the expedition to Poitou possible. Langton's influence was now very great. In January 1214 the king promised to enforce canonical elections, a promise formally confirmed later in the year—and assured the archbishop that there was no controversy between them.[3] During his absence the archbishop acted as adviser to the new justiciar, Peter des Roches, bishop of Winchester, and the baronial regents.[4]

The expedition was a failure. Fresh from his victory over John's allies at Bouvines, the king of France was able, with the mediation of Robert Curzon, to secure a long truce favourable to himself. John returned to England discredited, and the exaction of the scutage increased the unrest, intensified the desire, especially of the younger barons, to secure a more comprehensive settlement. They wanted to have England for the English, and murmured against the foreign justiciar. Influenced, perhaps, by the political discussions, of which the London collection of English law was a symptom, they wished to strengthen the powers of the great council. They hated the foreign mercenaries and longed to get rid of them. They resented the exactions of the officials and the bureaucratic indifference of the *curia regis*. There were hotheads and men nursing personal grievances among them, but it is a fatal mistake to imply that the English baronage was not an integral part of the state and versed in public affairs. Bracton, the greatest professional man of the century, reminds us that the vassals of the king were as free to disown

---

[1] Mitchell, *Studies in Taxation under John and Henry III*, pp. 109–15.
[2] *Histoire de Guillaume le Maréchal*, ll. 14701–3.
[3] Above, p. 105. [4] Norgate, p. 196.

a lord who did not fulfil his obligations as he was to disown a rebel.[1] A baron was accustomed in council to discuss politics, and by arbitration to decide knotty points which were transmitted by the judges. If and as he acquired a reputation, he might serve as a judge or baron of the exchequer.[2] In the administration of his lands, he had liberties of a semi-official kind, as much a part of acknowledged custom as the king's rights, and requiring for their exercise the same kind of experience as the king and his ministers possessed. He was not a stranger to the king, for he was not immersed in other interests. He was in constant contact with the system of government of which he formed a part, and with the local courts, the exchequer, the royal household. He could describe, for example, the marks which distinguished valid from incomplete letters of protection.[3] He would know quite well that in John's reign a freeman was any man whose name was inscribed on the roll of those who had to possess arms under the Assize of Arms.[4] He was not mentally incapable of discussing general customs with a bishop, or too proud to speak to a prosperous burgess. I have quoted Langton's words on the distinction between a commonwealth and a monarchy. In a monarchy the bulk of the people have no share, and therefore when they interpret their duty of obedience they must consider whether the king has or has not acted in accordance with proper judicial forms.[5] This was the root of the whole matter and it implies that those who had a share in affairs should help the king to govern in the

[1] *De Legibus Angliae*, lib. ii, c. xxxv, para. 11. Compare the passage from Matthew Paris on the death of Warin de Muntchenesy: 'in cuius obitu maxima regni columpna uacillauit . . . et ita diatim Anglorum nobilitas, proh dolor, expirauit', *Chronica Maiora*, v. 504.

[2] Some well-known barons acted as judges in John's reign; see the *Curia Regis Rolls*, Index of Subjects, s.v. Justices, in volumes i and ii (1922–5). In return for a loan William Brewer promised, in addition to repayment, that he would sit at the exchequer for a fortnight or three weeks when commanded (*Rot. litt. pat*, p. 55*b*).   [3] Cf. above, p. 43 n. 3.

[4] *Curia Regis Rolls*, i. 45: 'et dicit quod ipse liber homo est et in iurata domini regis ad arma habenda ut liber homo.'   [5] Above, p. 95.

general interest. The barons, not the people, were with the king responsible in God's sight.

Hence when we regard the events of 1214–15, let us call the charter a baronial document as much as we please, but do not let us imply thereby that it was a piece of selfish and reactionary class legislation. If we exclude the revolutionary security clause, and the temporary provisions, it was a statement of custom or of what was regarded as a legitimate restatement of custom, and as such it was accepted, with a few modifications, by all parties, the guardian of the realm, the legate, and at length by the pope himself.[1] It was regarded as a safeguard of ecclesiastical as well as of secular rights, and it took the place of the 'laws of the Confessor' as the guarantee of sound government. Much of it had long been needed, some of it restates earlier legislation, all of it was consistent with tradition. It must have been compiled—haphazardly, it is true—by men or with the assistance of men of the school of Glanvill and Hubert Walter, for it was a statement of common law no less than a piece of common sense.[2] The clause against excessive use of the writ *praecipe*, often described as the most reactionary sentence in a reactionary document, is a case in point. It expresses an objection to the arbitrary use of a writ, which was not apparently the outcome of general deliberation but an invention of the chancery, and which Glanvill himself clearly thought should be used with care. 'The aim of King and barons alike in the legal reforms of Henry II's reign, was', it has been well said, 'to secure quicker justice and thus maintain better order in the land.'[3] The writ *praecipe* might

---

[1] Faith Thompson, *The First Century of Magna Carta* (University of Minnesota, 1925), p. 7. It was a favourite contention of G. B. Adams that the security clause was in accordance with feudal usage and could not have been a special reason for papal disapprobation; this view appears to me to overlook the attitude to kingship which I have discussed earlier in this chapter.

[2] See the contemporary texts in Faith Thompson, op. cit., pp. 11–13. Cf. Léon Leclère, in the *Mélanges d'histoire offerts à Henri Pirenne* (Brussels, 1926), pp. 279–90.

[3] Doris Stenton, in the *Cambridge Medieval History*, v. 588. The chap-

or might not facilitate this object, whereas it certainly interfered with the powers of courts to which the barons had as much right by this time as the king had to his court.

The charter, it is true, reveals a tendentious regard for conciliar government, and for popular forms of justice. The tendency has been explained away in the interests of a theory and because modern writers do not sufficiently realize that a medieval baron in England was part of an administrative machine, and could not, even if he wished, escape from it.[1] And on these very points he would come under the additional influence of churchmen who believed that good and lawful counsel was the best safeguard of a prince, and of more popular thinkers who were beginning to draw a moral from the records of the past. Of the theological influence I have already said more than enough. Of the second kind of influence, I will give an example from the London collection of laws. There are some significant passages in the eighth section of the law tract, the *Leges Henrici*. One runs: 'Let every lord have with him such men as are responsible (*iusticiabiles*) to him, so that if they offend, he may have them to right, or, as it may be, answer for them.' Another says, 'Let a man of the better sort preside over each tithing and each hundred, to be

---

ter on private jurisdiction in the late G. B. Adams's *Council and Courts in Anglo-Norman England* (New Haven, 1926), pp. 151–78, should be studied in this connexion. It gives a remarkable analysis of the widespread activities of the baronial element in the life of the realm. From my particular point of view the problems in which Adams joins issue with Miss Reid (see next note)—the relative significance of what he calls baronial jurisdiction and franchisal jurisdiction—is not important; nor does it seem to me to matter whether the objection to the writ *precipe*, to which Glanvill devotes so much thought, was or was not justified. We cannot estimate progressive or reactionary elements in Magna Charta without implicit reference to our views about English history and the English constitution as a whole. The discussions of late years have helped us to get rid of the idea of a nation in arms against the Crown in 1215, but otherwise seem to me to have been beside the mark.

[1] Cf. Rachel Reid, 'Barony and Thanage' in the *English Historical Review*, xxxv (1920), 161 ff.

called the alderman, one who may study vigilantly to promote the laws of God and the rights of men.' [1] And, when
he came to this passage, the London writer made an un-
authorized and tendentious addition:

'For nothing should be exacted or taken save of right and reason,
in accordance with the law of the land and of justice and of the
judgement of the court without fraud, as has been decided after
careful deliberation by the best men of the whole realm in times
past, and approved by great gatherings of the servants of God and
the fathers of the Church (*bonorum patrum*) and of the wise men
of the whole kingdom.' [2]

In the opinion of the writer sound local administration,
judicial and financial, should be under the watchful care
of the leaders in Church and State.

If the charter was a statement of revised custom, an
elaboration of the coronation oath, why, it may be in-
quired, did it involve civil war, papal repudiation, and a
foreign invasion? And what was the archbishop doing to
allow developments of this kind? The questions are not
quite fair. Langton's influence with the barons began to
wane at the end of 1214, when they first contemplated the
use of force as a means of putting into effect their engagement with him and with each other. During the next six
months the archbishop was at John's side. He was certainly not out of sympathy with the demands of the rebels
so far as they professed to be a statement of custom or a
request for its observance. At Bury St. Edmunds in
November 1214 the barons took the charter of Henry I
as their guide; when they met the king in London they
reminded him of the oath which he had sworn at Winchester. So far Langton would be with them. After long

[1] Liebermann, *Die Gesetze der Angelsachsen*, i. 554.
[2] John Rylands Library, Latin MS. 155, f. 83: 'Quia nil a nullo exigi uel
capi debet nisi de iure et ratione per legem terre et iusticiam et per iudicium
curie sine dolo, prout statutum est maxima consideratione procerum et
baronum predecessorum totius regni et multa acgregatione seruorum dei
et bonorum patrum et sapientium totius monarchie approbatum.' This
differs slightly from the text printed from later manuscripts in Liebermann, *Leges Anglorum*, p. 75; Gesetze, i. 554 note.

negotiations he and the Marshal, who acted as intermediary, advised John to accept the demands. But he was
with equal certainty out of sympathy with the appeal to
force. He was probably responsible for the attempt, described by Matthew Paris, to place the ultimate authority
for the maintenance of the settlement in the hands of a
commission of thirty-eight barons, drawn from both sides,
just as he probably had a share in John's offer, on 10 May
1215, while the barons were gathering strength, to submit
the issue to the arbitration of four from each side under
the presidency of the pope. And when he realized that the
barons were determined to take ungenerous advantage of
their triumph, he joined with the legate, the archbishop
of Dublin, and seven other bishops in a manifesto to the
people on their refusal to give guarantees. Whether he
was right in thinking that his policy could be effectual
without the use of force I have not to determine.[1]

Stephen was thwarted during the spring of 1215 by the
calculated vacillation of the king. He believed in the justice of the baronial demands and was generally known to
be in sympathy with their promoters.[2] He hoped for a

[1] *Rot. litt. pat.*, pp. 141, 181; M. Paris, *Chronica Maiora*, ii. 604–6;
Norgate, pp. 229–36. During the lull in the summer of 1215, while the
harvest was being gathered, Langton and the bishops strove hard for
peace; see *Walter of Coventry*, ii. 222–4. The archbishop's share is emphasized in the Southwark annals (Cotton. MS., Faustina A. 8): 'conuenerunt
simul dominus Stephanus Cantuariensis archiepiscopus et omnes fere epi-
scopi Anglie et omnes barones apud Stanes coram Rege Iohanne ad tractan-
dum de magnis negociis et de stabilitate pacis regni, qui se absentauit
eodem die et noluit illuc uenire' &c. M. Tyson, 'The Annals of Southwark
and Merton' (p. 50), reprinted from the *Surrey Archaeological Collections*,
1925, vol. xxxvi.

[2] Roger of Wendover, although his tone becomes strongly anti-baronial
when he reaches the story of the gathering at Stamford in Easter week 1215,
still insists that the barons 'Stephanum, Cantuariensem archiepiscopum,
capitalem consentaneum habuerunt' (iii. 298). Again, both Gervase of
Canterbury (ii. 109) and Coggeshall (p. 172) believed that the final terms
of the Charter were arranged under the guidance of a middle part of
bishops and barons, headed by the archbishop. This raises the difficult
question, whether Langton did or did not approve of the security clause
and the committee of twenty-five. Probably clause 55, according to which

peaceful issue. John, on the other hand, while forced to use him as an intermediary, was not unnaturally suspicious, and at last, by taking the vows of a crusader, put himself under the protection of the Church.[1] His emissaries complained bitterly to the pope of the archbishop's independent attitude, of his refusal to take strong measures against the danger, and their complaints brought down upon him urgent reproaches from Innocent.[2] The barons, on their side, had realized their power. They repudiated all offers of a compromise, and, as their forces grew, braved the risk of the ecclesiastical censures which the pope ordered the leaders of the Church to pass upon them.

Their policy, eventually expounded in the security clause—by which John was compelled to recognize the right of rebellion, not in general, but as a permanent weapon at the disposal of the twenty-five barons—had been foreshadowed some months earlier, in the engagement made at Bury St. Edmunds, in November 1214.[3] At Stamford it was openly expressed in deed as well as in words.[4] An analysis of the names given by Wendover reveals several interesting facts about the party which gathered round Robert fitz Walter at Stamford. The centre of the movement was not the north of England, but, as Mr. Round has already shown, East Anglia, and especially Essex.[5] The northern barons in Yorkshire, for

he was to co-operate with the twenty-five in dealing with unjust fines and amercements reveals his attitude best. In the consideration of these cases interested parties among the twenty-five were to withdraw. Again, Stephen's independent position is illustrated by the fact that he received a safe conduct to come with his companions to Staines for the discussions between king and barons (27 May, *Rot. litt. pat.*, p. 142), and was entrusted with the Tower of London, when a dispute arose over its custody (*Walter of Coventry*, ii. 221: 'donec veritas plenius discuteretur). Similarly, in May, he surrendered Rochester castle to John, and in June received it back again.

[1] On Ash Wednesday, 4 March (*Walter of Coventry*, ii. 219).
[2] It is doubtful if these letters arrived in time to affect Stephen's policy. See below, p. 131.
[3] *Wendover*, iii. 294.   [4] Ibid., 297 for the 'exercitus inaestimabilis'.
[5] Round, 'King John and Robert fitzWalter' in *English Historical Review*, xix. 707–11 (October 1904).

example, had all refused to pay the scutage of 1214, or to speak more accurately, no scutage was paid in Yorkshire.[1] In 1215 the Yorkshire barons were about equally divided between the baronial and the royal parties. The barons in the area north-east of London, on the other hand, were, almost to a man, mustered against the king. As Stubbs pointed out many years ago, the northerners among the rebels were mainly drawn from old 'administrative' families.[2] This element gradually fell into the background. Further examination shows that the easterners were led by persons, chief among them being Robert fitz Walter of Dunmow, who had grounds for bitter personal resentment against John, that many of them were young men who had recently come into their inheritance—Geoffrey fitz Peter's son the young earl of Essex, the young constable of Chester, heir to Roger de Lacy (a Yorkshire baron), the eldest son of the Marshal, doubtless drawn in by his connexion with the Clares, John fitz Robert of Clavering, his step-brother Roger de Cressi, Richard de Muntfichet and others; also, that many of the eastern men composed a big family group, in which the wrongs of one would be the wrongs of all.[3] There were many older and more experienced heads among them, including the chiefs of the great house of Clare, enough to guarantee that their demands would be expounded with knowledge and derived from experience. The continuity with the little group which had talked with the archbishop in London in August 1213 was not broken. There was even one bishop among them, Giles of Briouze, of Hereford. But Giles had the foulest of wrongs to avenge[4]; and in general we can learn enough to be satisfied that the spirit which animated

[1] Mitchell, *Studies in Taxation*, p. 113.

[2] *Walter of Coventry*, ii, p. lxxv: 'the men who sprang from the chosen servants of Henry II and his most valued ministers.' At the same time Stubbs gives a misleading impression of the solidarity of the north. See Appendix V.

[3] See Appendix V.

[4] He was the brother of William of Briouze, whose wife and son had been starved to death in Windsor Castle.

the baronial party was not the spirit which animated the archbishop. That its programme was so moderate, so firmly grounded in fact, and so enduring, is of itself enough to show that it was the outcome of long deliberation, not solely concocted in haste or passion, but derived from saner counsels.

The archbishop, at any rate, was not disposed to assist in its destruction. He had deplored the methods of the barons, but he could not be indifferent to their demands, for they were the fruit of his own work at Winchester.[1] Rather than take responsibility for promulgating the papal sentence of excommunication against them, he was willing to incur the papal displeasure. He was suspended from the exercise of his functions and left England. It was the bitterest moment of his life, and he was sunk in the deepest depression. His search after truth in Paris, his successful fight for the cause of St. Thomas of Canterbury, his happy return, his hopes of a reorganized state, had ended in what? A king run wild, a vindictive and excommunicated baronage, anarchy in the administration, personal disgrace. He had thoughts of becoming a hermit or of entering the Carthusian, the most austere and remote of all the monastic orders.

But he might have said with the Psalmist : 'Neque iniquitas mea, neque peccatum meum, Domine: sine iniquitate cucurri et direxi.'

---

[1] His attempts and those of his fellow bishops at peace during the summer of 1215, after the issue of the Charter, are described by Norgate, pp. 239–43. It should be noted, in confirmation of the view that the text of the Charter was the outcome of careful and expert work, that several men who appear as judges in John's reign were involved in the rebellion.

VI

LANGTON AS ARCHBISHOP

I F we except the story, which is not free from perplex-
ity, of his share in the struggle for the Great Charter,
the material at our disposal for the biography of Langton
is meagre until we come to the last ten years of his life;
but when we come to these years, from his return to
England after civil war was over until his death in 1228,
our difficulty lies not in the paucity, but in the abundance
of material. For it is impossible to separate Langton's life
from the history of church and state during the minority
of Henry III, and this period is full of incident and movement, full of consequence for both the political and the
ecclesiastical life of England. We must do our best to look
at events through Langton's eyes and to disregard those
with which he had little or no concern.

In 1215 the archbishop found that he could not reconcile his policy as an Englishman with his duty to the
papacy. During the last seven years of his life (1221–8) he
was, on the whole, free from this dilemma. His emancipation from it must be our first concern.

As we have seen, misunderstanding began in 1214, before
the departure of the papal legate, Nicholas, who had been
sent to England to see that John's surrender of his kingdom was made formal and that reconciliation, on the basis
of an equitable restoration of ecclesiastical property, was
complete between the king and the clergy. Acting on
papal instructions, the legate had authorized ecclesiastical
appointments which, from the point of view of Langton
and his fellow bishops, were irregular in form and unwise
in substance—for the rights of the chapters had been
brushed aside and in some cases unsuitable persons had
been elected. Moreover, the careful arrangements, which
preceded the removal of the interdict, for the restitution
of the *ablata*, the property seized by John, appeared to

the clergy to bear too hardly upon the sufferers[1]; and Langton, rightly or wrongly, was believed at Rome to share this view. But the main ground of his unpopularity at the papal court was his supposed objection to the recognition of the pope as a feudal suzerain. Matthew Paris, later, asserts definitely that Langton felt it and makes it his chief claim to the gratitude of his fellow countrymen.[2] Langton, of course, had acquiesced—he could not do otherwise—and had attested the formal instrument of surrender,[3] just as he had co-operated loyally with the legate in the task of reconciliation and the proposals for the restitution of property; yet I am inclined to believe the statements of Matthew Paris, who had opportunities of knowing the archbishop's mind. The point to note, however, is that, before the end of 1214, Pope Innocent had more than one reason to believe that his old friend took a more provincial view of the situation in England than he did himself. We must remember that Innocent at this time was very busy and very concerned. He was preparing for the greatest manifestation of the unity of the Church since the days of the early councils—for that great Council of the Lateran, in which all the hesitations in dogma, all the vexed issues of recent years, would be decided, clearly, definitely, once for all; and a well-ordered Christendom be summoned to the crusade against the infidel and to the extirpation of heresy. To his mind in those days, social disturbance must have seemed petty and inopportune, and the countenance of local disturbance by the prelates of the Church peculiarly disloyal. He could not know, or be expected to appreciate the legal issues involved in John's demand for a scutage, nor the urgency of the demands upon John to give effect to his solemn promises

---

[1] For the *ablata* see Ramsay, *A History of the Revenues of the Kings of England, 1066–1399* (Oxford, 1925), i. 252; Mitchell, *Studies in Taxation under John and Henry III*, pp. 106–9; Norgate, *John Lackland*, p. 207.

[2] *Historia Anglorum* (ed. Madden), ii. 146, 147; Liebermann, *Ungedruckte Geschichtsquellen*, pp. 323, 326, 327.

[3] 3 October 1213, Rymer, *Foedera*, i. i. 115.

made at Winchester. He could only act and act quickly upon the information laid before him, and while the envoys passed to and fro events moved with bewildering rapidity.[1] In February 1215 he learned that a party of barons had joined in an illegal confederacy against the king and that the archbishop was aiding and abetting them. He wrote letters in March to king, archbishop, and barons; let the king see that justice was done in his court in all matters of dispute, let the archbishop and bishops be stern to restrain disorderly elements by ecclesiastical penalties, let the barons do nothing to disturb the recent settlement.[2] Next he learnt that John had taken the cross, and also that the archbishop had refused to support him, that the barons had gathered in arms. So in the middle of June he wrote strictly enjoining the publication of ecclesiastical penalties within eight days of the receipt of his letter, unless the barons submitted[3]; but even as he was deliberating, London had been occupied and the Charter extorted. It is even possible that, through some strange delays, his letters of March did not reach England before the seizure of London.[4] Innocent could not understand why the archbishop had done nothing. He was forced at

---

[1] G. B. Adams, 'Innocent III and the Charter', in *Magna Carta Commemoration Essays* (1917), pp. 26–45; Norgate, pp. 225, 226, 232, 242–6.

[2] Potthast, nos. 4960, 4961 (19 March 1215); *Foedera*, I, i. 127.

[3] Printed by Adams from the original in the Public Record Office, Papal Bulls, Box 52, no. 2, in the article cited, pp. 43–5. Adams considered that the bull 'Miramur plurimum' in *Wendover*, iii. 336–8, belongs to the same time (18 June). If these bulls were issued in reply to John's letter of 29 May (*Foedera*, I, i. 129) Innocent acted with most unusual promptitude, and John's messengers travelled at extraordinary speed. I doubt the connexion very much.

[4] Potthast, no. 4990; bull 'Etsi carissimi' of 24 August 1215 in *Wendover*, iii. 323 ff. The pope says that before his messengers arrived the barons had taken up arms, 'ita quoque quod civitatem Londoniarum, quae est sedes regni, proditione sibi traditam invaserunt (*Wendover*, p. 325). The reference is clearly to the letters of 19 March, but Innocent may not have intended to imply that the messengers did not arrive until after the occupation of London, but that the baronial movements which led to this event (17 May) had begun.

last, perhaps by John's letter of the end of May, to appoint commissioners who might insist upon the excommunication of the rebels and suspend any bishop who refused to co-operate. Even then he had not heard of the council at Runnymede and the issue of the Charter. He knew nothing of Langton's activities as mediator, of his efforts to prevent war. He could act only upon John's petulant criticism—criticism which is in strong contrast with the friendly relations outwardly observed between the king and his archbishop. Stephen was suspended in accordance with papal letters issued before the pope had heard both sides. He had received the king's consent to go to the great council at Rome and was about to sail when the papal commissioners, Peter, bishop of Winchester, and the papal deacon Pandulf, took action against him. He naturally took the view that the pope had acted without full knowledge of the facts (*tacita veritate*). He submitted with a good grace and a sad heart.[1]

In the bitterest moments of a man's life, there is generally some touch of lighter relief. During these dark days, Stephen received a letter from Gerald of Wales, with whom he had recently had a pleasant conversation at Guildford. Gerald, on the way from Guildford to Canterbury, had learned that the archbishop proposed to start for Rome about Michaelmas, the end of September, also that he would resign his see and either become a solitary or enter the Carthusian order. His letter of expostulation is highly characteristic and we can imagine Stephen's feelings as he read it. One must take the bitter with the sweet. The life of a prelate is much finer, in dignity and in influence, than that of a hermit. The one rules, the other is ruled; the one feeds, the other is fed, the one puts out his talents to useful service, the other hides his talent in the ground. St. Basil and St. Gregory were greater than Macarius or Anthony. The active life is not so safe as the contemplative, but in every way is much to be preferred. Stephen would remember how he had dealt with

[1] *Wendover*, iii. 338, 340; Norgate, pp. 244, 245.

this in his lectures at Paris, and, more solidly and im-
partially, had come to very much the same conclusion, so
far at least as he was concerned.[1] Then it would never do
to give up Canterbury, with its great traditions and
glorious opportunities, to another, less pleasing to God,
perhaps, less learned, less useful. He must hold on till
death. But Gerald would now like to touch on another
matter. The archbishop has in his company a monk—
would that his heart were not as black as his habit [2]—who
had raved wildly against one of Gerald's books, which
Gerald had presented to Stephen. He had spoken of it
as libellous, and had said that it and its author deserved to
be burned together. With the Pharisaism which one ex-
pects from a monk of Canterbury, he had expressed his
determination to burn the book if he got a chance. The
fellow does not see the difference between a libel (*scriptum
famosum*) and something written for the improvement of
a friend or neighbour.[3] The archbishop is requested to see
that the book does not come into the critic's hands. It may
be read aloud to him, for it might do him good; but if he
gets hold of it, he may alter it or add misrepresentations
to it. And so farewell, and may Stephen never desert his
post.[4] What a queer, egotistic old man he was—nearly
seventy years old by this time. He had left Paris about the
time that Stephen had gone there; Stephen had doubtless
heard about those lectures on law, of which he was afterwards to speak so boastfully in his autobiography.[5] How
excitable and fussy he was, with his royal Welsh ancestry
and his long record of wirepulling and controversy, yet
how loyal and affectionate. He had been staunch in the
days of the interdict and had refused to put his pen at the
king's service.[6] After all, the old man was right. It would

---

[1] Above, p. 12 n, 1; cf. below, Appendix III, p. 195 and note 2.
[2] 'monachus vester cubicularius pariter et commensalis, exteriore ni-
gredine fucatus et utinam non interiore contaminatus'.
[3] Corpus Iuris Civilis, Code ix. 36.
[4] Gerald of Wales, *Opera*, i. 401–7 (from Lambeth MS. 236, f. 157*b*).
[5] Ibid. 45–8, and above, p. 28 n. 5.   [6] Ibid. 150, 151.

never do to give up now, when England was—as Gerald feared his book might be—open to every envious and malicious man to besmirch and write what he liked upon.

As events were to prove, the situation was not so desperate as it must have seemed to be in the autumn of 1215. When the archbishop returned in the spring of 1218, he found a country purged of civil strife, the charter confirmed as part of the law of the land, and the affairs of the new boy-king in careful and capable hands. His life during the interval is almost a blank to us. Matthew Paris, in the fragment which alone survives of Stephen's biography, cannot be followed with confidence. He regards Stephen as a saint, who on the way to Rome startled the hard and half-pagan Italians by curing a demoniac.[1] On his arrival at Rome, he was upbraided by Innocent, 'who from of old hated and envied him', for his opposition to the payment of the annual tribute by England to the papacy. A section of the cardinals openly sympathized with him, the pope concealed his indignation and the archbishop tactfully forbore to press the point.[2] This is narrated on the authority of Gervase of Melkley, a contemporary of Stephen's, and doubtless contains a kernel of truth; but we get a more likely story from Roger of Wendover. Stephen submitted to the papal confirmation of his suspension, which was published on 4 November, just a week before the great council of the Lateran opened.[3] It must indeed have seemed too late to argue the matter. For the time John was triumphant in a divided land, the Charter had been invalidated by papal decree, and nothing would have been gained by resistance, especially at such a time of solemnity, when it behoved all prelates to rally round the great pope in the ordering of the Church. Stephen, after all, was a cardinal, and although he is said to have taken very little part in the council,[4] there was much to be done, full of

---

[1] Liebermann, op. cit., pp. 324–6.   [2] Ibid., pp. 326, 327.
[3] Potthast, no. 5006; *Wendover*, iii. 345.
[4] *Walter of Coventry*, ii. 228: 'sed quoniam intellexit gratiam domini papae sibi subtractam, pauca verba de caetero in con ilio fecit.'

interest to a mind trained in theology and canon law. In
due course the sentence was revoked on the understanding
that he stayed away from his see.[1] He won the favour of
Innocent's successor, Honorius III, and was permitted to
return. He made a leisurely journey homewards, preaching on the way against the heretics in north Italy, and the
usurers in Flanders.[2] The first papal letter now extant
addressed to him after his restoration to office is dated 27
April 1218, and must have been received by him shortly
after his arrival in England.[3]

One consolation was denied him, the presence of his
brother, Simon. Simon, so we may read between the lines,
was a more ardent, a less balanced man that the archbishop, inclined to headstrong speech and violent partisan-
ship. Like Stephen, he was a master of Paris and a canon
of Notre Dame and of York,[4] like him he was familiar with
the Roman courts, and as papal sub-deacon was a member
of the household of Honorius III.[5] During the negotia-
tion, which preceded the interdict, he had withstood King
John to his face; and during the crisis of 1215, he would
seem to have taken a strong line of his own; for when the
canons of York desired to elect him as their archbishop
in this year, his appointment was sternly vetoed by Pope
Innocent. The king, says Wendover, had urged the canons
to elect his old adviser and minister, Walter Grey, the
bishop of Worcester, who ultimately was elected. When
he heard that Grey had been passed over in favour of
Simon, he sent messengers to Rome to protest. The archbishop of Canterbury was a public enemy and had egged
on the barons against the king; if his brother Simon were
established in York, the peace of king and kingdom could

[1] *Wendover*, iii. 360.
[2] Liebermann, pp. 327, 328; Matthew Paris, on information of Gervase
of Melkley. Cf. above, p. 41.
[3] Bliss, *Calendar of Papal Letters*, i. 53.
[4] Guérard, *Cartulaire de l'église Notre-Dame de Paris*, iv. 105. In York
he had the prebend of 'Strenasham' (Strensall), *Rotuli litt. clausarum*, i.
178*b*.
[5] Honorius III refers to him as papal sub-deacon (Bliss, i. 55).

not possibly endure.[1] Simon, with some of the other canons of York, had come to Rome. He acquiesced in the pope's decision that he should not seek promotion, but was obviously suspected by Innocent of conniving at it; for in a letter of September, Innocent declares that if he had in fact consented to the election, he was to be ineligible for any episcopal dignity without papal dispensation.[2] Unlike his brother he did not endure disgrace quietly. He openly joined Louis of France, and presumably took an active part in the arrangements for the invasion of England. He crossed with Louis in the same ship and is said to have acted as his chancellor during the expedition. Along with the chancellor of St. Paul's, he openly spoke against the sentence of excommunication passed upon the rebels. Until the pope was properly informed of the facts, the sentence must be disregarded as void.[3] For a time in 1217 the negotiations for peace were delayed by the legate's refusal to include Simon and three other clerks, one of them Elias of Dereham, a clerk of Archbishop Stephen's household, in the terms of settlement.[4] He was deprived of his preferments, and remained in Louis's service. In May 1218 Pope Honorius allowed him to hold a prebend or other benefice in France, and as he had confessed his grievous sins, restored him to papal favour.[5] But, although Elias of Dereham was released from exile,

---

[1] *Wendover*, iii. 338. [2] Ibid., 339, 340.

[3] *Histoire des ducs de Normandie* (ed. Michel), pp. 165–7, 171, 172, &c. Wendover (iii. 369, 370) says that Louis made him his chancellor and speaks of his preaching in London with George Hobregge, chancellor (not precentor, as Wendover states) of St. Paul's. For Simon's relations with Louis see Petit-Dutaillis, *Étude sur la vie et le règne de Louis VIII* (1894), pp. 98, 161, 339, 511.

[4] *Wendover*, iv. 32, 33; Petit-Dutaillis, p. 161; Norgate, *Minority of Henry III*, p. 47 and note. Elias of Dereham had at one time been in the royal service; he was a clerk of Hugh of Wells, bishop of Lincoln, and was with him in exile; at this time he was one of Langton's clerks. See Armitage Robinson, *Somerset Historical Essays*, pp. 149, 154; Bliss, i. 63.

[5] Bliss, i. 55, 63. He was still receiving a pension in 1234; *Historiens de la France*, xxii. 566.

Simon was kept out of England until the summer of 1227, when, at the request of Henry III and the solicitation of the archbishop, he was allowed to return.[1] The brothers were together for only a few months before the archbishop died. Simon, now archdeacon of Canterbury, survived him for twenty years. He stood high in the favour of pope and king, and exerted an influence in England, France, and Rome far greater than an archdeacon of Canterbury—important though that dignitary was in those days—could usually hope to possess. He was a friend and patron of the Franciscans; but his actions alienated the monks, and he was execrated at St. Albans as whole-heartedly as the memory of Stephen was cherished.[2]

The conduct of Simon Langton and Elias of Dereham during the civil war of 1216–17, suggests two important inferences. In the archbishop's circle King John met with little sympathy. Although Stephen's public attitude was correct—for example, he surrendered his castle of Rochester in May 1215 at John's request, and when Louis of France entered London his servants at first refused to give up the Tower to the invader [3]—yet his private opinions of John's unreliability were doubtless well known. John was justified, not in regarding the archbishop as a treacherous envoy, but in regarding him as a hostile critic. But, in the second place, Simon's conduct at this time reminds us that the opposition to John was ecclesiastical, based upon moral considerations no less than baronial; it was an appeal to custom. The majority of the bishops acted together as mediators until civil war broke out, but when the prospect of a peaceful settlement disappeared, many of them joined

[1] *Royal Letters*, ed. Shirley, i. 548 (bull of 19 May 1227), cf. Bliss, i. 118; Gasquet, *Henry the Third and the Church* (1905), p. 112, quoting bulls of Gregory IX in the Public Record Office, Bundle XXXV, nos. 83, 84.

[2] For Simon's later life see Miss Norgate's article in the *Dictionary of National Biography*. For his protection of the Franciscans at Canterbury see Eccleston, *De adventu minorum*, ed. Little (Paris, 1909), p. 25 and Charles Cotton, *The Grey Friars of Canterbury* (1924), pp. 6, 7, 10.

[3] Petit-Dutaillis, p. 102. On Stephen's independent attitude see above, p. 125 and note 1.

Louis and with a large section of the clergy were involved in a common denunciation. One of these bishops was John's old servant, Hugh of Wells, bishop of Lincoln. It is perhaps significant that Elias of Dereham was in Hugh's company during the years of exile before 1213. He passed later from the service of Hugh to that of Stephen. Ecclesiastical opinion, and we may be sure academic opinion, was divided; in France it was undoubtedly on Stephen's side; and even in the college of cardinals Stephen had supporters. After John's death and the failure of Louis of France, the bitter feelings roused by rebellion and foreign invasion would naturally give way to the consideration that, in a very difficult situation, there was much to be said on both sides, and that Stephen had acted with great restraint. There was a return to the normal, strengthened by the acceptance on all sides of the essential elements of the Great Charter. If we start from this view of the position, we can appreciate Stephen's attitude to the papacy, to the relations between the papacy and England, and to the political and ecclesiastical problems with which he had to deal during the last years of his life. His standpoint was clear and consistent; it was characteristic of him. And, still more, it was the standpoint at which one would expect a theologian, versed in the practical work of Church and State, to arrive during this formative period in the history of the Church.

Langton dealt more than once, in the course of his teaching at Paris, with the papal power. As we have seen he taught that the pope could not use his authority to permit anything contrary to the law of nature, to the fundamental moral law expounded in the Scriptures.[1] On the other hand the supreme pontiff was the mouthpiece of God. Serious problems of interpretation, of the consistency of papal decree with traditional moral belief, were bound to arise. In a question on fasting such an issue is solved without much difficulty; a papal decree issued discreetly, with the counsel of the cardinals and in a good

[1] Above, p. 16.

cause (*ex honesta causa*), must be obeyed if it is a command (*mandatum*), and must be respected if it is advice (*consilium*). The establishment of a fast on the fourth, sixth, and seventh days of the week for five years on behalf of the Holy Land is a case in point. We read in the book of Judith that when a city was besieged the inhabitants decided to fast for five days on the understanding that, if the city were not delivered by the end of that time, it should be surrendered, and that Judith, inspired by the Holy Spirit, saw that they did evil and tempted God. It would seem that the papal decree was not lawful for the pope did evil. Langton explains:

'We say that the decree was lawful and that respect must be paid to the supreme pontiff, because who resists him resists the ordinance of God. Nor is the comparison a valid one, for [according to the book of Judith] they imposed a condition upon the fast and to set a term to the divine mercy is to tempt God, but the supreme pontiff did not do this. The difference is obvious.' [1]

Langton was more at a loss when he was trying to explain the papal dispensation from the payment of tithes, granted to the Cistercian [2] and the military orders. The duty to pay tithe is moral and formal, part of natural law. Any tithes for example paid by a layman belong to their appropriate parish. Langton argued that the exemption of the Cistercians could be justified, because the monastery can be made the mother church. Moreover, as was laid down by Alexander III in the decretal *Dilecti filii*, in a case of great need the tithes should be paid to the monastery to which they belong.[3] This argument, I may ob-

---

[1] Cambridge MS., f. 260^r. Langton's recollection of the narrative in the Book of Judith (chapters 7 and 8) was defective.

[2] J. T. Fowler, *Cistercian Statutes* (1890), pp. 36, 40. Cf. Alexander III in Decretals of Gregory IX, lib. iii, tit. xxx, c. 10.

[3] Cambridge MS., f. 340^v: 'Item Cistercienses non dant decimas de hiis que propriis sumptibus excolunt. Sed hoc miror, cum soluere decimam sit preceptum morale et indispensabile et de iure naturali, ergo si aliquis campus detur eis ab aliquo laico non debet perire parochia illa cuius decima erat [*altered in later hand* to ' decima illi in cuius parochia erat ']. Solutio: auctoritate apostolica datur priuilegium hoc predictis fratribus cisterciensis

serve, does not give an adequate interpretation of the decretal, which was clearly intended to distinguish lands acquired at farm by the Cistercians from those which they held and cultivated themselves.[1] Later in this very important discussion, Langton returns to the problem and faces the main issue. Why can the pope dispense from the payment of tithes? Could he extend the privilege to all laymen, as well as to the Templars and Hospitallers?

'We say that it is not our business nor is it possible to define how far (*quantum*) the pope can go. For who would have dared to say before the time of pope Alexander that a woman who had not consummated her marriage could transfer herself to the monastic life? Who would not have denied that the lord pope, in the light of the saying in the gospel, 'whomsoever God hath joined let no man put asunder,' could give dispensation in a matter of this kind? But afterwards when the decretal was issued, any man who had previously denied it would say that the lord pope could dispense. Similarly, I am at liberty to believe (*credibile est*) that the lord pope cannot dispense laymen from the payment of tithes, even small tithes, and Alexander's decretal on the question confirms this view ... but if the pope decreed otherwise I should say that I was in error' (*me fuisse deceptum*).

He proceeded to explain how the Templars and Hospitallers differed from ordinary laymen.[2]

This is a very frank statement. It shows us how a theologian and cardinal of strong personality, sane and inde-

ordinis et hoc potest facere papa, sicut de curiali ecclesia posset facere matricem. Si tamen ecclesia ad quam spectat enormiter ledatur, soluent decimas eidem monasterio, ut dicit Alexander in illa decretali Dilecti filii.'

[1] Decretals of Gregory IX, lib. iii, tit. xxx, c. 8; see the *Epistolae Gilberti Foliot*, ed. Giles, ii. 109. The abbot of Holy Cross had complained that the abbey of 'Neuden' was farming lands, and refusing to pay tithes which had formerly been paid to Holy Cross. Pope Alexander pointed out that the exemption from tithe was not intended to apply to lands held in this way (*quas conduxistis*). The parties were the Cistercian abbey of Holy Cross in Tipperary and the mother Cistercian house of Nenay or Maig in Limerick (cf. *Monasticon*, vii. 1137.).

[2] Cambridge MS., f. 341ʳ. Cf. Alexander III in Decretals, lib. iii, tit. xxx, c. 14. For the other point mentioned by Langton see Decretals, lib. iii, tit. xxxii, 'de conuersione coniugatorum'.

pendent in his thinking, accepted the doctrine of the *plenitudo potestatis* of the pope. It shows why, though at the time of his suspension he may have agreed, as he generally did agree, with his brother Simon, he could not bring himself, once the papal decision against him had been given, to resist further. But it shows also that the very reason which made him acquiesce forced him to consider all questions, as yet undecided, in the light of the natural, the moral, law. For the papal decisions, taken deliberately with the counsel and consent of the cardinals, were an exposition of the moral law. They could not be regarded as light or arbitrary, and a responsible person was not merely at liberty, he had a moral duty, to discuss and decide upon the issues of the day, to the best of his ability, in the light of the law of Scripture. This was the true academic view, and also the statesmanlike view. It was the view, later in the century, of Grosseteste, and is far removed both from the carping witticisms of a man like Matthew Paris and from the blind allegiance of time-serving papalists. Langton lived at the most critical period in the history of the Church. The future alone could decide whether the achievement of theological unity under the direction of the papal power would be followed by a finer, more delicate, yet closer moral harmony, or lead to a moral cleavage. Langton was not a subtle thinker. It would be absurd to suppose that he speculated on the problem of development. Yet, as many other passages in his *Sentences* show, he was quite alive to the fact of development. He realized that, throughout history, the process of adjustment had been necessary and persistent. While, for example, he approached every subject from the starting-point of Scripture, he delighted to show how the law of the Old Testament had been rightly modified or abridged in matters of detail.[1] But only a solemn papal

[1] Compare the questio 'utrum antiqui patres crediderint eosdem articulos penitus quos et nos credimus' (Cambridge MS., f. 210ʳ; MS. latin, 14556, f. 228ʳ). In the discussion of fasting Langton explains why in some respects the Church regards the night as belonging to the previous day, and

decree could shake his interpretation of fundamentals; and we may be sure, I think, that until some decisions were taken he worked for a contrary result and that, in his acquiescence, his reason lagged behind his faith.

Langton's *questiones* are of value to us because they reveal the working of an orthodox, steady mind during a formative period in the history of the Church. There was nothing peculiar, of course, in the teaching that the exercise of papal authority must be guided by the law of nature. William of Drogheda, Langton's younger contemporary, who wrote his *Summa Aurea*—a text-book of canonical practice—at Oxford about 1239, discussed the question whether a papal rescript which is *contra ius commune*, is valid. He showed that it is invalid if it is contrary to natural law or revelation, and should be safeguarded by a *non obstante* clause if it conflicts with *ius pontificale*.[1] The canons of the councils of the Lateran in 1179 and 1215, the decretals of Alexander III and Innocent III expounded the wisdom and experience gained by masters at Paris and Bologna, by cardinals in counsel, by prelates face to face with the problems of the Christian society. Langton, theologian, cardinal, and archbishop, lived in the centre or centres of the movement. He was not an agent or spectator—he was one of those who exerted an influence upon the life and thought of the Church. And, in addition, he has an interest for us because he was, by race and birth, an Englishman, singularly clear-sighted and honest, filled with affection for his native land; and had the duty of bringing all his varied experience to bear upon the problems which beset England in his day. His responsibility was great, for his opportunity was unique.

in others adopts the opposite practice and begins the day with the preceding vigil (Cambridge MS., f. 338ʳ). In the discussion of tithes he touches on the difference between the city life of the Levites and the agricultural surroundings of the clergy and regulars of his day (f. 341ᵛ).

[1] *Summa Aurea*, ed. Wahrmund (Innsbruck, 1914), pp. 322, 342; F. de Zulueta, 'William of Drogheda', in the *Mélanges de droit romain dédiés à Georges Cornil* (Ghent, 1926), pp. 641–57.

For two and a half years after his return to England, that is to say, from the late spring of 1218 to the autumn of 1220, the archbishop took a secondary place in the administration of the kingdom. His public appearances, when mentioned by the annalists, were, for the most part, on great ecclesiastical occasions. For example, when the great earl William the Marshal, the *rector* of the kingdom, died, the legate Pandulf immediately took counsel with Hubert de Burgh and the officials of the exchequer.[1] The archbishop was apparently not consulted. He supervised the arrangements for the Marshal's funeral in the New Temple, and preached the funeral sermon, drawing the old moral that death the leveller reduces us all to dust, all that remained of him who was as good a knight as had ever lived upon the earth.[2] About this time Stephen received the papal commission, addressed to himself and to John, abbot of Fountains, later bishop of Ely, to investigate the life and miracles of Hugh of Lincoln. The inquiry, if we may judge from the fragments which survive, was conducted with great care, and must have involved considerable trouble. The commissioners ordered local investigations to be made about every alleged miracle, and detailed reports were sent to them.[3] The process was completed at Rome by the middle of February 1220, when Pope Honorius issued the bill of canonization.[4] An incident which occurred some years later illustrates the care observed by the archbishop in work of this kind. In March 1224 the pope sent a mandate to the archbishop, archdeacon and official of Canterbury to give licence to the abbot and convent of Dorchester-on-Thames to translate

[1] *Royal Letters*, ed. Shirley, i. 112–13, 117–21. For the dates see the *English Historical Review*, xxiii (April 1908), 229, 230. .

[2] *Histoire de Guillaume le Maréchal*, ll. 19022–84 (ed. Meyer, ii. 324–6).

[3] Potthast, no. 6053, mandate 27 April 1219. The procedure of inquiry is shown in a record of two miracles, printed in the *Opera Giraldi Cambrensis* (vii. 188–92) from a Harleian manuscript.

[4] The bull of canonization of 17 February 1220 (Potthast, no. 6195) is in *Wendover*, iv. 64, 65.

to a more worthy place the body of St. Birinus, the apostle of Wessex. The archbishop and his colleagues went to Dorchester and opened the tomb, which, they reported to the pope, appeared to be that of St. Birinus. But they were puzzled by the passage in Bede's history, in which it is said that the body of St. Birinus had been translated to Winchester. The pope, writing in August 1225, empowered Stephen to make inquiry at Winchester, but at the same time authorized him to pronounce that the body of St. Birinus actually was at Dorchester. Bede, he remarks, says many things on hearsay. Moreover, as the bodies of two bishops, Birinus and Bertinus, were buried at Dorchester, Bede may really have been referring to Bertinus. By the carelessness of copyists his words may have been transferred to Birinus.[1] I can find no evidence that a bishop Bertinus lived in England before the time of Bede, and while Bede's statement may have been erroneous it is certainly explicit. Stephen's gentle scepticism is more satisfying than the historical criticism of the papal curia. However, the canons of Dorchester got their desire, and later fragments of the shrine of St. Birinus can still be seen, I think, in the abbey church.

The year 1220, opened by the canonization of that austere champion of the faith, St. Hugh of Lincoln, might be described as a period of ceremonial stocktaking in the Church in England. The restoration of peace and unity in the country was symbolized by the solemn coronation of the young king at Westminster on Whit-Sunday, 17 May, when the archbishop took the opportunity to proclaim the bull of canonization and to summon the faithful to the Crusade.[2] But the year 1220 was also the fiftieth anniversary of the martyrdom of St. Thomas of Canter-

[1] Bliss, i. 95, 103, papal letters of March 1224 and August 1225. The passage to which Langton referred in the *Historia ecclesiastica* (iii. 7) will be found in *Baedae Opera Historica*, ed. Plummer, i. 140.

[2] *Chronicon Rad. Coggeshall*, ed. Stevenson (Rolls Series), p. 188. The Dunstable annalist says that he preached *ad populum* (*Annales Monastici*, iii. 57). The day before (16 May) the king laid the foundation stone of the Lady Chapel of the new abbey. Its site is now uncertain.

bury, and a few weeks after the coronation, on 7 July, the long-awaited translation of the saint's body was made to its beautiful shrine behind the new choir of the cathedral church. The chief place was given on the great day to the archbishop of Rheims, but it was Stephen's day. He had made the preparations, he provided the hospitality and entertained the visitors in the great hall of the palace, begun by Hubert Walter and finished by himself. His address in honour of his famous forerunner has come down to us, and his name was henceforth to be associated in prosperity, as it had been linked in adversity, with that of St. Thomas. The story of the translation has frequently been told, and may be passed over here.[1] Its importance lies in the symbolism of all this pomp and magnificence. St. Thomas had at last come to his own. The liberties of the Church had been secured. The right to free canonical relations by the chapters had been acknowledged. The ecclesiastical courts were busy, the canon law was seriously taught and studied. The daily life of the Church was fully and freely open to the inspection and intervention of the Universal Ordinary. On the other hand, the period of tutelage was drawing to a close. The archbishop was no longer on probation. When he went to Rome in October of this year, carrying with him portions of the sacred relics of St. Thomas, he received no half-hearted welcome. He was asked to preach a sermon to the Roman people on St. Thomas.[2] He was able to represent to the papal court that England was now at peace, and that the archbishop of Canterbury need no longer be subordinate to a legate who ought, as bishop-elect of Norwich, to behave as one of his suffragans. He asked for papal recognition of the new

---

[1] See especially the texts translated in A. J. Mason's 'What became of the bones of St. Thomas?' (Cambridge, 1920), pp. 69–83, and his note on the archbishop's palace, pp. 56–60. Langton's 'tractatus de translatione' will be found in Giles, *Vita S. Thomae* (1845), ii. 269–97. Other contemporary incidents of a similar nature were the translations of St. Wulfstan (1218), and St. Hugh (1220), the canonizations of St. William of York (1227, after inquiry 1223–4) and St. Laurence O'Toole (1226).

[2] *Walter of Coventry*, ii. 246.

order: that the legate should be withdrawn, that the old tiresome claim, so often rejected, of the archbishop of York to carry his cross as an equal in the southern province, should be stopped. He pointed out also that, if there was to be harmony in English society, the rights of patrons and the freedom of the English to find promotion in their own land should be respected. The right of the pope to nominate or to guide nominations to canonries and livings was undoubted, but if it were exercised as it had been exercised of late, it would create an unhappy division of sympathies in England. To override the normal procedure without grave cause, and to encourage foreign ecclesiastics, especially Italians, to seek preferment in England, was unwise. Langton got his way on most points, and before he reached England again in August 1221, Pandulf had ceased to be legate.[1] On the way home Stephen spent some time in his old haunts at Paris. Since his day the schools had developed into a university, and the issues raised on the relations which should exist between the bishops and cathedral church on the one part, and the self-conscious corporation of masters on the other, were fre-

---

[1] Annals of Dunstable in *Annales Monastici*, iii. 74, 75; cf. Gasquet, op. cit., p. 54. The pope in 1224 reproached Langton for representing that the peaceful condition of England made the presence of a legate no longer necessary (*Royal Letters*, i. 543). Conditions were perhaps more serious in 1224; but Honorius cannot have been ignorant of the serious disturbances of the year 1220-1, on which see Norgate, *Minority of Henry III*, c. 3. In the end of April he was writing about the danger of civil war (Potthast, no. 6643; Bliss, i. 80), yet Pandulf resigned in July. The dispute with York was, of course, a very old one and had been decided already in favour of Canterbury; see the papal mandate of Feb. 1218 in accordance with the decisions of popes Alexander and Innocent (Bliss, i. 52). The controversy was still causing inconvenience in the royal councils in 1237 (ibid., p. 160). See Makower, *Constitutional History of the Church of England*, p. 290. Lastly, the limitation of papal provisions does not seem to have been so complete as is frequently suggested, in spite of the specific bull of 26 February 1221 (Potthast, no 6569; Wilkins, i. 584). At any rate an indult to the archbishop, dean, and chapter of York of 18 February promised only that the pope would not provide to prebends, &c., on the next occasion of vacancy (Bliss, i. 79).

quent and acute. Stephen came to Paris as one of a papal commission to settle some disputes,[1] then passed on to England to resume, without any local superior, his duties as archbishop and chief adviser to the Crown.

It would be a mistake to regard the change in the archbishop's position as a victory for an insular policy. There is no evidence that the papacy ever regarded the surrender of the kingdom by John to Rome as in itself involving the right to keep a legate permanently in England.[2] A legate was sent on ecclesiastical business when particular conditions required his presence. Thus the cardinal Nicholas came to reconcile John with the clergy, arrange the restitution of ecclesiastical property and to remove the interdict. These duties accomplished, he returned. The cardinal Guala was sent to protect a son of the Church, a Crusader, against the attacks of a foreign prince and a rebellious baronage; he remained to guide a helpless child, who was peculiarly a charge of the papacy. It is impossible, indeed, to distinguish Guala's ecclesiastical duties from his responsibilities as political adviser in a vassal state. That he took a decisive and predominant share in the government of England is beyond dispute. From a 'feudal' standpoint the legate's presence might have been justified on the ground that he was the warden of a minor. But the pope appears to have taken a more elastic view. His letters emphasize not the king's feudal dependence, but his claim, as an infant, upon spiritual protection. Lordship, we must remember, was a wider conception than the feudal relation. *Dominium* had its precedents in scripture, in law and history, long before the days of Dante and Wyclif, and the pope had no need to explain his relation to his ward and vassal with arguments drawn from local feudal custom. When arguments of this kind were used, they were used by

---

[1] *C.U.P.* i, part i, p. 98, no. 41. For the points involved see Rashdall, *Universities of Europe in the Middle Ages*, i. 311 note, 318, 457 note.

[2] Langton is not known to have exercised legative powers as archbishop, but his successors did: Stubbs, *Constitutional History*, iii. 307, 308. On the whole subject see Makower, op. cit., pp. 232–4, 284–9 with notes.

interested parties in England, more familiar than Rome was with customary ideas. For example, the king and his great council of barons and prelates argued in 1226 that, as England paid an annual tribute of 1,000 marks, she ought to be exempted from any other permanent claims upon English revenues, lay or clerical, and a few months earlier the king's advisers ordered the ecclesiastical council which was to debate the papal request for a fixed revenue from the whole Church in the West, to grant nothing which would diminish the resources of the Crown.[1] Considerations of this kind may appropriately be described as feudal—they apply arguments drawn from the relations between a lord and his vassal. The papacy was not concerned to discuss its relations with England on this ground, just as, because England was now part of the 'Patrimony of St. Peter', it did not pretend to govern England as it governed the neighbourhood of Rome. When England was freed from the invader and Louis of France had made peace, Guala withdrew, as Nicholas had withdrawn. His successor, Pandulf, was a person of different status. He was not a cardinal but a member of the papal household, and is variously described as the pope's sub-deacon and familiar, as notary and chamberlain. In September 1218 he was granted legatine powers and, although bishop-elect of Norwich, was exempted from the jurisdiction of Canterbury because the pope still desired to keep England under supervision. On the death of the Marshal he became the actual head of the State, more influential than the justiciar and the archbishop. But the very fact that he intervened in the ordinary administration, and had no special task of

---

[1] *Wendover*, iv. 116; Barnwell annalist in *Walter of Coventry*, ii. 279. The Barnwell writer says that the king and his council actually met the nuncio Otto, whereas Wendover says that Otto had left the country earlier (iv. 124). For the dates see Barker, *The Dominican Order and Convocation*, p. 46 note. The record evidence supports Wendover, for about 17 March 1226, the sheriff of Kent was ordered 'quod habere facias Magistro Ottoni nuncio domini Pape *versus suas partes eunti* unam bonam nauem ad transfretandum in ea ad custum nostrum'; *Rotuli litterarum clausarum*, ii. 102*b*.

magnitude to perform, emphasized the anomaly of his position. Moreover, King Henry was nearing the age of fourteen (Oct. 1221) when he could be emancipated from his tutors and begin to learn the duties for which he would be held responsible when he came of age. So Pandulf was withdrawn in his turn.

During the next few years—the last of Langton's life and of the king's minority—Pope Honorius and his successor Gregory IX exercised a real lordship over England, but they acted in general on the advice of the king's counsellors. The consent of Honorius was required before any fundamental change could be made. He granted Henry the 'dispositio regni' and the control of the great seal at the end of 1223, and at the same time he authorized the king to resume the possession and disposition of the royal castles; but it is clear that he acted in response to advice from England, and probably on the advice of the archbishop and bishops; and the distinction drawn at this date between the control of the seal and the right to affix it to royal charters was obviously made by the council.[1] The pope's policy is defined in another letter in which he announced to Henry that he had rescinded his instructions to certain barons to surrender the royal castles in their keeping. Henry was not to regard this action as binding upon him, for the pope had issued his earlier instructions on the petition of parties speaking on the king's behalf. Honorius would not intervene lightly.[2] If Henry finds that it is unwise to act upon the original letters ordering the surrender of the castles, he should await more stringent orders regarding them. The pope did not know how the land lay; he was prepared to act upon the deliberate

---

[1] For these changes in Henry's status see Norgate, *Minority of Henry III*, pp. 202–7 and the important note on pp. 286–90, with the articles of Turner and Powicke there cited. The share of the archbishop and bishops was later alleged against them by Fawkes de Breauté; see his *querimonia* in the Barnwell annals (*Walter of Coventry*, ii. 261, 262). The annalist, in speaking of Henry's second coronation in 1220 refers to the archbishop's affection for the king (ibid., 245). See also *Wendover*, iv. 88.

[2] *Royal Letters*, i. 539: 'ne aliqua interuenisse leuitas uideatur'.

advice of Henry and his counsellors, but he would not be rushed by either party. The tone of his letters, indeed, is that of a benevolent and anxious parent, rather than of a feudal suzerain. Their phraseology smacks of the moral theology of the schools—so familiar to Langton—rather than of the law book. He calls Henry his 'specialissimus filius'; he is giving the most careful consideration, with the cardinals, for suggestions from England; let Henry avoid all scandal to his subjects and choose a really suitable time for securing the restitution of his property. And when he had occasion to write sharply to Langton, he rebukes him for his forgetfulness of those moral considerations which we know the archbishop made his political guide.[1]

If a papal legate were not required to maintain the papal *dominium* over England, he was still less necessary to maintain ecclesiastical dependence upon Rome. Here the issues raised by John's surrender of his kingdom did not arise. John's submission had removed an external obstacle to the smooth working of the canonical system; it had done nothing to establish it. No pope of this period had any need to write to an archbishop as Alexander III wrote to archbishop Richard in his famous letter *Qua fronte,* 'with what face you dare to consult us about questions of law we cannot understand, since you are said to be perverting the order of justice in matters which are plain and free of doubt.'[2] Archbishop Stephen felt no difficulties, had no need to hesitate about his duty here, for the Lateran Council of 1215, which he had attended, had issued a programme which he could whole-heartedly approve. His differences with Rome in matters ecclesiastical were few, and were differences, not on any point of principle, but on details of policy. He had disliked the interference with canonical appointments, he disliked the

---

[1] *Royal Letters,* i. 544: 'ubi est enim tue abundantia sapientie? . . . sicut maior habes locum in Anglia, ita si status eius malus fuerit tibi specialiter imputabitur'.

[2] Decretals, Greg. IX, lib. ii, tit. xxviii, c. 25, translated in part by Maitland, *Canon Law in England,* pp. 126, 127.

tendency to increase the numbers of foreigners provided
to canonries and other benefices, but, as an old teacher at
Paris and a cardinal, he appreciated as well as any man the
conception of a united Church, bound together under the
headship of the pope, by a common law inspired by the
law of God.

The history of the reconstruction of the Church in
England after the Interdict, in accordance with the
Lateran decrees, has yet to be written. Historians of the
English Church tend to overlook the fact that this was no
insular movement, but a general attempt to give force to
the decrees of a great council. And these decrees were not
councils of perfection issuing from the brain of a great
pope; they summed up the work of previous councils, of
a generation of papal legislation, and of ceaseless discussion
by theologians, of whom Langton had been one, on the
sacraments, the details of ecclesiastical discipline, monastic
administration, the duties of prelates and officials, current
heresies and moral questions. And, more than this, they
opened a new era in which the Church was free to develop
the intricacies of its administrative and financial system,
to devise new methods of work, to enrol new types of re-
cruits, such as the Mendicant Orders, in the fight against
the infidel, the heretic and the backslider. English experience had provided much of the material, suggested
many of the problems which had led to the great work of
definition,[1] and now England was open to its full effects.

The archbishop was hardly in a position to take the lead
until Pandulf had resigned in July 1221, a month before
Stephen returned from his last visit to Rome. He must
have set to work at once, for the provincial council met at
Osney in April 1222. This was the council whose canons,
applying the Lateran decrees, mark a new starting-point
in the history of canon law in England. It is the council
familiar to us all from Maitland's paper on 'The Deacon

---

[1] I need merely recall the 'lengthy examination paper' as Maitland
calls it, which Bishop Eustace of Ely presented to Pope Innocent III in
1204. Analysed by Maitland, op. cit., pp. 124–6.

and the Jewess'.[1] A critical edition of the canons is badly needed, if only to bring them into relation with the constitutions issued during the period by the English bishops.[2] We have the constitutions issued for the clergy of the dioceses of Salisbury, London, and Durham[3] and whether they were independent or applications of the Osney canons is still an open question. During the last few years the popes had brought particular decrees of the Lateran Council to the attention of this bishop or that, and asked him to enforce them in his diocese.[4] The bishops, again, were busy in framing concordats with their cathedral chapters,[5] and the chapters in defining their customs or compiling their liturgical uses.[6] In some dioceses, notably in Lincoln, the parochial system was overhauled, and the mutual obligations of monasteries and their vicars in appropriated churches were defined.[7] The archdeacons must have been busy on their visitations and in the compilation of their registers of the utensils and ornaments of churches, and one can get some idea from the writings of William of Drogheda of the activities of the Church courts. The Benedictines and orders of regular canons were organizing themselves in general chapters,

---

[1] Maitland, op. cit., pp. 158–79.

[2] Wilkins, i. 585 ff. There are many manuscripts which require classification. On some liturgical problems see Bradshaw and Wordsworth, *Lincoln Cathedral Statutes*, iii. 543, 544.

[3] Richard Poore's constitutions for Salisbury and Durham, the latter ascribed to Richard Marsh, are in *Sarum Charters and Documents* (Rolls Series), pp. 128–63; Wilkins, i. 572–83, cf. 599 ff.; the diocesan constitutions for London (Lincoln Chapter Library MS., B. 6, 7a) have been edited by R. M. Woolley in the *English Historical Review*, xxx. 288–302 (April 1915).

[4] The papal registers contain many letters addressed to bishops ordering the enforcement of the decrees about married clerks, the succession of sons of clerks to their fathers' livings, pluralists, absentees, &c. See Bliss, i, pp. 78, 79, 84, 85, 86, 90, 91, 105 for the years 1221–6.

[5] e.g. Bath, Carlisle, Coventry, Worcester.

[6] See the list in Bradshaw and Wordsworth, *Lincoln Cathedral Statutes*, iii. 831 ff.

[7] A. Gibbons, *Liber antiquus de ordinationibus vicariarum tempore Hugonis Wells* (Lincoln, 1888), with the introduction.

as prescribed by the Lateran Council.[1] And, all the while, and in all parts of England, dignitaries on papal commissions were investigating special cases which had been brought to the notice of the pope, the universal ordinary. As archbishop, Langton was involved in all this work, although, in the absence of registers and of nearly all the correspondence of his chancery, we cannot follow him from day to day.[2] He must have been amazingly busy, apart from his political responsibilities, and we can sympathize with him when we find Pope Honorius reminding him in 1222 that he had neglected to make a formal visitation of his province.[3]

We do get two or three glimpses of Stephen, very intimately and humanly concerned in the new life around him. In 1221, from his second and last general chapter, St. Dominic sent out a mission to England. The mission, Gilbert of Fresnay as prior with twelve companions, reached Canterbury in the company of the bishop of Winchester. Stephen can have been back home only a few weeks when they arrived and were presented to him. He immediately invited brother Gilbert to preach before him in the church where he had himself arranged to preach that day.[4] Three years later the first Franciscans reached England, a few days before their master endured the agony of the stigmata far away in the Apennines. They settled in Canterbury and in later years received much kindness from Simon, the archbishop's brother. It is unlikely that Stephen—in this busy year—was there to welcome them, but Eccleston tells a pleasant story of his courtesy to a brother Solomon, who was sent to him for

---

[1] See H. E. Salter's introduction to *Chapters of the Augustinian Canons* (Canterbury and York Society, part 70, 1922); Edmund Bishop in the *Darnside Review*, xlv (1925), 217–19, and W. A. Pantin in *Trans. R. Hist. Soc.* (4th Ser. X. 1928). Mr. Pantin dates the first English Benedictine Chapter, September 1218.

[2] See Appendix VI.   [3] Bliss, i. 86 (26 March 1222).

[4] Trivet, *Annales* (ed. Hog), p. 209. St. Dominic had died a few weeks before.

ordination as an acolyte: 'Accedat frater Salomon de ordine apostolorum'.[1] And again, we see Stephen on Michaelmas Day, 1225, preaching a fine sermon to the people outside the new Lady Chapel at Salisbury—the first building
of the new cathedral—and entering to celebrate mass.[2]
The rise of this lovely church was symbolic of the new
order—for the removal from Old Sarum was a deliberate
act of emancipation from the cramped and disturbing
neighbourhood of a royal castle to a spacious site where
the canons could live with more freedom.

In the work of ecclesiastical reconstruction papal policy
was sure and vigorous, a striking contrast to the uncertain
touch with which Pope Honorius handled the affairs of
the realm. Langton, on the contrary, in ecclesiastical administration a willing instrument of the Church, took his
own line as the chief counsellor of the king. He seems to
have had no hesitation and he maintained his position
with independence and energy. Henry would soon be of
age, and parties at court began to form. The issues were
very much the same as they had been in John's reign, but
the centre of gravity had shifted. Now the supporters of
the charter were in the ascendant, while the old friends of
John—the earl of Chester, William Brewer, Fawkes de
Breauté, and the rest were in opposition. The maintenance
of peace depended on the control of the royal castles. In
the crisis of 1224, memorable for the siege of Bedford, the
archbishop took a clear line. There is a clause in the Constitutions of Clarendon—a clause to which Alexander III
had not taken exception—to the effect that if any man de-
prives the king of his right, the archbishop and bishops and
archdeacons ought to force him to make satisfaction—they

---

[1] Eccleston, *De adventu minorum*, ed. Little (Paris, 1909), p. 16. Eccleston
proceeds: 'Hoc ideo dixerim, ut innotescat quantae reverentiae fuerit apud
sapientes fratrum primordialis simplicitas'. After eating at the archbishop's
table, Solomon and his companions went off barefooted in the snow.

[2] *The Register of S. Osmund*, edited W. H. Rich Jones (Rolls Series), ii.
39. The 'noua basilica' was the Lady Chapel and its two side aisles 'all
probably that was then completed of the new cathedral' (ibid., p. cxx).

must use spiritual weapons, in this war, to bring him to reason. And, as we know, Langton used to teach at Paris that, whatever they may think of the justice of the King's cause, the king's subjects ought to follow him against a castle, if its lord had been adjudged by lawful process.[1] Now it is evident from the protests of the bishop of Winchester, the earl of Chester and others, from the papal letters, and the pamphlet prepared on behalf of Fawkes de Breauté by his clerk, Robert Passelew, that Stephen's interpretation of his duty in cases of this kind was strongly resented. The pope upbraided him for reckless disregard of the danger which threatened the king in Poitou, for conniving at civil disturbance, for forgetfulness of the principles which should guide a scholar of his reputation, and of the conciliatory sagacity required of the chief counsellor of the Crown. The bishop and his friends complained that their motives had been misrepresented and the loyalty of Fawkes de Breauté wrongly suspected. Fawkes and his advisers charged Stephen with abusing his powers of excommunication. The archbishop, they suggested, was the real ruler in the land, and he was bringing it to ruin. They begged the pope to send a legate. Stephen's letters are lost, but the letters of Honorius show that the pope was sufficiently persuaded to leave him in control. He would send a nuntio, not a legate. The crisis

---

[1] Above, p. 95. According to one account, Langton in the year 1215 refused to surrender Rochester castle until he had been deprived of it by legal process (*nisi per iudicium*); *Chronicon Rad. Coggeshall*, ed. Stevenson (R.S.), p. 173. This was after his earlier surrender of the castle, and during the negotiations of the summer. During the proceedings against Fawkes de Breauté a curious incident occurred in Devon (August 1224). The feudal tenants, summoned by the sheriff by royal command, refused to blockade the castle of Plympton, on the ground that 'se nec posse nec debere huiusmodi custodiam facere, cum domini sui sint [in exercitu] uestro, quibus sua debent seruitia'; the sheriff of Devon to the King, *Royal Letters*, i. 232. The men of Devon carried Langton's line of argument farther; unusual service, the justification for which was unknown, should not be exacted in the absence of their lords. There was perhaps the additional consideration that the military service due was already being performed.

passed, the castles were distributed among safe guardians, Peter des Roches and the earl of Chester were worsted and Fawkes de Breauté died in exile.[1]

Langton's success was due, I think, to the fact that he had on his side men of administrative experience. The justiciar, Hubert de Burgh, was a somewhat uncertain element, and may have been swayed by mixed motives, but he had everything to gain by falling into line. The bishops were more to be relied upon, and throughout this time were very active in political affairs. It is noteworthy that many of them had been trained in the royal household or exchequer, and came of administrative families—Richard Poore of Salisbury, Hugh of Wells of Norwich, Richard Marsh of Durham, till his death William of Sainte-Mère-Église of London, and Archbishop Walter Grey of York, were men of this type. Old servants of John, they had outgrown any narrow curialism. They had taken the lead in the reorganization of the Church, and had rallied to the principles of the charter. They assumed the temporary charge of royal castles and of the proceeds of taxes,[2] advised the council and the pope on policy, threatened recalcitrant barons with excommunication, and they acted as a group, under Langton's guidance. Against them even men like William Brewer were powerless; with them Langton was able in 1225 to provide for a solemn reissue of the charters. The Great Charter, I have argued, was a

[1] *Royal Letters*, i. 224–6, 234, 543, 544. Annals of Dunstable in *Annales Monastici*, iii. 89. See Norgate, c. 5, *passim*.

[2] The redistribution of royal castles in December 1223 and the following months was really carried through by Langton, and most of them were for a time entrusted to bishops. See Norgate, pp. 210–14, 290–2; and the entries from the Patent Roll collected by Shirley, *Royal Letters*, i. 508–16. The proceeds of the fifteenth of 1225 were entrusted to the care of the bishops of Bath and Salisbury, who kept them in the castles of Devizes and Winchester: see Mitchell, *Studies in Taxation*, p. 167. It should be noted that the action of Langton and the bishops, in taking the responsibility in these important matters, relieved the justiciar and maintained the solidarity of the council. Cf. the later defence of Hubert de Burgh (Matthew Paris, *Chronica Maiora*, vi. 65–6 in the liber Additamentorum).

statement of custom; but whereas ten years before it had been forced upon a reluctant king, and an occasion of strife, it was now the symbol of unity and sound government. Langton had not changed, he had lived to see his idea of kingship realized. In 1215 rebellious barons had fought for the charter; in 1225 they had been defeated by it. Fortune was to turn again, but the lesson of 1224 was not forgotten.

The reissue of the charter, of course, meant more than this. Money had been needed for the war in Poitou, and in granting it the great council, led by the archbishop, induced the king and his ministers to take this step. And as a result the position of the great council as a national body, acting for the whole community, was strengthened. It could be argued—and actually was argued—that any one who refused to pay the fifteenth granted on this occasion could not expect to enjoy the liberties secured by the charter. If the charter belonged to all, all must share in the responsibility assumed by the Great Council. In course of time this view naturally encouraged the tendency to make the Great Council representative of every interest. It is unlikely that Langton thought of this; but it is certain that at this time the Justinian tag 'what touches all should be approved by all' was very present to the minds of the clergy. During the years 1224–6 Langton had to face the problem of the taxation of the clergy. It will be remembered how clearly and also how moderately he had discussed this problem in his Paris days. The secular power had no right to tax the clergy, but the Church should give its aid in a just and urgent cause, provided that nothing was done—we may interpret, no precedent created—to prejudice its liberty or harm its interests.[1] A just occasion arose in 1224, when the prelates 'of their mere grace and liberality' provided men and money from their demesnes for the siege of Bedford. The king's letters patent declared that this assistance was not to be regarded

[1] Above, p. 92.

as a precedent.¹ The clergy contributed to the fifteenth in 1225, but only from their temporalities. The pope, however, had urged on the clergy the duty of a general contribution, in view of the king's needs in Poitou, and in October 1226, a sixteenth was granted—and the grant was followed as in 1224 by royal assurances that it was freely given, and no precedent²—on all property not assessed for the fifteenth of the preceding year. This was a very grave act. It was a grant of a tax on spiritualities for a secular purpose. The principle, rather than the amount, had been long and solemnly debated in the cathedral chapters. The assembly which granted the tax had been summoned by the archbishop with great care. It contained representatives of all the chapters and the archdeacons or their proctors. Precautions were taken that all the chapters should join and speak with one voice. In the preliminary discussions at Salisbury, at this time a particularly well-informed and enlightened chapter, questions like the right of a majority to bind the whole body had been debated.³ By a fortunate coincidence, the issue was raised at the same time as the pope's well-known request for the provision of a permanent papal revenue from the whole Church. Honorius had revived the suggestion, said to have been originally made by the emperor Henry VI,⁴ for the allocation of a prebend in each cathedral church, and he had added a demand for allocations from episcopal and monastic revenues, and from each collegiate church. The

---

¹ References in Norgate, p. 239.

² The pope's letters of 3 February 1225 explain the position clearly and should be compared with Langton's treatment of the subject: 'cum ecclesia secularium principum in necessitatibus sponte communicat, necessarium eis subsidium liberaliter impendendo, non est libertatis ecclesie preiudicium, sed officium potius caritatis. . . . Nolumus autem quod hec uestra gratia, uestraque caritatiua subuentio, trahatur in consequentiam uel exemplum' (Wilkins, i. 603; *Walter of Coventry*, ii. 256). The royal letters patent declaring that the grant should not form a precedent are in *Patent Rolls*, Henry III, ii. 64.

³ *Register of St. Osmund* (Rolls Series), ii. 55–70; Mitchell, op. cit., 169–71.   ⁴ See above, p. 83.

legate Romanus laid this request before a council of French clergy at Bourges, the papal subdeacon Otto brought it to England. At Bourges proctors of the chapters had claimed to be heard. They quoted the famous phrase 'quod tangit omnes'. Their protest was soon known in England. Langton acted upon it. He summoned a council—to which, as Dr. Ernest Barker has pointed out, all the ecclesiastical corporations and persons mentioned in the papal letter were asked to send representatives, and in the meantime he got the pope to recall his agent.[1] Now this council had met five months before the council which granted the sixteenth. It refused to accede to the pope's suggestion unless the whole Church acceded. Representing the local corporations, it insisted upon its unity with the rest of the Church.[2] And in doing this it maintained a principle, which had some sanction from no less a person than Innocent III. For when Innocent summoned the Lateran Council he had commanded the chapters to send representatives, on the ground that matters which affected them would be discussed.[3] Great and wonderful were the possibilities in 1215. If the action taken ten years later by Langton and the English clergy had become general, if the principle of representation had become, not merely a principle of local organization, but one of the marks of a united and universal Church, history might indeed have been changed.

The ecclesiastical councils of 1226, following upon the assertion of the royal power on the basis of the Great

---

[1] *Walter of Coventry*, ii. 274–9; *Wendover*, iv. 123, 124; *Register of St. Osmund*, ii. 51; also above, p. 148 note. See especially E. Barker, *The Dominican Order and Convocation* (Oxford, 1913), pp. 34–6, 44–8. Dr. Armitage Robinson points out that this was not a provincial council, for the bishop of Durham died on his way to it; but the form of summons helped to define the procedure of convocation, illustrated by the later council of this year. See his article 'Convocation of Canterbury: its early history', *Church Quarterly Review*, October 1915, lxxxi. 87–9.

[2] *Wendover*, iv. 124.

[3] Barker, op. cit., p. 32; Hefele-Leclercq, v. 1317.

Charter in the previous years, brought Langton's public life to a close. Henry III acquired full independence early in 1227; the archbishop died in July 1228. In 1223 he had once more seen Paris[1] and had doubtless talked once more with his brother Simon. In the last months of his life he had Simon beside him as archdeacon of Canterbury, and was able to make him one of the executors of his will.[2] He died at his manor of Slindon in Sussex and was buried in his cathedral at Canterbury.[3]

The annalist of Waverley noted down the following epitaph :

> Presul uirtutis Stephanus documenta salutis
> Viuens multa dedit, moriens a morte recedit.
> Forma gregis, clerique decus, uite speculator
> Et speculum, Christique fuit deuotus amator.[4]

In the course of this study of Stephen Langton, I have tried to present his life as a unity. The crowded activity of the last few years, when he had more freedom and responsibility than he had ever had before, recalls at every turn some phase or other of his teaching at Paris, some incident or other of his thwarted efforts during the struggle for the charter. I have tried to describe a great man, with a clear, sensible, penetrating, but not original mind, at work in a time more important, more critical,

---

[1] He went in August with two bishops on a vain endeavour to persuade Louis, now king of France, to restore Henry's rights in the lands across the sea; Norgate, pp. 188, 190; Petit-Dutaillis, *Louis VIII*, p. 232.

[2] See letters patent of the king, declaring Simon restored to royal favour, 28 July 1227, *Patent Rolls*, 1225–32, p. 136, and above, p. 137. The other executors of Stephen's will were Alexander of Stavenby, bishop of Coventry, Henry of Sandford, bishop of Rochester, Master Thomas of Freckenham and Master Elias of Dereham, *Close Rolls*, 1227–31, p. 110.

[3] For the dates of his death and burial (July 9–15, 1228) see the *Dictionary of National Biography*. A curious tomb, half inside and half outside the east wall of St. Michael's chapel is said to be his. It is depicted in J. Dart's *The History and Antiquities of the Cathedral Church of Canterbury* (1726), p. 134.

[4] *Annales Monastici*, ii. 305. Was this one of the efforts of Gervase of Melkley?

more full of opportunity, than any other period in the history of the medieval Church. And above all, I have tried to bring him into relation both with the common man in England and with the intellectual life of Europe, to break down the barriers which prevent us from considering as a whole, in the light of the influences which played upon them, the men and affairs of politics and religion. A vision or an idea is not to be judged by its value for us, but by its value to the man who had it. And only if we can understand, though it may be but dimly, how a man thought and felt in the presence of the daily task or in times of stress, can we hope to interpret his work. The hope may never be attained, but it remains true that, just so far as we avoid easy going and conventional interpretations, are we likely to make significant to others what has become intelligible to ourselves.

APPENDICES

APPENDIX I

The Langtons of Langton-by-Horncastle and of Langton by-Wragby

As I have explained in the first chapter (above, p. 6) Henry Langton, the father of Stephen and his brothers, must be distinguished from a Henry Langton who was prominent in Lincolnshire during the first quarter of the thirteenth century. I am indebted to Canon Foster for the information collected in this Appendix from local deeds.

A. Henry Langton of Langton-by-Horncastle.

Henry Langton in 1219 had lands in Woodhall, a village which adjoins Langton-by-Horncastle on the south-west. For he made a final concord with his niece Agnes Duce, regarding a meadow called Brademore in Woodhall, before Hugh, bishop of Lincoln, and his fellow justices in Lincolnshire. The bishop, as is well known from his letter of expostulation to William the Marshal,[1] acted as justice in this year. Henry later gave part of this meadow to the monastery of Kirkstead, as appears from the following charter. The inscription upon the seal shows that he was the son of Alan of Woodhall.

before 1232

B.M., Cart. Harl. 52, I. 26.

Vniuersis sancte ecclesie filiis presentibus 7 futuris Henricus de Langeton' salutem. Noueritis me dedisse concessisse 7 hac mea carta confirmasse deo 7 ecclesie sancte Marie 7 monachis de Kẏrkested' totum pratum illud sine retinemento in territorio de Wdehall' in prato quod dicitur Brademor'. quod michi remansit per finem 7 concordiam factam in Curia domini regis coram Hugone de Well' Episcopo Lincolniensi Iohanne Marescall'. Waltero Maucler' iusticiariis itinerantibus in comitatu Lincolnie 7 aliis domini regis fidelibus. inter me 7 Agnetem duce neptem meam. scilicet illud pratum

---

[1] Royal Letters, edited Shirley, i. 20.

quod iacet inter pratum quod fuit eiusdem Agnetis 7 quod ipsa dedit eisdem monachis 7 pratum Willelmi de Winceby. Hoc siquidem pratum habebunt 7 tenebunt predicti monachi cum liberis introitibus 7 exitibus ad falcandum. fenum leuandum 7 inde cariandum 7 cum omnibus aliis pertinenciis. in liberam. puram 7 perpetuam elemosinam. Et ego, H. 7 heredes mei hoc pratum sicut predictum est predictis monachis warantizabimus. 7 de omnibus rebus acquietabimus. Hiis Testibus. Ricardo de rouell' tunc decano Hornecast' Willelmo de rouell' Petro de Edlincton'. Iohanne de Thimelbÿ. Petro 7 Willelmo filiis eius. Ricardo clerico de Barden'. Spirwi de Langetona. Willelmo de Halton' 7 aliis.

Endorsed. lx. [13c.]

Seal on tag, round, 1⅞", green, a fleur-de-lis + SIGILLVM HENRICI F' ALAIN DE WDEHALE.

The charters in the Kirkstead cartulary (Cotton MS. Vesp. E. xviii) give a good deal of information about Henry, son of Alan, and his family tree can also be compiled to some extent from the original deeds edited by Professor Stenton in the *Danelaw Charters*. His brother William of Woodhall, who had land in Roughton, a few miles south of Horncastle,[1] his nephew Rolland of Woodhall, William's son, and his niece Maud appear frequently. Henry described himself indifferently as Henry of Langton and Henry of Woodhall. He is styled sometimes as a knight and was, therefore, one of those freemen who rose in the social scale.[2] In a dated charter of 1222 he attests as Henry of Langton[3], but he probably attained knighthood before this date. Canon Foster dates the various charters attested by him to various periods between 1175 and 1230.

This Henry Langton had a son Eudo.[4] By the name of his son, his connexions in the Horncastle area, and by the length of his life, he is clearly to be distinguished from Henry of Langton-by-Wragby.

---

[1] Cf. Stenton, no. 196, p. 136.
[2] Kirkstead cartulary, Wildmore section, nos. 70–4 (early Henry III).
[3] Ibid., no. 67.
[4] Ibid., no. 55; also in the Great Sturton and Langton-by-Wragby section of the cartulary, f. 164, no. 35.

Canon Foster has compiled the following genealogical table:

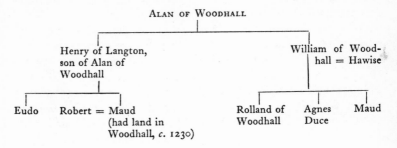

ALAN OF WOODHALL

Henry of Langton, son of Alan of Woodhall

William of Wood-hall = Hawise

Eudo   Robert = Maud
                (had land in
                Woodhall, *c.* 1230)

Rolland of   Agnes   Maud
Woodhall   Duce

B. *The Langtons of Langton-by-Wragby.*

The existence of a Henry Langton in this neighbourhood is shown by several deeds and by attestations of the late twelfth century of Bullington charters.[1] Henry of Woodhall, who appears to have had interests here, occasionally appears as a witness, as also do other members of the Woodhall family. It is not always possible to distinguish the two Henries. The following charters are especially noteworthy.

1. Charter of John Flandrensis, granting land in Langton, including the land which Ulfric held between the land of Henry of Langton and of Robert son of Gosse. Among the witnesses are Henry, parson of Langton, and Henry of Woodhall. Late twelfth century. (Kirkstead Cartulary, ff. 163*d*, 164, no. 34 = Stowe charter 459.)

2. Charter of Master Simon of Langton, son of Henry of Langton, granting a toft on the west side of Langton church, *c.* 1235. (Harleian Charter, 52, I. 30.)

This grant by Simon was presumably made after he succeeded his brother Walter, and may be connected with the suit between the prior of Bullington and Walter Langton regarding a toft in Langton (see above, p. 6).

I add a genealogical table to illustrate the brief connexion between the Langton and Anesty families.

---

[1] Danelaw Charters, no. 22, p. 16 (1187); Transcripts of Charters relating to Gilbertine Houses, p. 98 (Henry II).

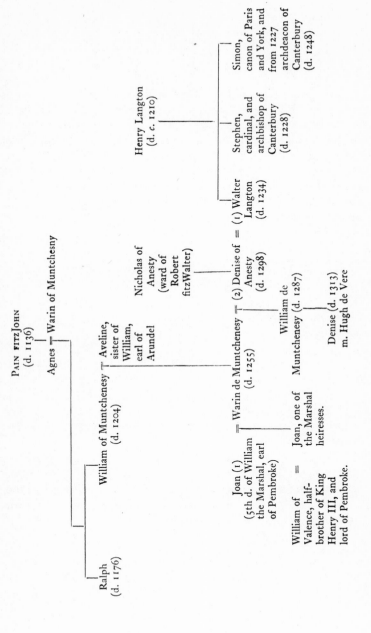

APPENDIX II

Langton's Sermons

In the previous pages I have referred to Langton's reputation as a preacher. It is attested by James of Vitry and by Matthew Paris. The annalists occasionally refer to particular sermons, e.g. the sermon ad populum on 25 August 1213, the sermon at the funeral of William the Marshal, the sermon, already in print, on the occasion of the translation of St. Thomas of Canterbury, 9 July 1220, the sermon in Rome on St. Thomas, the sermon on Michaelmas Day 1225 at Salisbury.[1] The tract on the hymn 'Ave maris stella'[2] is described as a sermon, as is also the commentary on the two verses, said to have been composed by himself, which were sung at vespers on the vigil of the feast of St. Peter:

> Solue, iuuante Deo, terrarum, Petre, catenas
> Qui facis ut pateant celestia regna beatis.

This sermon begins 'Cathene ille quas Ecclesia rumpi orat'.[3]

I add here a list of some of the chief manuscript collections which contain sermons ascribed to Langton.

Paris

Bibliothèque Nationale, MS. lat. 14859. Thirty-five sermons ascribed to Langton, mingled with others. See Lecoy de la Marche, *La chaire française au XIIIe siècle*, p. 89.

— MS. lat. 12420, ff. 55, 92, 101, &c. See Hauréau, *Notices et extraits*, ii. 114.

Ste. Geneviève, MS. no. 1422 (D. 1 in 4°, 27²), f. 4. Incipiunt sermones magistri Stephani de Linguatonante (Ch. Köhler, *Catalogue des MSS. de la Bibliothèque Sainte Geneviève*, ii, 1896, p. 16. The first sermon begins 'Circumdederunt me gemitus mortis . . . Apostolus dicit quiddam . . .'

---

[1] Above, pp. 42, 115, 143, 145 154.   [2] Above, p. 47.

[3] Bibliothèque Nationale, MS. lat. 12420, f. 101, for which see Hauréau, *Notices et extraits*, ii. 115; Reims MS. 582, f. 54 (*Catalogue générale: Départements* xxxviii. 741). The verses are imitated from some ascribed to Helpidia, the wife of Boethius.

Arsenal MS. 400, f. 179. Forty sermons ascribed to Langton, as in Bruges MS. 278 (H. Martin, *Cat. des MSS. de la Bibl. de l'Arsenal*, i. 1885, p. 267). The first sermon is on the words 'Afferam paxillam aque . . .' Thirteenth century.

TROYES

See the *Catalogue générale*, ii. (1850), under the following numbers. All these manuscripts came from Clairvaux, and were written in the thirteenth century.

Troyes, 862. After the Verbum abbreviatum of Peter the Chanter, a collection of sermons, including three definitely ascribed to Langton. The first of these was the sermon preached in London after his return to England, in August 1213.

1. ad populum. Begins, 'In Deo sperauit cor meum etc. . . . Audiuimus, fratres karissimi, et bene scimus quod optimis plena est ciuitas ista doctoribus, qui uobis sepe uerba uite disseminant.'

On this manuscript and on other collections of Langton's sermons in Bruges MSS. 28, 93, *see* A. de Poorter, 'Catalogue des MSS. de prédication médiévale de la Bibliothèque des Bruges', in the *Revue d'histoire ecclésiastique* for January 1928, vol. xxiv, pp. 64, 68, 92.

2. For feast of St. Martin. Begins 'Iustum deduxit Dominus per uias rectas, etc. . . . Vellem, karissimi, ad uos uenire frequentius, si temporis oportunitas se offeret.'

3. On the Passion. Begins 'Cum uenisset Saul . . .'

Troyes, 1100. After Langton on Kings and other items, seventy sermons attributed to him (no. 8). Begin 'Viderunt eum hostes et deriserunt, etc. . . . Scitis, patres, quod licet uinum in se bonum sit.'

Troyes, 1367. A quarto manuscript, containing seventy-nine sermons by masters of Paris, with no distinction of authors. Title: 'Magistri Stephani Lingetonantis et quorundam aliorum magistrorum Parisiensium Sermones ad populum'. For Sundays and festivals.

(The title suggests that such of Langton's sermons as are contained in this collection were preached before he left Paris.)

Troyes, 1227. Between Langton on Exodus and on the Minor Prophets, eleven sermons by Langton. Not ascribed to him, but see Hauréau ii. 111 for the first of them, a sermon in an ecclesiastical synod, recalling bishops to their duties (also in MS. lat. 12420, f. 55). Begins 'Attendite uobis et uniuerso gregi in quo uos Spiritus Sanctus posuit episcopos regere ecclesiam Dei . . . Terret [me] latebras conscientie mee scrutantem illud psalmiste.'

LONDON

British Museum, Royal MS. 2 D. xxxvii, f. 142. Fifteen sermons, after Langton on the Minor Prophets. They apparently form a series (see Warner and Gilson, *Catalogue of the Royal MSS.*, i. 61) and the first is generally attributed to Langton. Begins, 'Sacerdotes nescientes Dominum neque officium suum'.[1] Thirteenth century.

OXFORD

Magdalen College MS. 168, a small 4° volume of 162 folios, written in the thirteenth and fourteenth centuries. It consists of sermons, and the various items are described in Coxe, *Catalogus codicum MSS. collegii B. Mariae Magdalenae*, pp. 77, 78). On f. 50^v–f. 51^v is a table of seventy-eight sermons,[2] including eighteen definitely ascribed to Langton. The text follows of numbers 1–19 (middle) and from the middle of the 'capitulatio bibliothece' (no. 31) to the middle of no. 38. I print this table, also the beginnings of the surviving sermons ascribed to Langton, from a transcript kindly made for me by my friend, Mr. W. A. Pantin.

Magdalen Coll: Oxon: MS. clxviii.

fo. 50^v.

In hoc volumine continentur sermones modernorum magistrorum quorum nomina subscribuntur. Magistri videlicet Stephani Cant' In festo s. Mathei.

.j. Vidit ihc hominem etc'. *Eiusdem in apparitione Domini.*

.ij. Transeamus usque Bethleem.

.iij. *Eiusdem de beata virgine Maria.*   Extendit Rex virgam auream.

---

[1] Cf. Pits, 304 'De sacerdotibus Deum nescientibus', librum vnum.

[2] Including, as no. 31, the 'capitulatio bibliothece secundum M. Stephani', afterwards given in part on ff. 78 onwards. See above, p. 35.

.iiij. *Item eiusdem in pascha.*

Maria Madagl' (*sic*) et Maria Iacobi etc'.

.v. *Sermo magistri Iohannis de Abbatisvilla.*

Amen amen dico vobis quia plora[bitis].

.vj. *M. Stephani Cantur' vnius confessoris.*

Sint lumbi vestri precincti et lucerne.[1]

.vij. *Cuiusdam magistri Ludonen'.*

Sp̄c oris nostri xp̄c Dominus.

.viij. *Magistri Nicholai de Turnaco.*

Preceptor tota nocte labora-[ntes].

.ix. *Item eiusdem in nativitate s. Iohannis baptiste.*

At tu puer propheta altissimi vo[caberis].

.x. *M. Stephani in festo beate Marie Madagl' (sic).*

Gaude et letare filia Edom.

.xj. *Item eiusdem in adventu Domini.*

Rorate celi desuper et nubes.

.xij. *Item eiusdem in unius confessoris.*

In omni ore quasi mel indulcabitur.

.xiij. *M. I. de Abbatisvilla ad clericos.*

Ambulate in lucem ut filii lu[cis].

.xiiij. *Item eiusdem in ramis palmarum.*

Cum appropinquasset ih̄c iherosolimis.

.xv. *Item eiusdem in pascha.*

Pascha nostrum immolatus est xp̄c.

.xvj. *Sermo cuiusdam in dedicatione.*

Terribilis est locus iste non est.

.xvij. *M. Odonis abbatis Morimundi.*

Opus gratie eius qui operatur omnia.

.xviij. *Eiusdem in festo s. Benedicti abbatis.*

Dilectus a Deo et hominibus cuius me[moria].

.xix. *Sermo cuiusdam.*

Ero quasi ros. Israel germinabit quasi lil'.

.xx. *Cuiusdam abbatis in natali Petri et Pauli.*

Elegit sibi suspendium anima mea.

.xxj. *Eiusdem abbatis in visitatione.*

Reverendi patres et fratres diligendi.

.xxij. *Item eiusdem in visitatione.*

Creabit Dominus et cetera.

---

[1] Cf. Bibliothèque Nationale, MS. lat 14859, f. 267 (ad populum).

.xxiij. *Item eiusdem in visitatione.*   Ponat vir gladium super femur.

.xxiiij. *Cuiusdam in purificatione.*   Hodi[e] beata v. Maria.

.xxv. *Cuiusdam in visitatione.*   Cum accesseris ad expugndā ei (*sic*).

.xxvj. *Item eiusdem in visitatione.*   Sophon'. In tempore illo scrutabor.

.xxvij. *Item eiusdem in pascha.*   Ihm̄ queritis Nazarenum cru[cifixum]

[fo. 51.]

Epistola M. Alexandri ad quemdam discipulum.   Sibi predilecto quondam .xxviij. discipulo.

Sermo eiusdem in octavis pasche.   Quasi modo geniti in- .xxix. fantes.

Item eiusdem in natali Domini.   In sole posuit tabernacu- .xxx. lum suum.

Capitulatio bibliothece secundum M. Stephanum.   In principio erat verbum. .xxxj. (*sic*).

Expositio M. P. Blesensis de transfiguratione Domini.   Reverendo domino et patri .xxxij. karissimo.

Sermo magistri Stephani in passione Domini.   Qui xp̄i sunt carnem suam. .xxxiij.

Item eiusdem in annuntiatione dominica.   O radix Iesse qui stas in .xxxiiij. sig[num].

Sermo eiusdem Stephani de Trinitate.[1]   Benedicat nos Deus Deus .xxxv. noster.

M. Nicholai de Turnaco in natali Domini.   Nolite timere ecce ewan- .xxxvj. gel'.

Sermo . . .[2] *in annuntiatione dominica.*   Descendet sicut pluvia in .xxxvij. vellu⁹ (*sic*).

Item sermo in die sancto Penthecostes.   Veni sancte Spiritus reple .xxxviij. tuorum.

---

[1] Cf. the 'meditaciones Stephani Archiepiscopi de misterio trinitatis', in the medieval catalogue of St. Augustine's, Canterbury (James, *The Ancient Libraries of Canterbury and Dover*, p. 280, no. 798).

[2] Blank in MS.

M. Iohannis in cena Domini ad sanctum Germanum.	Ecce ego sto ad ostium	.xxxix.
In annuntiatione dominica.	Brachium Domini cui reve[latum].	.xl.
M. Stephani Cantur' in unius confessoris.	Iustus cor suum tradidit ad.	.xlj.
Magistri Danielis in pascha.	Vespere comeditis carnes.	.xlii.
M. Stephani Cantuar'.	Estote imitatores mei sicut.	.xliij.
Sermo magistri Nicholai de Turnaco.	Mulier quam dedisti mihi.	.xliiij.
M. Iohannis in die sancto Penth'.	Manda Deus virtuti.	.xlv.
M. Nicholai de Turnaco in u[nius] confessoris.	Sobrii estote et vigilate.	.xlvj.
Item eiusdem in adventu Domini.	Excutere de pulvere consurge.	.xlvij
Sermo in annuntiatione dominica.	Mulierem fortem quis inve[niet].	.xlviij.
In assumptione beate Marie.	Mulier gratiosa inveni.	.xlviiij.
In nativitate beate Marie.	Orietur stella ex Iacob et consur[get].	.l.
In nativitate beate Marie.	Beata progenies unde x̄ natus est.	.lj.
In sollempnitate omnium sanctorum.	Gaudent in celis anime sanctorum.	.lij.
M. Stephani in Nativitate Domini.	Vidi angelum fortem descen[dentem]	.liij.
In apparitione Domini.	Parum est ut sis mihi servus.	.liiij.
Sermo in assumptione beate Marie.	Tenuisti manum dexteram.	.lv.
In nativitate sancti Iohannis baptiste.	Ecce ego mitto angelum.	.lvj.
Item sermo in eadem sollempnitate.	Quis dimisit onagrum.	.lvij.

.lviij.   *M. Stephani in die Penth'.*   Veni sancte Spiritus reple tuorum.

.lix.   *Eiusdem in festo apostolorum Petri et Pauli.*   Bonum certamen certavi cursum.

.lx.   *Lectio M. Stephani Cantuar' in exodo.*   Legimus filios Israel profectos de Eg[ipto].

.lxj.   *M. Iohannis dominica in passione Domini.*   Ẏsaẏas. levabit Dominus signum in nationibus.

.lxij.   *Eiusdem in pascha.*   In Zach' propheta. Si bonum est in oculis afferte m'.

.lxiij.   *M. Stephani in sollempnitate apostolorum Petri et Pauli.*   In ingressu oraculi.

.lxiiij.   *In resurrectione Domini.*   Si consurrexistis.

.lxv.   *Item in resurrectione Domini.*   Vidi hostium apertum.

.lxvj⁹.   *In assumptione beate Marie.*   Tronus meus sicut sol.

.lxvij.   *In dedicatione ecclesie.*   Domus mea domus orationis.

.lxviij.   *Sancti Benedicti.*   Iustum deduxit Dominus per vias.

.lxix.   *In die Penth'.*   Cum venerit Paraclitus.

.lxx.   *In nativitate Domini.*   Gloria in excelsis Deo.

.lxxj.   *In nativitate beate Marie.*   Iamque advenerat vigilia.

.lxxij.   *Ad claustrales.*   Abicite deos alienos.

.lxxiij.   *De beata virgine.*   Ego quasi fluvius dorix (*sic*).

.lxxiiij.   *De misericordia Domini.*   Multitudo miserationum.

.lxxv.   *Ad crucissignatos.*   Quis miserebitur tui.

.lxxvj.   *In dedicatione ecclesie.*   Nescitis quia estis templum.

.lxxvij.   *Ad claustrales.*   Cum transieritis Iordañem.

lxxviij.   *Miraculum de duobus clericis.*   Ea tempestate qua ph⁹.

Of the sermons ascribed to Langton, eleven survive in the Magdalen MS. They begin as follows:

(fo. 54.)

j⁹. *Sermo Magistri Stephani Cantuʀ in festo Mathei.*
  Vidit iħc hominem . . . [etc.].
  Sala[mon] dicit verbum quoddam. ex quo magnam spem possunt concipere qui verbum Dei audiunt et faciunt. . . .

(fo. 55ᵛ.)

ij⁹. *Item sermo eiusdem in apparitione Domini.*
  Transeamus usque Bethleem . . .
  Sicut vir quidam sapiens attestatur dicens. qui interrogationem manifestat . . .

(fo. 57.)

.iij⁹. *Item eiusdem de beata virgine Maria.*
  Extendit rex virgam auream . . .
  Rex iste est Deus Pater. virga aurea virgo Maria.
  Manus regis Filius Dei. Hester anima a Deo per peccatum separata . . .

(fo. 57ᵛ.)

.iiij⁹. *Item eiusdem in pascha.*
  Maria Magd' . . .
  Per os sapientis sp̄c locutus est dicens. Homini est linguam preparare, Dei autem gubernare. Igitur . . .

(fo. 59ᵛ.)

.vj⁹. *M. Stephani Cantur' unius conf.*
  Sint lumbi vestri . . .
  Filiis Israel exeuntibus de Egipto precepit Dominus facere farinam . . .

(fo. 65.)

.x⁹. *Stephani Cantuʀ . In festo beate Marie Magđ.*
  Gaude et letare filia . . .
  Cum sol vitream quandam tenuem et lucidam penetrat et illuminat . . .

(fo. 67^v.)

.xj^9. *Item sermo in adventu.*

Rorate celi desuper . . .

Sancta mater ecclesia hiis diebus prophetarum recitat suspiria . . .

(fo. 68.)

.xij^9. *M. Stephani Cantur̃. unius conf.*

In omni ore quasi mel . . .

Vere felix est sanctorum memoria que nulli dulcedini comparatur . . .

(fo. 78.)

[part of xxxi.] Capitulatio Bibliothece *giving the books of the bible with the initia of the chapters, according to Stephen Langton's divisions.*

e.g.

> *cantica canticorum.* Osculetur me.
>> .ij. ego flos campi.
>> .iij. in lectulo meo.
>> .iiij. quam pulcra es amica.
>> .v. veniat dilectus meus.
>> .vj. Quo abiit dilectus meus (? tuus. Now v. 17).
>> .vij. q*uid* videbit in Sunamite.
>> .viij. t (*sic*) quid michi det.

(fo. 86.)

.xxx[iij^9.] *M. Stephani Cantur' in passione Domini.*

Qui ẋ sunt carnem . . .

Vox Domini hodie insonuit in c^a. p^o. Hodie si vocem eius . .

(fo. 88^v.)

.xxxiiij^9. *Item eiusdem in annuntiatione dominica.*

O radix Iesse . . .

Si quis pauper regem in multis offendisset . . .

(fo. 90^v.)

.xxxv. *De trinitate.*

Benedicat nos Deus . . .

Intuens Iob incomprehensibilem diei maiestatis excellenciam . . .

APPENDIX III

A. *The manuscripts of Langton's Questiones*

C. Cambridge, St. John's College, MS. 57, f. 147ʳ–f. 345ʳ. 13th century.

This is described by James, *A Descriptive Catalogue of the manuscripts in the library of St. John's College, Cambridge*, pp. 74, 75. The manuscript is written in double columns of sixty-six lines in several small neat hands. Langton's short summa and questiones are described below. They are preceded by the questiones of Master Martin (see above, p. 52) and are followed by a contemporary index, which James does not describe quite correctly. A list of questiones, which apparently were at one time part of these miscellaneous collections, but which are not now bound up with the rest, is followed by a list of these which do exist, in twenty-two quires. See above, pp. 63–5.

V. Paris, Bibliothèque Nationale, MS. latin 14556, f. 165ʳ–f. 266ʳ. 13th century, formerly in the library of the regular canons of St. Victor, Paris.

Title: Incipit summa magistri Stephani Cant. archiepiscopi.

Begins: Latria est cultus soli deo siue creatori exhibendus, dulia est cultus creature exhibendus. Sed queritur utrum Iohannes uoluerit angelum adorare dulia an latria.

There are 163 questiones. Most of them have titles which were inserted later. The last questio, *de extrema unctione*, begins: Circa sacramentum extreme unctionis primo est uidendum quid sit ipsum sacramentum in . . .

Ends: Expliciunt questiones magistri Stephani Cant. archiepiscopi. Deo gratias.

S. Paris, Bibliothèque Nationale, MS. latin 16385, 117 folios. 13th century. On the verso of the last folio: Iste liber est collegii pauperum magistrorum Parisius in theologia studentium ex legato magistri Geraudi de Abbatisuilla, precii xxxs.[1]

[1] This book is described in the catalogue of the Sorbonne library, compiled in 1338, in the class 'summe questionum', no. 25: Summa Stephani de Longotona

Title, f. 2: Incipit summa magistri Stephani de Longuetona.
Begins: Q. 1ª. Utrum homo possit resurgere in tanta caritate a quanta cecidit. Quod homo possit resurgere in tanta caritate. . . .
The last questio, f. 117: *Quo modo petitio debet fieri*, begins: Solet dici in petitione hec obseruanda ad hoc ut optineatur. . . .
Ends: petit ergo pie, etc. ut deus det ei. Explicit summa magistri Stephani de Longetona.

Arras MS. 965. 14th century. From St. Vedast, Arras. See *Catalogue générale*, iv (1872), p. 382. After the summa of Prepositinus.

Title: Incipit summa magistri Stephani de Langhothonia.

Begins: Queritur utrum homo possit resurgere in tanta caritate a quanta cecidit.

The manuscript stops short in the questio *de pari cremento uirtutum*.

Avranches MS. 230. 13th century.[1] See *Catalogue générale*, Départements, x. 109, 110; Ravaisson, *Rapports au ministre de l'instruction publique sur les bibliothèques des départements de l'Ouest* (1841), p. 407.

Title, f. 212: Incipit summa magistri Stephani de Longuotona.

Begins: Queritur utrum homo possit resurgere in tanta caritate a quanta cecidit. Quod homo possit resurgere in tanta caritate . . . (as in S. and Arras).

Rome, Vatican Library, MS. latin 4297. 13th century.

Title: Incipit summa magistri b. de Lang, qua queritur utrum homo possit resurgere in tanta caritate a quanta cecidit. Quod homo possit resurgere in tanta caritate . . . (as in the three preceding manuscripts.)

utrum homo possit resurgere in tanta caritate a quanta cecidit, ex legato magistri G. de Abbatisuilla. Incipit in 2º fol. *pena*, in pen. *eam*. Precium xxx sol. Delisle, *Le cabinet des manuscrits de la bibliothèque nationale*, iii (1881), p. 30. By his will, dated 1271, Gerard of Abbeville left 300 books to the Sorbonne (op. cit., ii. 148–9).

[1] The manuscript is bound up with an important twelfth-century MS. of John Scotus Erigena's 'De divisione naturae', or 'Perifision', the work which was condemned to be sought out and burned in 1225 by Pope Honorius III (Potthast, *Regesta*, i. 634, no. 7348, 23 Jan. 1225; cf. de Wulf, *History of Medieval Philosophy*, second English edition, i. 138, 140).

Grabmann, *Geschichte der scholastischen Methode*, ii. 500, describes this as a unique manuscript of an unknown writer B. de Lang, but it is obviously a copy of Langton's questiones, in the form found in S, Arras, and Avranches. The similarity was noted by A. Landgraf, *Das Wesen der lässlichen Sünde in der Scholastik bis Thomas von Aquin* (Bamberg, 1923), pp. xiii–xv. I owe this reference to the work of P. Amédée Teetaert, *La confession aux laïques dans l'église latine depuis le viiie jusqu'au xive siècle* (Brussels, 1927), pp. 180–2. Teetaert makes use of the Vatican MS. as Langton's.

This text comprises 137 questiones. The 135th, *quod uterque gladius sit ecclesie*, is also the last questio but two in S.

Bamberg MS. Q, vi. 50. 13th century. Formerly in the cathedral library. See Friedrich Leitschuh and Hans Fischer, *Katalog der Königlichen Bibliothek zu Bamberg* (1895–1906), i. 523.

Title, f. 1: Summa magistri Stephani [1] cantuariensis archiepiscopi.

Begins: Breues dies hominis sunt et numerus mensium.

The last questio, *de extrema unctione*, ends: de ea participatione fidei, spei, caritatis. This is the ending of the questio on extreme unction in C., f. 214^v. V ends with the same questio, below, p. 204. Explicit summa magistri Stephani cantuariensis archiepiscopi.

Rouen MS. 657. 13th century. See *Catalogue générale, Départements*, Rouen, i, 170. A fragmentary text, followed on f. 25 by a commentary on the minor prophets. It originally contained 102 questiones or chapters.

Begins on f. 1 in the middle of c. 46: Exodus. Residuum grandinis (*sic*) comedit locusta.

Ends (c. 102): ut manifestaretur per legem.

Explicit summa magistri Stephani Cantuariensis archiepiscopi de uitiis et uirtutibus.

Laon MS. 133. 14th century. See *Catalogue générale*, i (1849), p. 110. Formerly belonged to the abbey of St. Vincent. After St. Augustine on the Trinity.

Title: Incipit conflictus uicium et uirtutum Parisius elucidatus

---

[1] On an erasure.

secundum magistrum Stephanum de Longue Toune Cantuariensem archiepiscopum de uiciis capitalibus et surculis eorum, de uirtutibus et surculis eorum.

Begins: superbia, inobedientia, presumptio.

Douai MS. 434. 13th century (end). A manuscript in three volumes, formerly in the library of the abbey of Anchin. See *Catalogue générale*, vi (1878), pp. 246–9. The second item in volume iii, ff. 28–61 is thus described:

Title: Compilatio aut summa per magistrum Stephanum de Languetona.

Begins: Cum penitens accessit ad sacerdotem.

Ends: Glorificetur Deum in die iustificationis.

Erlangen MS. 353. Questiones diversae, ff. 65^r–100^v, are ascribed to Langton by Denifle and Chatelain, *C.U.P.*, i. 99, but Grabmann, op. cit., ii. 501 note, denies that they are his. The first questio begins, 'Queritur quid sit uotum'.

In April 1713 the Maurists saw a Summa of Stephen Langton at the Cistercian abbey of Royaumont. See *Voyage littéraire de deux religieux bénédictins de la congrégation de Saint Maur*, Paris, 1717, i, p. 153.

B. *The contents of the Cambridge MS.*

In the third chapter of this study I have given a brief description of the Cambridge MS. (C). Langton's short summa is followed by five collections of questiones, which are carefully indexed. The index shows that the latter were originally preceded by another collection of 114 questiones, which are now lost. The surviving questiones, 252 in number, begin abruptly on f. 170. I hope to arrange for a complete account of the manuscript, but in the meantime the list of the chapters of the short summa and of the 252 questiones may be found useful. I have followed the index, and added some notes and references to corresponding questiones in the Paris MS. latin 14556 (V) of which the University of Manchester possess a copy in rotograph. What follows is based very largely upon the investigations of Miss A. Gregory, to whom I am deeply indebted.

f. 147ʳ. Incipit summa magistri Stephani.

    1. de hiis que dicuntur de deo. Cum diuersa dicionum genera dicantur de deo primo dicendum est de illis que predicant diuinam essentiam.¹

f. 147ᵛ. 2. utrum deus misericordia sit iustus. Item deus misericordia est iustus probatio. Deus iusticia est iustus et supposita iusticia supponitur et misericordia.

    3. utrum deus ex misericordia puniat. Item deus ex misericordia punit minus quam iste meruerit.

f. 148ʳ. 4. an deus ex misericordia uel iustitia remuneret. Item utraque istarum uera est.

    5. [an deus misericordius uel iustius agat cum uno quam cum alio. *In the margin*]² Sed queritur de hac, iustius agitur cum isto quam cum illo.

f. 148ᵛ. 6. an iustius fuerit coronari Petrum quam Linum. Item maius fuit meritum Petri quam Lini.

    7. de hac dictione talis. Item deus est iustus et Petrus est talis.

f. 149ʳ. 8. Eadem. Item cum dicitur hec res est eadem.

    9. alius. Item cum dicitur fortes est alius a Platone.

    10. equalis. Item patris et filii et spiritus sancti equalis est gloria.

    11. unus. Item unitas est diuina essentia.

f. 149ᵛ. 12. trina. Item queritur de quo dicatur hec dictio trina.

    13. trinitas. In *quicunque vult* dicitur trinitas in unitate.

    14. triplex. Item non ualet hoc argumentum, essentia est trina, ergo est triplex.

    15. deus. Item hec dictio deus restringitur.

f. 150ʳ. 16. deitas. Item cum utraque istarum dicionum sit essentialis deus. deitas quare non potest restringi hoc nomen deitas.

    17. omnipotens. Item due res omnipotentes procedunt a patre.

¹ Cf. below, no. 34, also questiones nos. 47, 58, and V, nos. 67, 69, 105.
² From this point there is a tendency to break up the argument by means of headings which are not descriptive and do not introduce new subjects. They are rather notes of indication. A few other rubricated words come in the text or margin.

f. 150ʳ. 18. generat. Item deus generat deum ergo se deum uel alium deum.

19. creans genitus. Item deus et creans et genitus differt a patre.

20. solus. Item unus solus deus non generat.

f. 150ᵛ. 21. potens. Item hec dictio potens.

22. spirat. Item cum dicitur deus spirat.

23. res. Item addidit sic. Sit hoc nomen res.

f. 151ʳ. 24. hec. Item simus in incarnatione.

25. Christus. Item queritur de hac Deus non est pater et Christus est genitus.

26. iustum. Item idem est iudicium.

27. deus de deo. Item filius est deus de deo.

f. 151ᵛ. 28. ens. Item cum dicitur deus est pater.

f. 152ʳ. 29. enunciabile. Item et deum et deum spirare est enunciabile.

30. Sapientia. Item sapientia genita et sapientia ingenita sunt.

f. 152ᵛ. 31. diligit spiritu sancto. Item pater diligit filium spiritu sancto.

32. pater operatur per filium. Item in secundo libro sententiarum[1].

f. 153ʳ. 33. per. Item queritur cum uere dicatur pater operatur per filium.[2]

f. 154ʳ. 34. de nominibus infinitatis. Item queritur utrum iste terminus non generans.[3]

f. 155ʳ. 35. de potentia gubernandi. Item cum dicitur pater potest gubernare.[4]

f. 155ᵛ. 36. de notionibus. Item queritur utrum proprietates sint in personis.[5]

f. 157ᵛ. 37. de spiratione. Consequenter dicendum est de spiratione.

38. de principio. Item dicit Augustinus quod sicut pater et filius et spiritus sanctus sunt unum principium creaturarum.

---

[1] Cf. questiones, no. 19, and V. 52.
[2] Rubricated sub-headings in the margins of f. 153ᵛ and f. 154ʳ.
[3] Cf. questiones, no. 47, and V. 105.   [4] Cf. questiones, no. 89.
[5] Cf. questiones, no. 127, and V. 53.

f. 159ʳ. 39. de persona. Post predicta dicendum est de persona. prenotandum ergo quod quedam nomina sunt apud Grecos.¹

f. 161ʳ. 40. de uirtutibus an una habita habeantur omnes. Multimenbris diuisio uirtutum solet poni.

f. 161ᵛ. 41. Utrum omnes uirtutes sint pares. Postmodum queritur utrum omnes uirtutes sint pares.²

f. 162ᵛ. 42. an omnes uirtutes simul habeantur in usu. Item dictum est superius quod omnes uirtutes simul habeantur in habitu sed non omnes in usu. Sed quod omnes simul habeantur in usu, sic uidetur posse ostendi.

f. 163ᵛ. 43. de perseuerantia. Item dictum est quod qui habet unam uirtutem habet omnes, ergo qui habet unam habet perseuerantiam.³

f. 165ʳ. 44. utrum naturalia fiant gratuita. Postmodum queritur utrum naturalia fiant gratuita et utrum fides informis sit formata. Super hoc duplex est opinio.⁴

f. 170ᵛ. Explicit summa magistri Stephani.

[*Group A. Quire I.*]

f. 171ʳ. Incipiunt questiones Magistri Stephani de Longoton Cantuariensis archiepiscopi.

f. 171ʳ. 1. de correptione fratris. (V. 74; cf. below, no. 131.)
f. 172ʳ. 2. de timore seruili. (V. 151.)
f. 173ᵛ. 3. de timore initiali et filiali. (V. 152.)
f. 174ᵛ. 4. de originali peccato.
f. 175ᵛ. 5. utrum omnia opera ex eadem caritate non crescente [siue in eodem statu manente, *in margin*] procedentia sint equalis premii meritoria siue opera sint paria siue non. (Cf. below, no. 64.)
f. 176ᵛ. 6. utrum potentia credendi sit naturalis an gratuita. (V. 65; cf. below, no. 63.)

¹ This chapter appears twice among the questiones, nos. 20, 143.
² Cf. questiones, no. 224, and V. 159.
³ Cf. questiones, no. 99; V. no. 78.
⁴ Cf. questiones, no. 56.

f. 177ᵛ.   7. utrum aliquis pro ueniali puniatur eternaliter.[1] (Cf. V. 156, and below, no. 185.)

f. 178ʳ.   8. de fictione et quare eucharistia iteretur et non baptismus [de effectu baptismi—*index*]. (V. 86, de eucharistia; cf. below, nos. 61, 190.)

[*Quire II*]

f. 179ʳ.   9. quare non quantulacumque caritas nisi crescat sufficit ad plene resistendum quantecumque temptationi.[2] (Cf. V. 28.)

f. 180ʳ. 10. quod quantulacumque caritas non crescens sufficit ad resistendum.[3]

f. 180ᵛ. 11. de dupplici missione filii et spiritus sancti. (Cf. V. 89.)

f. 181ᵛ. 12. utrum temporalia absolute an sub conditione sint petenda. (V. 163, and cf. below, no. 94.)

f. 182ʳ. 13. de stimulo Pauli et oratione ut stimulus amoueretur. (V. 76, and cf. below, no. 95.)

f. 182ᵛ. 14. quare nullus ex condigno meretur uitam eternam.

f. 183ᵛ. 15. quod licet uirtutes sint simul tempore non tamen natura, immo est ibi ordo naturalis.[4]

f. 184ʳ. 16. utrum omne illud sit simpliciter possibile quod est possibile secundum superiores causas. (V. 87.)

f. 184ᵛ. 17. utrum Christus, secundum quod homo, possit mundare a peccato et creare et similia facere. (V. 85.)

f. 185ᵛ. 18. de latria et dulia. (V. 1.)

f. 186ʳ. 19. cum pater operetur per filium quare non e conuerso. (V. 52, and cf. Summa, nos. 32, 33.)

[*Quire III*]

f. 187ᵛ. 20. de persona. (Cf. Summa, no. 39, and below, no. 143.)

f. 189ᵛ. 21. de gemina scientia Christi. (V. 88.)

---

[1] One of the marginal notes in another hand begins: dicebat Magister Simon bene.

[2] The index is rather different and repeats the opening words of the questio: 'utrum quantulacumque caritas sufficiat sine augmento ad plene.' This suggests that the rubrics were inserted after the quires were put together and the index was compiled.

[3] Not indexed.

[4] A space of four lines is left in the first column of f. 184ʳ.

f. 190ʳ. 22. ad quid ualeant bona opera facta extra caritatem.[1]
(Cf. V. 147, and below, nos. 41, 43, and 222.)

f. 191ʳ. 23. secundum quid attendatur intensio caritatis. (V. 111,
de ordine caritatis; cf. 127, and below, no. 219.)

f. 191ᵛ. 24. de dilectione proximi et ordine diligendi.[2] (V. 112.)

f. 192ᵛ. 25. de prima morte Lazari et eius suscitatione.[3]

f. 193ᵛ. 26. utrum deus in gehenna puniat aliquem pena condigna.
(V. 114.)

f. 194ᵛ. 27. quomodo corpora glorificata uideantur et de dotibus
eorum. (V. 138.)

[*Quire IV*]

f. 195ʳ. 28. utrum bona ecclesie a prelatis ecclesiasticis iure proprietatis an ex dispensatione possideantur. (V. 141.)

f. 196ʳ. 29. utrum prelatus plusquam alii ad opera misericordie
teneatur. (V. 140.)

f. 196ᵛ. 30. utrum opera ceremonalia tempore legis fuerint meritoria. (V. 139.)

f. 198ʳ. 31. quid sit reatus et an sit differentia inter maculam et
reatum. (Cf. V. 137, and below, no. 177.)

f. 199ʳ. 32. de uoto Iepte. (Cf. V. 99, and below, no. 210.)

f. 199ᵛ. 33. utrum peccatum sit causa uel pena peccati. (V. 115.)

f. 200ᵛ. 34. utrum ueniale sit uitandum et quomodo transeat in-
mortale. (V. 24, de sobrietate.)

f. 201ʳ. 35. quomodo sit intelligendum illud ius naturale, scilicet
quecunque uultis ut faciant nobis homines etc.
(V. 15.)

f. 201ᵛ. 36. utrum omnes uelint esse beati. (V. 16.)

f. 202ʳ. 37. de angelis ad custodiam antichristi [MS. exerticium]
deputatis. (Cf. V. 23.)

f. 202.ᵛ. 38. quid magis obliget ad diligendum deum.[4]

---

[1] Part of the second column on f. 190ʳ is marked 'hoc interpositum est'.

[2] A long footnote to f. 192ᵛ, in the corrector's hand is marked 'hoc interpositum est'.

[3] A later hand has inserted a passage which fills a gap or erasure of five lines (lines 10–14 of the text) and the lower right-hand margin. It is continued on a small schedule which was at one time stitched into the quire. This is the passage, noted above, p. 69, which contains references to Prepositinus and Peter of Corbeil. As it begins in the text, it was clearly taken from Langton, perhaps from another copy. [4] The foot of the last column of the quire is blank.

[*Quire V*]

f. 203ʳ. 39. [utrum ueniale sit aliud quam pene obnoxietas et qualiter habeat dimitti et utrum ueniale habeat reatum.]¹ (Cf. V. 149, 157, and below, no. 186.)

f. 204ʳ. 40. qualibus danda uel deneganda sit eucharistia. (V. 90.)

f. 204ᵛ. 41. [de bonis operibus extra caritatem factis ad quid ualeant].² (Cf. V. 147, and above, no. 22, and below, nos. 43 and 222.)

f. 205ᵛ. 42. de uoluntate dei et signis beneplaciti.³ (Cf. V. 26, and below, nos. 149, 160.)

f. 206ʳ. 43. utrum bonum opus factum extra caritatem uel etiam penitentia facta ab eo qui nullius peccati est sibi conscius, uiuificetur per caritatem aduenientem. (Cf. V. 147, and above, nos. 22, 41, and below, no. 222.)

f. 206ᵛ. 44. de transubstantione et de quibusdam dubiis in canone misse. § Arnuldus de sacramento eucharistie.⁴ (V. 64; cf. below, no. 205.)

f. 207ᵛ. 45. de immolatione ysaac et precepto Abrahee ⁵ [dato Abrahe—*index*]. (V. 103.)

f. 209ʳ. 46. utrum circumstantia agrauet peccatum et de circumstantiis circa bonum opus. (V. 104; cf. below, no. 172.)

f. 209ᵛ. 47. de infinitatis nominibus in trinitate. (V. 105; cf. 67, 69, Summa, 1, 34, and below, nos. 58, 157.)

¹ No rubric, but the opening words of the questio have been repeated in the space left for it, as in the index.

² No rubric, but a complete rubric indication in the same hand as that of the text.

³ The index adds 'infra de eodem', a cross reference to no. 149, the 11th questio of the 13th quire.

⁴ The index says simply 'de transubstantione'. The meaning of the latter part of the rubric is not clear from the text, which does not appear to refer to any *Arnaldus*, but the point requires more investigation than can be given to it here. The Cistercian Ernald of Bonneval (d. 1186) discussed the doctrine of the eucharist in his 'De cardinalibus operibus Christi'. The reference can hardly be to Arnulf of Rochester. For these and for Langton's use of the word *transubstantiari*, see Ghellinck, 'Eucharistie au xiiᵉ siècle en occident', in Vacant and Mangenot's *Dictionnaire de théologie catholique*, v, cols. 1244, 1247, 1262.

⁵ Two passages are marked in the margin as added: f. 207ᵛ, 'istud totum superadditum est', and f. 208ᵛ, 'hoc totum interpositum est'. It will be noticed that nos. 45–52 correspond in identical order with nos. 103–10 in the St. Victor MS.

f. 210ʳ. 48. utrum antiqui patres crediderint eosdem articulos penitus quos et nos credimus [de articulis fidei, *index*]. (V. 106.)

[*Quire VI*]

f. 211ʳ. 49. utrum quatuor cardinales uirtutes sint in patria. (V. 107.)

f. 211ᵛ. 50. utrum omnis motus meritorius sit motus iusticie. (V. 108, de iusticia.)

f. 212ʳ. 51. quare potius dicantur esse vii dona spiritus sancti quam patris et filii [de donis—*index*]. (V. 109, cf. 71.)

f. 213ʳ. 52. utrum bonum naturale per peccatum corrumpatur [de corruptione naturalium—*index*]. (V. 110, de malo, etc.)

f. 213ᵛ. 53. de extrema unctione. (V. 171; Bamberg, f. 98.)

f. 214ᵛ. 54. de circumcisione et differentia inter sacramenta noue legis et ueteris [de effectu circumcisionis et baptismi—*index*]. (V. 12; cf. 132, and below, nos. 82, 188, 195.)

f. 215ᵛ. 55. quare omnis actio est a deo ¹ [utrum mala actio sit a deo—*index*].

f. 216ʳ. 55a. quod non omnis actio est a deo.²

f. 216ᵛ. 56. quod naturalia non efficiuntur gratuita.²
            56a. quod naturalia efficiuntur gratuita.

f. 217ʳ. 57. de occulte peccante.

f. 218ʳ. 58. de hoc nomine deus.³ (Cf. V. 67, 69, Summa, 1, 34, and below, 157; also above, 47, and V. 105.)

[*Group B. Quire VII*]

f. 219ʳ. 59. de penitentia.⁴ (Cf. V. 136.)

f. 219ʳ. 60. de battismo [baptismo—*index*]. (Cf. V. 8, 101, and below, nos. 189, 194.)

---

¹ The ink changes at this part in the Cambridge manuscript.

² This is not indexed, though rubricated in the text. It was apparently regarded at first as a part of no. 55 and the title was inserted later. No. 56a is indexed.

³ This questio is indexed, but is written in a different hand from that of the preceding text, apparently by the corrector, whose hand in these six quires (ff. 171–218) is very similar. f. 218ᵛ is blank. This section (A) ended half-way down the second column of f. 217ᵛ.

⁴ Here a new set of questiones begins, occupying eight quires. The section

f. 219ᵛ. 61. de fictione (cf. above, no. 8, below, no. 192.)

f. 220ʳ. 62. de liberatione humani generis.

f. 220ᵛ. 63. de potentia credendi que est in homine an sit naturalis. (Cf. V. 65, and above, no. 6.)

f. 221ʳ. 64. utrum qui faciunt opera ex pari caritate pariter mereantur. (Cf. above, no. 5.)

f. 221ʳ. 65. de scándalo. (V. 158.)

f. 221ᵛ. 66. an caritas semel habita possit amitti. (V. 91.)

f. 222ʳ. 67. de reditu peccatorum.

f. 222ᵛ. 68. an caritas uel virtus possit minui. (V. 154.)

f. 223ʳ. 69. de creatione angelorum.¹

f. 223ᵛ. 70. de predestinatione. (Cf. V. 164, and below, no. 162.)

f. 224ʳ. 71. de peccato in spiritum sanctum. (V. 40, cf. 39.)

f. 224ᵛ. 72. de frui et uti.

f. 225ʳ. 73. utrum homo teneatur facere ex caritate quicquid tenetur facere.

f. 225ᵛ. 74. de raptu Pauli. (V. 41.)

f. 225ᵛ. 75. quod non aliquis mereatur uitam eternam ex condigno.

f. 226ʳ. 76. quod aliquis potest mereri uitam eternam ex condigno.²

f. 226ᵛ. 77. de passionibus sanctorum.

[*Quire VIII*]

f. 227ᵛ. 78. utrum sancti antiqui meruerint uitam eternam. (V. 2.)

f. 228ʳ. 79. de pena antiquorum patrum qui erant in limbo inferni. (V. 3.)

f. 228ᵛ. 80. an aliquis possit mereri predestinationem. (V. 119; below, no. 164.)

f. 229ʳ. 81. de actionibus [diuina—*index*].

f. 229ᵛ. 82. de ueteri lege et euangelio. (Cf. V. 12, 132; cf. above, no. 54, and below, nos. 188, 195.)

originally ended on the first column of f. 278ᵛ. See no. 153 below. The handwriting seems to be the same as in the previous section (excluding no. 58). The first column of f. 219ʳ contains a gloss within the width of the text, showing that the gloss is copied from the manuscript before the scribe. The gloss reappears elsewhere, e. g. f. 231ᵛ.

¹ The last sixteen lines of the first column (f. 223ᵛ) are marked 'hoc superadditum est'.

² A diagrammatic exposition of 'meritum' in the right-hand margin of f. 226ʳ.

f. 230ʳ. 83. de fide. (Cf. V. 94, 95, and below, no. 93.)

f. 230ᵛ. 84. an quidam teneantur deum magis diligere.

f. 230ᵛ. 85. de duabus uoluntatibus in Christo.

f. 231ʳ. 86. de primis motibus. (Cf. V. 102, and below, no. 98.)

f. 231ᵛ. 87. de ignorantia. (V. 18–21, and below, nos. 173–6.)

f. 232ᵛ. 88. de collatione boni et mali. (V. 63.)

f. 234ʳ. 89. de potentia gubernandi. (Cf. Summa, no. 35.)

[*Quire IX*]

f. 235ʳ. 90. utrum uoluntas et actus sint diuersa peccata uel idem.
(Cf. below, no. 184.)

f. 235ᵛ. 91. de iuramento.

f. 236ᵛ. 92. de obedientia. (Cf. V. 128, and below, no. 231.)

f. 237ᵛ. 93. de fide. (See above, no. 83, and cf. V. 94, 95.)

f. 238ʳ. 94. utrum temporalia sint absolute petenda¹. (Cf. V. 163,
and above, no. 12.)

f. 238ᵛ. 95. de stimulo Pauli et eius petitione. (V. 76; above, no.
13; S., f. 116ᵛ.)

f. 238ᵛ. 96. de ordine uirtutum. (V. 82.)

f. 239ᵛ. 97. an qui habet unam uirtutem habeat omnes.

f. 240ʳ. 98. de primis motibus. (V. 102, cf. above, no. 86.)

f. 240ᵛ. 99. de perseuerantia. (V. 78.)

f. 241ʳ. 100. de iustificatione. (V. 117.)

f. 241ᵛ. 101. de ligno, feno et stipula. (Cf. V. 66, and below, no.
218.)

f. 242ʳ. 102. an eadem actio sit meritoria et demeritoria. (V. 134.)

f. 242ʳ. 103. de fine actionum.

f. 242ᵛ. 104. de prophetia. (Cf. V. 118, and below, no. 165.)

[*Quire X*]

f. 243ʳ. 105. utrum resurrectio corporum sit naturalis uel miraculosa. (V. 70.)

f. 243ᵛ. 106. de libero arbitrio. (Cf. V. 146, and below, no. 171.)

f. 244ᵛ. 107. de sinderesi. (Cf. V. 145, and below, no. 170.)

f. 245ʳ. 108. de illo uerbo apostoli *coartor e duobus*. (Cf. V. 36, and
below, no. 238.)

---

¹ The whole of this and the next questio is marked 'supra', i.e. a cross reference
to nos. 12, 13.

f. 246ʳ. 109. [utrum aliquod nomine Christi dicatur de deo—
           marginal note in index] begins: Iohannes Dama-
           scenus ait.

f. 246ʳ. 110. de suffragiis ecclesie. (Cf. V. 116, and below, no. 212.)

f. 246ᵛ. 111. quod furiosus peccet [peccat—*index*]. (Cf. V. 84, and
           below, no. 136.)

f. 247ʳ. 112. de uirginitate.

f. 248ʳ. 113. utrum mali angeli demereantur usque ad diem iudicii.

f. 248ᵛ. 114. de mercenariis: begins, apostolus dicit ad philip-
           penses, *siue per ueritatem, siue per occasionem*, as in
           V. 55, cf. 54, and below, no. 182.

f. 249ᵛ. 115. utrum quicunque habet caritatem sciat se habere.
           (V. 100.)

[*Quire XI*]

f. 251ʳ. 116. de contemptu. (Cf. V. 49, and below, no. 178.)

f. 251ᵛ. 117. utrum Christus fuerit homo in triduo. (Cf. V. 166,
           and below, no. 214.)

f. 252ʳ. 118. de satisfactione iniuncta ab indiscreto sacerdote. (V.
           37.)

f. 252ᵛ. 119. de contritione. (V. 48; cf. 142, and below, nos. 152,
           197, 198.)

f. 253ʳ. 120. de confessione. (V. 153; cf. 29 and below, no. 199).

f. 253ᵛ. 121. utrum homo licite possit uelle contrarium eius quod
           scit deum uelle. (Cf. V. 50.)

f. 254ᵛ. 122. utrum Christus omni opere suo meruerit equaliter
           nobis. (Cf. V. 72).

f. 255ᵛ. 123. de dispensatione eucharistie.

f. 256ᵛ. 124. de principio.

f. 257ʳ. 125. [de peccato Luciferi. *Index, in later hand*].

f. 257ᵛ. 126. de *deus est ubique*. (Cf. V. 123.)

f. 258ʳ. 127. de notionibus. (V. 53; cf. Summa, no. 36.)

[*Quire XII*]

f. 259ʳ. 128. de relaxationibus. (Cf. below, no. 204.)

f. 259ʳ. 129. de ieiunio.[1] (Cf. V. 47 and below, no. 239, also 204.)

---

[1] This questio ends with twenty-two lines identical with part of no. 204 below
(de relaxationibus). No. 239 (de ieiunio) comprises 129*a* followed by 129 but
without the addition from 204. See above, p. 66.   The lower half of the second

f. 260ʳ. 129*a* de ieiunio. (Cf. V. 47, and below, no. 239.)

f. 260ʳ. 130. quomodo dicatur unum genus operum magis bonum uel malum alio.

f. 261ʳ. 131. de correctione fratris. (Cf. V. 74, and above, no. 1.)

f. 262ʳ. 132. de crucifixione Christi.

f. 262ʳ. 133. quare diabolus fuit motus ad liberandum Christum.¹

f. 262ᵛ. 134. de descriptione sacramenti. (Cf. V. 58.)

f. 263ᵛ. 135. de oratione. (V. 59; cf. 125, 143.)

f. 264ᵛ. 136. utrum furiosus peccet. (Cf. V. 84, and above, no. 111.)

f. 266ʳ. 137. quomodo dicatur *homo factus est ad ymaginem dei* (V. 60.)

f. 266ᵛ. 138. de spe. (V. 42.)

[*Quire XIII*]

f. 267ʳ. 139. de preceptis decalogi et additionibus. (V. 168.)

f. 268ᵛ. 140. de simbolo et oratione dominica quare potius in completorio dicantur.² (Cf. V. 43.)

f. 269ʳ. 141. de hoc nomine *eternus*.

f. 269ᵛ. 142. de elemosina. (Cf. below, no. 240.)

f. 270ʳ. 143. de usia, usiosis, ypostasis, prosopa, de essentia subsistentia, substantia et persona. (Cf. above, no. 20, and Summa, no. 39.)

f. 271ᵛ. 144. de quantitate caritatis et premii.

f. 272ʳ. 145. de acceptione personarum. (Cf. below, 249.)

f. 273ʳ. 146. de capite ecclesie. (Cf. V. 122, and below, no. 215.)

f. 273ʳ. 147. de hoc uerbo *dixit deus fiat lux et facta est lux.* (Cf. V. 120, and below, no. 156.)

f. 273ᵛ. 148. de Leui decimato in Abraham.

f. 273ᵛ. 149. de uoluntate dei et signis.³ (Cf. V. 26, and above, no. 42, and below, no. 160.)

f. 274ʳ. 150. de ira dei. (V. 121.)

f. 274ᵛ. 151. de perplexitate.

column of f. 259ᵛ is blank. No. 129*a*, which is not indexed, begins at the top of f. 260ᵛ: summus pontifex instituit.

¹ Rubricated as a sub-heading to 132 (f. 262ʳ): quare diabolus fuit motus ad liberandum Christum. The index reads *de uerbis permissionis*, to cover both.

² Heading in *brown* ink, and a later hand.

³ A later hand has added in the index 'supra de eodem'.

[*Quire XIV*]

f. 275ᵛ. 152. de contricione. (Cf. V. 48, 142; above, no 119, below, nos. 197 and 198.)

f. 276ᵛ. 153. de peccato ad mortem.[1] (Cf. V. 57 and 80.)

f. 278ᵛ. [154. *begins*: quare, cum baptizatus puer, ad quem dirigatur sermo, cum dicitur *credis in deum*.]

f. 279ᵛ. [155. *begins*: questio est de libro uite].

[*Group C. Quire XV*]

f. 283ʳ. 156. de hoc uerbo *dixit deus fiat lux*.[2] (V. 120; cf. no. 147.)

f. 283ᵛ. 157. de nominibus essentialibus, ut de hoc nomine deus. (Cf. V. 67, 69, Summa, 1, 34, and above, no. 58; also above, no. 47 and V. 105.)

f. 284ʳ. 158. utrum essentia possit demonstrari.

f. 285ʳ. 159. de similitudine patris ad filium. (V. 62.)

f. 286ʳ. 160. de uoluntate diuina. (V. 26; cf. above, nos. 42, 149.)

f. 286ᵛ 161. de prescientia. (V. 92.)

f. 287ʳ. 162. de predestinatione. (V. 164; cf. above, no. 70.)

f. 287ᵛ. 163. de predestinatione Christi.

f. 288ʳ. 164. de predestinatione sanctorum. (V. 119; above, no. 80.)

f. 288ᵛ. 165. de prophetia. (V. 118; above, no. 104.)

f. 289ʳ. 166. quid sit prophetia.

f. 290ʳ. 167. de officio prophetiarum et propter quid dicendus sit aliquis prophetia et de quanto sit ei credendum.

f. 290ᵛ. 168. de statu angelorum ante casum. (V. 6.)

[*Quire XVI*]

f. 291ʳ. 169. de statu Ade ante peccatum. (V. 61.)

f. 292ᵛ. 170. de sinderesi. (V. 145; cf. above, no. 107.)

f. 292ᵛ. 171. de libero arbitrio. (V. 146; cf. above, no. 106.)

f. 294ᵛ. 172. utrum euentus sequens agrauet peccatum. (Cf. V. 104; above, no. 46.)

f. 295ʳ. 173. Quando habeat esse ignorantia et utrum paruulus dicatur ignorare. (V. 18; cf. above, no. 87.)

[1] This questio (f. 276ᵛ–f. 278ᵛ) ends the second collection. The next two questiones were added later, after the index had been made, on the blank folios. f. 282 is altogether blank.   [2] Section C, of three quires, begins here.

f. 296ʳ. 174. utrum scientie naturali contraria sit ignorantia. (V.19.)
f. 296ᵛ. 175. de ignorantia inuincibili. (V. 20.)
f. 296ᵛ. 176. de ignorantia affectata. (V. 21.)
f. 297ʳ. 177. de reatu. (V. 137, and cf. above, no. 31.)
f. 298ʳ. 178. de contemptu. (V. 49, and cf. above, no. 116.)
f. 298ᵛ. 179. utrum mala actio sit remuneranda temporaliter. (V. 81.)

[*Quire XVII*]

f. 299ʳ. 180. utrum omnis actio de genere bonorum existenti in mortali sit mortalis.
f. 299ᵛ. 181. De operibus que fiunt ministerio alterius.
f. 300ʳ. 182. De hoc quod dicit apostolus *siue per ueritatem siue per occasionem*. (V. 54; cf. 55, and above, no. 114.)
f. 300ᵛ. 183. utrum peccata dimissa rederint.
f. 301ʳ. 184. utrum uoluntas et actus sint idem peccatum uel diuersa. (Cf. above, no. 90.)
f. 301ᵛ. 185. utrum ueniale peccatum puniatur eternaliter. (V. 156; cf. above, no. 7.)
f. 302ʳ. 186. utrum ueniale habeat reatum. (V. 149; cf. 157, and above, no. 39.)
f. 302ʳ. 187. de omissionibus et tentoribus.[1]

[*Group D. Quire XVIII*]

f. 307ʳ. 188. utrum opera legalia iustificarent.[2] (V. 132; cf. 12, and above, nos. 54, 82, and below, no. 195.)
f. 308ʳ. 189. de baptismo. (Cf. V. 8, 101; cf. above, no. 60, and below, no. 194.)
f. 308ᵛ. 190. de effectu baptismi. (Cf. above, no. 8.)
f. 309ᵛ. 191. utrum intentio baptisantis uel baptisati sit necessaria in baptismo.
f. 309ᵛ. 192. de fictione. (Cf. above, nos. 8, 61.)
f. 310ʳ. 193. de exorcismo et catecismo. (V. 155.)
f. 310ʳ. 194. de baptismo Iohannis. (Cf. V. 8, 101, and above, nos. 60, 189.)
f. 310ʳ. 195. de circumcisione. (Cf. V. 12, and above, no. 54.)

[1] End of the third section. f. 306 is blank.
[2] The next two quires form a fourth section (D).

f. 311^r. 196. de sacramento circumcisionis.

f. 311^r. 197. utrum sola contritione delatur peccatum. (Cf. V. 142; S., f. 6, and above, nos. 119, 152.)

f. 312^r. 198. utrum contricio sit sacramentum. (Cf. V. 48, 142; above, nos. 119, 152.)

f. 312^v. 199. de confessione. (V. 29; cf. 153, and above, no. 120.)

f. 313^r. 200. utrum penitentia facta in mortali sit iteranda.

f. 313^v. 201. de restitutione et utrum sit pars satisfactionis.

f. 314^v. 202. quomodo sacerdos dimittit peccata uel retinet. (Cf. S., f. 4^v de potestate ligandi.)

[*Quire XIX*]

f. 315^v. 203. quid sit clauis. (V. 14; S., f. 7^v.)

f. 316^v. 204. de relaxationibus que fiunt in ecclesia.[1] (Cf. above, nos. 128–9a.)

f. 317^r. 205. [de sacramento eucharistie—*index*]. (Cf. V. 64, and above, no. 44.)

f. 318^r. 206. utrum caracter conferatur in ordine.

f. 318^v. 207. de matrimonio. (V. 4.)

f. 319^r. 208. de redditione debiti coniugalis. (V. 5.)

f. 319^v. 209. de uoto. (V. 162.)

f. 320^v. 210. de uoto Iepte. (V. 99; cf. above, no. 32.)

f. 321^r. 211. utrum in omni opere domini sit misericordia et iusticia. (V. 27.)

f. 322^r. 212. de suffragiis ecclesie.[2] (V. 116; cf. above, no. 110.)

[*Group E. Quire XX*]

f. 323^r. 213. de homine assumpto et utrum Christus sit duo.[3]

f. 323^v. 213a. utrum Christus sit filius adoptiuus.

f. 323^v. 214. utrum Christus fuerit homo in triduo passionis. (V. 166; cf. above, no. 117.)

f. 324^r. 215. de Christo capite, quot modis dicitur caput ecclesie. (V. 122; cf. above, no. 146.)

---

[1] See note on no. 129 above. A note in right-hand margin of f. 317^r begins: audiui magistrum Stephanum [. . .] mensem dicentem quod.

[2] f. 322^v is blank.

[3] The last section, comprising three quires, begins here. The new hand is like that of the index.

f. 325^r. 216. qualiter Christus post resurrectionem apparuit. (V. 17.)

f. 325^v. 217. utrum falsum subsit fidei. (V. 96.)

f. 325^v. 218. de ligno, feno et stipula. (V. 66; cf. above, no. 101.)

f. 326^r. 219. de ordine caritatis. (V. 127; cf. 111 and above, no. 23.)

f. 327^v. 220. de responsione Pharisaei *cui plus dimissum est* plus diligit *begins*: duo debitores erant cuidam senatori (V. 35.)

f. 328^v. 221. utrum homo possit resurgere in tanta caritate a quanta ceciderit uel in maiore.[1] (V. 113, S. 1, Arras 1, Avranches 1, Vatican 1; cf. V. 77.)

f. 329^r. 222. quare bonum factum extra caritatem non ualeat isti quando habebit caritatem. (Cf. V. 148, and above, nos. 22, 41.)

f. 329^v. 223. utrum quantulacunque bonitas sit magis bona quam malitia sit mala.

f. 330^v. 224. utrum omnes uirtutes sint pares. (V. 159, cf. Summa 41.)

f. 330^v. 225. utrum paruuli habeant uirtutes. (V. 160.)

[*Quire XXI*]

f. 331^r. 226. penes quid distinguuntur timores substantialiter. (V. 167.)

f. 331^v. 227. de additionibus.

f. 332^r. 228. de mendatio. (V. 165; cf. 22.)

f. 333^r. 229. de benedictione Iacob. (V. 126.)

f. 333^v. 230. de ypocrisi. (V. 30.)

f. 334^r. 231. de obedientia. (V. 128; cf. above, no. 92.)

f. 334^v. 232. de usu obedientie. (V. 129.)

f. 335^r. 233. de negligentia in opere. (V. 144*a*; cf. V. 93, 144.)

f. 335^v. 234. de fraude in opere.

f. 336^r. 235. de contemplatiua et actiua.[2] (V. 161).

f. 336^r. 236. de hoc quod dicitur *quicquid petieritis patrem in nomine meo dabit uobis.*

---

[1] See above, pp. 68, 178–9.

[2] This questio is printed in Ravaisson's *Rapports* from the Avranches MS. See above, p. 12 n.

f. 336ᵛ. 237. quid est perseuerant petere.

f. 337ʳ. 238. de hoc quod dicit apostolus *Coartor e duobus.* (V. 36; cf. above, no. 108.)

f. 337ᵛ. 239. de ieiunio. (V. 47; cf. above, no. 129 and note.)

f. 338ʳ. 240. de elemosina. (Cf. above, no. 142.)

[*Quire XXII*]

f. 339ᵛ. 241. quid sit sanctos orare pro nobis.

f. 339ᵛ. 241a. utrum sit preceptum uel consilium hoc quod dicitur *qui habet duas tunicas det non habenti.*

f. 340ᵛ. 242. de decymis et primitiis. (V. 34, 131.)

f. 341ᵛ. 243. de ira per zelum.

f. 342ʳ. 244. quomodo istud sit intelligendum *omnia sunt iustorum.*

f. 342ᵛ. 245. de usura. (V. 98.)

f. 342ᵛ. 246. de symonia. (V. 75.)

f. 343ᵛ. 247. utrum si aliquis meruit, necessarium sit illum meruisse.

f. 344ʳ. 248. de officio ecclesie in aduentu. (V. 7.)

f. 345ʳ. 249. de acceptione personarum. (Cf. above, no. 145.)

f. 345ᵛ. Index.

f. 346ᵛ. Expliciunt tituli questionum Stephani de longoton Cantuariensis Archiepiscopi.

It will be seen that, of the 250 questiones (a number which includes some duplicates) a very large proportion can be traced in the St. Victor manuscript. Some of the parallels are almost exact, more show a greater or less degree of correspondence. Moreover, groups or blocks of questiones occur in both manuscripts, e.g. V. 103–10 correspond to C. 45–52, V. 137–41 to C. 27–31 (in a different order), V. 18–21 to C. 173–6. Undoubtedly we have to do with the same work in each case. No counterpart of any kind has been traced to V. 9–11, 13, 25, 31–3, 38, 44–6, 51, 56, 68, 73, 83, 97, 124, 130, 133, 135, 144, 148, 150, 169, 170, but further investigation would probably reduce this list. Of the 170 or so questiones of V, about thirty do not seem to be contained in C, about 115 can find fairly exact parallels in C, and about twenty-five deal with matters also treated in C. These conclusions are somewhat tentative and require further investigation, but they are sufficient to show the general relation between the two manuscripts.

C.

It may be of assistance to scholars to have a list of the questiones of V, with their parallels in C.

[*Quire I*]

f. 165ʳ.   Incipit summa magistri Stephani Cantuariensis archiepiscopi.[1]

f. 165ʳ.   1. Latria est cultus soli deo siue creatori exhibendo. *Inc.*[2] (C. 18.)

f. 165ᵛ.   2. de statu antiquorum patrum. (C. 78.)

f. 165ᵛ.   3. de patribus qui erant in limbo inferni. (C. 79.)

f. 166ʳ.   4. de matrimonio. (C. 207.)

f. 166ʳ.   5. de redditione debiti [coniugalis]. (C. 208.)

f. 166ᵛ.   6. de statu angelorum [ante casum]. (C. 168.)

f. 167ʳ.   7. de officio ecclesie in aduentu domini. (C. 248.)

f. 167ᵛ.   8. de potestate baptismi. (Cf. C. 194, also 60, 189, and below, 101.)

f. 168ʳ.   9. de impossibili.

f. 168ᵛ.   10. de merito domini per suum.

f. 168ᵛ.   11. de hoc siue manducauitis.

f. 169ʳ.   12. de differentia legum. (C. 54; cf. 82, 188, 195, and below, 132.)

f. 169ᵛ.   13. de remissione.

f. 170ᵛ.   14. de clauibus. (C. 203.)

f. 171ʳ.   15. de iure naturali. (C. 35.)

f. 171ᵛ.   16. vtrum omnes homines uelint esse beati. (C. 36.)

f. 172ʳ.   17. qualiter Christus apparuerit post resurexionem. (C. 216.)

f. 172ᵛ.   18. de ignorantia. (C. 173, and cf. 87.)

[*Quire II*]

f. 173ʳ.   19. Postea queritur vtrum scientie naturali contraria sit ignorantia aliqua. *Inc.* (C. 174.)

f. 173ʳ.   20. de ignorantia. (C. 175, and cf. 87.)

---

[1] A table of contents, 'incipiunt tituli questionum' precedes. The order is not identical with that followed here from the text.

[2] *Inc.*, i.e., no rubric.

f. 173ᵛ. 21. de ignorantia affectata. (C. 176, and cf. 87.)

f. 174ᵛ. 22. de mendatio. (Cf. C. 228, and below, 165.)

f. 175ᵛ. 23. vtrum deputente (*sic*)¹ angelis ad custodiam antichristi. (Cf. C. 37.)

f. 176ʳ. 24. de sobrietate. (C. 34.)

f. 176ᵛ. 25. vtrum Christus sit aliquid secundum quod homo.

f. 177ʳ. 26. de uoluntate diuina et signis eius. (C. 160; cf. 42 and
149.)

f. 177ᵛ. 27. In omni opere domini misericordia et ueritas. (C. 211.)

f. 178ᵛ. 28. vtrum quelibeι parua caritas sufficiat ad resistendum
cuilibet temptationi. (C. 9.)

f. 179ʳ. 29. de confessione in generali. (C. 199; cf. 120, and
below, 153.)

f. 179ʳ. 30. de ipocrisi. (C. 230.)

f. 180ʳ. 31. de caritate utrum conferatur in ordine.

f. 180ʳ. 32. de superfluis.

f. 180ᵛ. 33. de predicabilibus de deo.

[*Quire III*]

f. 181ʳ. 34. de decimis. (C. 242; cf. below, 131.)

f. 181ᵛ. 35. de hac parabola duo debitores erant cuidam senatori.
(C. 220.)

f. 182ᵛ. 36. de hoc uerbo coartor ex duobus. (C. 238; cf. 108.)

f. 183ᵛ. 37. de satisfactione. (C. 118.)

f. 183ᵛ. 38. de comparatione in generali.

f. 184ᵛ. 39. de peccato in spiritum sanctum. (Cf. C. 71, and below,
40.)

f. 184ᵛ. 40. Peccatum in spiritum sanctum dicitur abstinatio. *Inc.*
(C. 71, and cf. above, 39.)

f. 185ʳ. 41. [de raptu P[auli]].² (C. 74.)

f. 185ᵛ. 42. de spe. (C. 138.)

f. 186ʳ. 43. de simbolo fidei. (Cf. C. 140.)

f. 186ᵛ. 44. de paritate uirtutum.

f. 187ʳ. 45. de merito martirum in pacientia.

f. 188ʳ. 46. vtrum homo potestate naturali possit.

f. 188ᵛ. 47. de ieiunio. (C. 239; cf. 129, 129*a*, and note.)

¹ So MS., *qu.* deputetur?
² Title supplied from rubric indication at foot of the folio.

[*Quire IV*]

f. 189ᵛ. 48. de contricione. (C. 119; cf. 152, 197, 198, and below, 142.)

f. 190ʳ. 49. de contemptu. (C. 178; cf. 116.)

f. 190ᵛ. 50. vtrum teneamur uelle quicquid scimus domini uelle. (Cf. C. 121.)

f. 191ʳ. 51. de hoc uerbo ex ipso et per ipsum et qualiter filius aparitur per patrem.

f. 191ʳ. 52. Terminos quos nulli transgredi licet posuerunt patres sancti nobis dicentes. *Inc.* (C. 19, and cf. Summa, nos. 32, 33.)

f. 192ʳ. 53. de nocionibus. (C. 127; cf. Summa, no. 36.)

f. 193ʳ. 54. de hoc uerbo apostoli siue per accionem (*sic*) etc. (C. 182; cf. 114.)

f. 193ʳ. 55. Ad Philippenses. siue per occasionem. *Inc.* (Cf. C. 114 and 182.)

f. 193ᵛ. 56. de hoc uerbo dictum est antiquis diliges proximum et odio etc. (Cf. below, 79, 112.)

f. 194ʳ. 57. vtrum peccator in peccato mortali existens non possit. (Cf. C. 153, and below, 80.)

f. 194ᵛ. 58. de sacramento in generali. (Cf. C. 134.)

f. 195ʳ. 59. de oratione. (C. 135; cf. below, 125, 143).

f. 196ʳ. 60. de hoc uerbo faciamus hominem ad imaginem. (C. 137.)

f. 196ᵛ. 61. de statu primo ade utrum interfuerit peccatum in isto statu. (C. 169.)

[*Quire V*]

f. 197ʳ. 62. de similitudine patris ad filium. (C. 159.)

f. 197ᵛ. 63. de conparatione boni et mali. (C. 88.)

f. 198ᵛ. 64. de sacramento altaris. (C. 44; cf. 205.)

f. 199ᵛ. 65. de potentia credendi. (C. 6; cf. 63.)

f. 200ᵛ. 66. Super illum locum apostoli ubi loquitur de **edificione** ligni. *Inc.* (C. 218; cf. 101.)

f. 200ᵛ. 67. de nominibus que predicantur de deo. (Cf. Summa, 1, 34, C. 58 and 157, and below, 69; also below, 105, and C. 47.)

[*Quire VI*]

f. 205ʳ. 68. de missione (?) spiritus sancti.[1]

f. 205ᵛ. 69. de su*ppo*sitione nominum. (Cf. Summa, 1, 34, C. 58 and 157, and above, 67; also below, 105 and C. 47.)

f. 208ᵛ. 70. de resurrexione utrum futura sit miraculosa **an** naturalis. (C. 105.)

f. 208ᵛ. 71. de septem donis. (Cf. C. 51, and below, 109.)

f. 209ʳ. 72. de merito Christi. (Cf. C. 122.)

f. 209ᵛ. 73. vtrum omnes motus fuerint pacati in Christo.

f. 210ʳ. 74. de hoc uerbo si peccauerit in te frater tuus. (C. 1, and cf. 131.)

f. 211ʳ. 75. de simonia. (C. 246.)

f. 211ᵛ. 76. de stimulo Pauli. (C. 13, and cf. 95; S., f. 116ᵛ.)

f. 212ᵛ. 77. Certum est quod homo possit resurgere in equali caritate uel in maiori quam habuit ante lapsum. *Inc.* (Cf. C. 221, and below, 113.)

f. 212ᵛ. 78. de perseuerantia. (C. 99.)

[*Quire VII*]

f. 213ʳ. 79. de hoc uerbo dictum est diliges proximum tuum et odio habebis inimicum. (Cf. above, 56, and below, 112.)

f. 213ᵛ. 80. vtrum existens in peccato mortali indignus sit omni bono. (Cf. above, 57, and C. 153.)

f. 213ᵛ. 81. vtrum actio mala sit remuneranda. (C. 179.)

f. 214ʳ. 82. de ordine uirtutum. (C. 96.)

f. 214ᵛ. 83. vtrum deus creauit omnia simul.

f. 215ʳ. 84. vtrum furiosus peccet. (Cf. C. 111, 136.)

f. 216ʳ. 85. vtrum Christus secundum quod homo habuerit potentiam dimittendi peccata. (C. 17.)

f. 216ᵛ. 86. de eucaristia. (C. 8.)

f. 217ᵛ. 87. vtrum sit possibile tamen quod est possibile secundum causas superiores. (C. 16.)

f. 218ʳ. 88. duplex est et fuit ab eterno scientia. *Inc.* (C. 21.)

f. 218ᵛ. 89. de missione spiritus sancti. (C. 11; cf. above, 68.)

---

[1] MS. inusicione.

f. 219ᵛ. 90. quibus danda sit eucaristia. (C. 40.)

f. 220ᵛ. 91. quod caritas non possit amitti semel habita. (C. 66.)

f. 220ᵛ. 92. hoc uerbo prescit dictum de deo. *Inc.* (C. 161.)

[*Quire VIII*]

f. 221ʳ. 93. Qualiter fiat opus dei negligentia. (Cf. C. 233; cf.
         below, 144, 144a.)

f. 221ᵛ. 94. Dicturi de fide primo distinguendum est. *Inc.* (Cf.
         C. 83, 93.)

f. 221ᵛ. 95. de fide. (Cf. C. 83, 93.)

f. 222ʳ. 96. vtrum falsum subsit fidei. (C. 217.)

f. 222ᵛ. 97. de illo uerbo quantum iurendis tantum fatis.

f. 223ʳ. 98. de usura. (C. 245.)

f. 223ʳ. 99. de uoto iepte. (C. 210; cf. 32.)

f. 223ᵛ. 100. vtrum aliquis sciat se habere caritatem. (C. 115.)

f. 224ᵛ. 101. de baptismo. (Cf. C. 60, 189, 194, and above, 8.)

f. 224ᵛ. 102. de primis motibus. (C. 98; cf. 86.)

f. 225ʳ. 103. de precepto domini ad abraam de imolatione ysaac.
         (C. 45.)

f. 226ᵛ. 104. de circumstantia. (C. 46; cf. 172.)

f. 227ᵛ. 105. de infinitis nominibus predicati de deo. (C. 47; cf.
         58, 157; Summa, 1, 34, and above, 67, 69.)

f. 228ʳ. 106. de antiquis patribus utrum crediderint eosdem ar-
         ticulos quos et nos. (C. 48.)

f. 228ᵛ. 107. de uirtutibus cardinalibus utrum sint in patria.
         (C. 49.)

[*Quire IX*]

f. 229ʳ. 108. de iustitia. (C. 50.)

f. 229ᵛ. 109. de septem donis. (C. 51; cf. above, 71.)

f. 230ᵛ. 110. de malo quid mali in*fenit* (*sic*). (C. 52.)

f. 231ʳ. 111. de ordine caritatis et de caritate ipsa et eius motu.
         (C. 23.)

f. 232ʳ. 112. de dilectione proximi et inimicorum. (C. 24.)

f. 232ᵛ. 113. vtrum homo possit in tanta caritate resurgere in
         quanta cecidit uel in maiori. (C. 221; cf. above, 77.)

f. 234ᵛ. 114. vtrum deus puniat condigna in gehenna. (C. 26.)

f. 235ʳ. 115. vtrum peccatum sit pena peccati. (C. 33.)

f. 236ʳ. 116. de suffragiis. (C. 212; cf. 110.)

f. 236ᵛ. 117. de iustificatione impii. (C. 100.)

f. 236ᵛ. 118. de prophetia. (C. 165; cf. 104.)

[*Quire X*]

f. 237ᵛ. 119. Augustinus dicit Deus predestinat iustos quia uult et
eius uoluntas non est iniusta. *Inc.* (C. 80, 164.)

f. 237ᵛ. 120. de hoc dixit deus fiat lux. (C. 156; cf. 147.)

f. 238ʳ. 121. de ira. (C. 150.)

f. 238ᵛ. 122. vtrum Christus sit caput ecclesie. (C. 125; cf. 146.)

f. 239ʳ. 123. Qualiter deus sit ubique. (Cf. C. 126.)

f. 239ʳ. 124. vtrum tota [. . .] malorum sit peccatum.

f. 239ᵛ. 125. de oratione unde habuerit originem. (Cf. C. 135,
above, 59, and below, 143.)

f. 240ʳ. 126. de benedictione iacob. (C. 229.)

f. 240ᵛ. 127. de ordine caritatis. (C. 219; cf. 23, and above, 111.)

f. 241ᵛ. 128. de obedientia. (C. 231; cf. 92.)

f. 242ʳ. 129. de usu obedientie. (C. 232.)

f. 242ᵛ. 130. vtrum diabolus uelit se esse deum et utrum omni
motu suo peccet.

f. 243ʳ. 131. de decimis. (C. 242; cf. above, 34.)

f. 243ᵛ. 132. de differentia ueteris legis et noue. (C. 188; cf. 54,
82, 195, and above, 12.)

f. 244ᵛ. 133. de restitutionibus.

[*Quire XI*]

f. 245ᵛ. 134. vtrum motus idem possit esse meritorius et demeri-
torius. (C. 102.)

f. 246ᵛ. 135. de quibusdam que queruntur circa passionem domini.

f. 246ᵛ. 136. vtrum penitentia facta in mortali iteranda sit. (Cf.
C. 59.)

f. 247ʳ. 137. de differentia macule et reatus. (C. 177, and cf. 31.)

f. 247ᵛ. 138. de dotibus glorificati corporis. (C. 27.)

f. 248ʳ. 139. de cerimonialibus utrum fuerint meritoria. (C. 30.)

f. 249ʳ. 140. vtrum prelatus teneatur ad opera misericordie et
utrum teneatur habere perfectam caritatem. (C.
29.)

f. 249ᵛ. 141. vtrum bona ecclesie possideantur a prelatis. (C. 28.)

f. 250ʳ. 142. de contricione. (Cf. C. 119, 152, 197, 198, and above, 48.)

f. 250ᵛ. 143. de oratione. (Cf. C. 135, and above, 59 and 125.)

f. 251ʳ. 144. de hac auctoritate ieremie maledictus qui facit opus dei negligenter. (Cf. above, 93.)

144*a*. Ieremias, Maledictus qui opus dei facit negligenter. *Inc.* (C. 233; cf. above, 93, 144.)

f. 251ᵛ. 145. Ieronimus dicit quod in nullo uiuente extincta est sinderesis. *Inc.* (C. 170; cf. 107.)

f. 252ʳ. 146. de libero arbitrio. (C. 171; cf. 106.)

[*Quire XII*]

f. 253ᵛ. 147. queritur ad que ualeant opera facta extra caritatem. (Cf. C. 22, 41, 43, and 222.)

f. 254ʳ. 148. de predictis operibus iterum.

f. 254ᵛ. 149. de ueniali peccato. (C. 186; cf. 39, and below, 157.)

f. 255ʳ. 150. de remissione peccati.

f. 255ᵛ. 151. de vi speciebus timoris. (C. 2.)

f. 257ᵛ. 152. de timore initiali. (C. 3.)

f. 258ʳ. 153. de confessione. (C. 120; cf. 199, and above, 29.)

f. 258ʳ. 154. vtrum caritas possit minui. (C. 68.)

f. 258ᵛ. 155. de catacismo. (C. 193.)

f. 259ᵛ. 156. de ueniali utrum puniatur in inferno. (C. 185; cf. 7.)

f. 259ʳ. 157. de ueniali. (Cf. C. 39, 186.)

f. 259ᵛ. 158. de scandalo. (C. 65.)

f. 260ʳ. 159. de equalitate uirtutum. (C. 224; cf. Summa, 41.)

f. 260ʳ. 160. vtrum paruuli habeant uirtutes. (C. 225.)

f. 260ᵛ. 161. de conparatione actiue et contemplatiue. (C. 235.)

f. 260ᵛ. 162. de uoto. (C. 209.)

[*Quire XIII*]

f. 261ʳ. 163. vtrum liceat petere temporalia. (C. 12, and cf. 94.)

f. 261ᵛ. 164. de predestinatione. (C. 162; cf. 70.)

f. 262ʳ. 165. de mendatio. (C. 228; cf. above, 22.)

f. 263ʳ. 166. vtrum Christus fuerit homo in triduo. (C. 214; cf. 117.)

f. 263^v. 167. de timore et speiebus eius. (C. 226.)

f. 263^v. 168. de preceptis x. (C. 139.)

f. 263^v. 169. de secundo membro mandati.

f. 264^v. 170. de fomite.

f. 265^v. 171. de extrema unctione. (C. 53.)[1]

f. 266^r. Expliciunt Questiones Magistri Stephani Cantuariensis archiepiscopi. Deo Gratias.

---

[1] See above, p. 179. In his valuable paper, ' La somme theologique d'Etienne Langton ' (*Recherches de science religieuse*, iv (1913) 255–61), which I was not able to study before this work was put into proof, Father Ghellinck concludes that the Bamberg MS. contains a more articulated and later *summa*, which may not be Langton's. This problem requires further examination, with special reference to the short provisional *summa* in the Cambridge MS. I am at present inclined to think that the Bamberg MS. contains the latest form or edition of the *questiones*, worked up into a more systematic whole, possibly by a man who had more legal knowledge than Langton had. But, in spite of the differences in treatment, both the Bamberg and the MSS. in Cambridge and Paris seem to be recensions of the same teaching.

MS. *Bodley* 57, f. 66ᵛ

Documenta clericorum Stephani de Lanketon'

.i. Non te lusisse pudeat,   *primus*
sed ludum non incidere
et que lusisti temere
ad vite frugem regere
magistra morum doceat
te racio,
ut dignus pontificio
diuini dono muneris
ad laudem Christi nominis
fungaris sacerdocio.

.ij. Sis pius, iustus, sobrius,   ij[us]
prudens, pudicus, humilis,
in lege Dei docilis,
et ne sis arbor sterilis,
tuo te regas apcius
officio.
expulso procul vicio
munderis labe criminis,
ut mundus munde virginis
ministres in altario.

.iij. Pius protector pauperum   iij[us]
omni petenti tribue:
malos potenter argue,
manusque sacras ablue
a sordidorum munerum
contagio.
nullus te palpet premio:
quesita gratis gracia
largite beneficia
sed dignis beneficio.

.iiij. Ministros inmundicie.   iiij[us]
a te repellas longius:
bonorum vitam forcius[1]
pravus depravat socius,
et afficit infamie

    [1] Corrected from 'pocius'.

dispendio.
sic trahitur presumpcio
a convictu similium ;
prelati vita milium[1]
vilescit contubernio.

.v. Non des ministris scelerum   v^us
non tua ecclesie[2]
sub pietatis specie:
non abutaris inpie
commisso tibi pauperum
suffragio.
nil a te ferat ẏstrio,
et tibi non alicias
infames amicicias
de Christi patrimonio.

.vj. Caute dispone domui,   vj^us
pauca set vera loquere,
verba confirmes opere,
quia non decet temere
os sacerdotis pollui
mendacio.
prudencium te consilio[3]
fratrum non displiceat,[3]
nec te sinistre moveat
salubris exortacio.

.vij. Teneris ut abstineas   vij^us
ab omni mala specie.
sub freno temperancie,
magistra pudicicie
sobrietate floreas:
ne vario
vagoque desiderio
declines ad illecebras,
set tue mentis tenebras
purga virtutum radio.

---

[1] So the MS. Qu. 'vilium'?
[2] (*Sic*). The metre demands an extra syllable. Qu. read 'bona tue ecclesie'?
[3] (*Sic*). 'consilium' would make better sense than 'consilio'. Both these lines are faulty in metre: probably 'te' should come in the second line.

APPENDIX V

The Twenty-Five Barons of the Charter

THE personnel of the opposition to King John in 1215 requires much detailed investigation. Local connexions and the evidence given in the Fine Rolls and other records of personal grievances have never been thoroughly examined. In this appendix I desire merely to offer some tentative conclusions, based upon Matthew Paris's list of the twenty-five, and upon Wendover's list of those who, with many more, gathered at Stamford in Easter week.[1]

1. The centre of power and, I believe, the immediate reasons for resistance had changed since 1213. As I have tried to show, the programme was continuous. The barons who talked with Langton in August 1213 were clearly not the northerners, who at that time were withdrawing to the north, but a group which had no intentions of rebellion and centred in the returned exile, Robert fitz Walter. But for some months the interests of the northerners were the chief consideration; and attention was concentrated upon the three issues: foreign service, scutage, illegal attacks by the king. Hence in the 'unknown charter' the revision of points in Henry I's charter was followed by declarations on these issues. It is noteworthy that the group which later gathered around Robert fitz Walter from the eastern counties seems to have had no objection to the Poitevin campaign. The long list of barons and others who were allowed their scutage—i.e. who either went or sent their sons or knights to Poitou—contains the names of many of the later rebels: earl Roger Bigod, the earl of Winchester (Saer de Quinci), William Malet, William de Beauchamp the lord of Bedford, Geoffrey de Sai, William de Lanvallei, William de Huntingfield, Richard de Montfichet.[2] It looks as though John's failure abroad, and, doubtless, new experiences of which we have no record, had determined these and others to adopt more drastic methods in the pursuit of the policy begun in 1213. Hence the gathering at Stamford included, not only the northerners, but a still larger number of

---

[1] *Wendover*, iii. 297. Dr. Round led the way in the *English Historical Review*, xix. 707–11.   [2] *Rot. litt. claus.* i. 200–1 (16 John, m. 24d).

barons drawn from the circle of Robert fitz Walter.[1] Only five northerners in the strict sense appear in the later committee of twenty-five: Eustace de Vesci, William Mowbray, Robert de Ros, Richard Percy, Roger de Montbegon. Two of these, Eustace de Vesci, lord of Alnwick, and Robert de Ros, lord of Helmsley and Wark, were brothers-in-law of the young King Alexander of Scotland.[2] William Mowbray of Thirsk should perhaps be regarded as a Lincolnshire baron, for in 1215 his most important barony was apparently not in the vale of York, but in the isle of Axholme. The Lancashire baron, Roger de Montbegon of Hornby, had other connexions and stands by himself. Moreover, Eustace de Vesci had been for many months in close touch with Robert fitz Walter, whose exile he had shared, and had been to Rome to appeal to Pope Innocent against John. He can be classed with Saer de Quinci, another member of the twenty-five, also an old associate of Robert fitz Walter,[3] and, as lord of Leuchars in Fife, an associate of the Scottish king. A seventh member of the committee, the young John de Lacy, constable of Chester and lord of Castle Donington (Leicestershire) and Pontefract, may be regarded as a link between north and south.

Wendover mentions other northerners who were at Stamford at Easter 1215: Peter Bruce of Skelton in Cleveland, Nicholas de Stuteville of Kirby Moorside and of Cottingham near Beverley, G(ilbert) de Laval and Thomas of Moulton. The Lancashire baron Robert Grelley was also important in Lincolnshire, and may be grouped with Simon de Kyme and Gilbert de Gant.

This brief analysis is sufficient to show that it is quite erroneous to regard the northern group as a distinct or predominant factor in the rebellion of 1215. Its leader, Eustace de Vesci, had wider

---

[1] If this argument is sound, it gives additional force to the view that the 'unknown charter' belongs to 1213–14, not to 1214–15. See above, p. 119. A certain lack of cohesion between the northerners and easterners is illustrated by a curious incident. Robert de Ros, recently sheriff of Cumberland, had received certain royal manors in Cumberland and Westmorland only a week or so before he joined the assembly at Stamford; and shortly afterwards the king tried to prevent the election of Robert fitz Walter's sister as the abbess of Barking by supporting the candidature of the aunt of Robert de Ros (*Rot. litt. claus*, i. 194, 202).

[2] Invested at Scone, 6 Dec. 1214, aged seventeen. He was very hostile to John.

[3] E.g. in the defence and surrender of Vaudreuil, the great Norman fortress, in 1203. See Powicke, *Loss of Normandy*, pp. 239, 240.

interests and connexions; and, if report spoke the truth, had the strongest grounds for personal hatred of the king.[1] Most of the others—and there were not so many others as the nickname of the party, 'the Northerners', would suggest—had other connexions which would induce them to co-operate with the baronage in the midlands and the east. They had no territorial cohesion and John had no difficulty, after the war broke out, in asserting his power in the north. His friends, Robert of Vieuxpont and Hugh Balliol controlled the Eden valley and Teesdale, and the road from Carlisle into Yorkshire by way of Brough. In the West Riding of Yorkshire, the king's cousin, the earl of Warenne, held Conisbrough and Sandal. The earldom of Lincoln was in abeyance, and John was lord of Lancaster, and at this time in control of the palatinate of Durham, the lands of the archbishopric of York and the honour of Richmond. When he was joined by William de Fors, the son of the Poitevin who had become count of Aumâle in right of his wife, he was still stronger, for William—the only one of the twenty-five who deserted to the king—was lord of Holderness.

2. We have accounted for eight of the twenty-five.[2] Four others stand apart from the rest—the mayor of London, the earl of Hereford, William Malet, and William de Albini. The mayor of London and Henry de Bohun, first earl of Hereford, had close connexions with the easterners. The mayor represented interests which had been captured by Robert fitz Walter, who had Baynard Castle to the west of the city walls, and hereditary claims to share in the administrative life of the city. The earl of Hereford was the brother-in-law of the young Geoffrey fitz Peter, earl of Essex, and through him closely connected with the group round Robert fitz Walter. The other two, William Malet and William de Albini, belonged to well established territorial families of administrative experience. The former, lord of Shepton Mallet in Somerset, had been sheriff of Dorset and Somerset and had joined in the expedition to Poitou. He had come to Stamford with William de Montacute, another Somersetshire baron. William de Albini, lord of Belvoir, who had

---

[1] See Norgate, *John Lackland*, p. 289, for the story of John's relations with Eustace's wife.

[2] Eustace de Vesci, William Mowbray, Robert de Ros, Richard Percy, Roger de Montbegon, Saer de Quinci (earl of Winchester), John de Lacy (constable of Chester), William de Fors (count of Aumâle).

in his time administered at least four shires, threw in his lot with
the rebels and distinguished himself by his defence of Rochester.

3. The remaining thirteen were all closely connected with eastern families, and especially with Essex. It is clear that Robert fitz
Walter relied upon a group of neighbours and relatives, and, with
them by his side, co-operated with the great houses of Clare and
Bigod. The easterners had as much political capacity and administrative experience to draw upon as the northerners; but, as their
conduct after the charter had been issued was to show, they had
become inflamed by personal feeling and were unable to retain
their hold in England. In London, their head-quarters, they revealed little military capacity and behaved like an irresponsible
family.

The earl of Norfolk, Roger Bigod, with his son Hugh Bigod, and
the earl of Clare and Hertford, with his son Gilbert, later earl of
Gloucester in right of his mother; and the young William the
Marshal, who had perhaps been drawn into the movement through
his Clare cousins, were the chief among the East Anglian and east
midland elements. William of Huntingfield had his chief seat in
Suffolk.[1] The remaining seven of the twenty-five were Essex
barons, or closely connected. The earl of Gloucester, as Matthew
Paris styles him, was the younger Geoffrey fitz Peter or de Mandeville, earl of Essex, in 1215 the husband of Isabella of Gloucester,
John's discarded wife. The earl of Oxford, Robert de Vere, had
his chief seat at Hedingham in Essex. He was, like Geoffrey de Sai,
related to the Mandevilles. Robert fitz Walter of Dunmow was
closely related to the Mandeville or fitz Peter family. John fitz
Robert was lord of Clavering in Essex. William de Lanvallei's
honour had been formed of various scattered manors in various
counties, all parcels of the old honour of Eudo the Sewer[2]; but his
family had acquired an hereditary claim to the custody of the castle
of Colchester. Richard de Montfichet was lord of Stanstead Montfichet in Essex.

The accompanying table illustrates the family relationships of
the greater barons: Robert fitz Walter, Geoffrey earl of Essex,

---

[1] *G. E. C. Complete Peerage*, ed. Vicary Gibbs, vi. 671.

[2] Chalk (Kent), Hamerton (Huntingdon), Wakeley (Northampton), &c. See
Farrer, *Honours and Knight's Fees*, iii. 168.

Geoffrey de Sai,[1] Robert de Vere, and Henry de Bohun. Further study of the barons who came to Stamford would reveal other relationships. For example, the fitz Alans of Oswestry and Clun in Shropshire were related through marriage to Simon de Kyme of Lincolnshire[2]; William Beauchamp of Bedford was married to Gunnora, the sister of William de Lanvallei II (d. before 1205) and aunt of the young William de Lanvallei III, the charter baron[3]; and Roger de Cressi was the half-brother of John fitz Robert.[4]

4. It is important to notice that a considerable number of the twenty-five had but recently come into their inheritance, and that most of these were young men, who, when the issue was joined, would have less sense of responsibility than their elders had. They had been children when King John came to the throne. Geoffrey de Sai and Robert de Vere, earl of Oxford, were middle-aged men in 1215, but had only recently (in 1214) succeeded to their lands. Geoffrey de Mandeville, son of Geoffrey fitz Peter, had succeeded his father as earl of Essex in 1213, and must have been about thirty years of age in 1215. The king had lately exacted a fine of no less than 20,000 marks for his consent to Geoffrey's marriage with Isabella of Gloucester. In 1242 this fine was still largely unpaid, and Geoffrey's nephew, Humphrey de Bohun, earl of Essex and Hereford, was allowed to allot the earl's third penny in Essex to the gradual liquidation of the debt.[5] Geoffrey's first wife, a daughter of Robert fitz Walter, is said on good authority, the contemporary *Histoire des ducs de Normandie*, to have been one of the victims of the king's lust.[6] John de Laci, constable of Chester, whose father Roger had been one of the king's most valiant and faithful friends, was a minor in 1212, when his father died, and was not permitted to take possession of all his lands when he came of age. The king had retained the great castle of Pontefract.[7] John fitz Robert of

---

[1] Geoffrey had, among other fiefs, Sawbridgeworth in Hertfordshire, on the Essex border.

[2] *Rot. litt. claus.*, i. 140. [3] Farrer, op. cit., iii. 289, 290.

[4] Ibid., p. 316; Stapleton, *Rotuli scaccarii Normanniae*, ii, pp. cxviii, cxix.

[5] Bémont, 'Un *Rotulus finium* retrouvé (1242–3)' from the *Bulletin philologique et historique (jusqu'à 1715)* for 1924 (Paris, 1926), pp. 3, 4; no. 2. For the fine see Round's remarks in the *English Historical Review*, xix. 707, 708.

[6] See Norgate, *John Lackland*, pp. 289–91.

[7] See in particular the king's instructions of September and October 1213,

Clavering was still a minor in 1211, and had received his lands in 1212.[1] William de Lanvallei was a minor in 1205, but was in possession of his lands in 1212.[2] Richard de Montfichet was a ward in 1207 of the constable of Chester, who gave 1,000 marks for the wardship, and Richard was still a minor in 1212.[3] William de Fors, count of Aumâle, was born in 1191 or later, and had married Avelina de Montfichet.[4] This connexion with the Essex baron may have been one of the reasons for his brief rally to the baronial cause in 1215.

Three of the twenty-five were the sons of great barons and had not yet come into their inheritance. The young William the Marshal was born about 1190, Hugh Bigod was the son of earl Roger, and Gilbert of Clare, who had reached middle age, was the son of the elderly earl of Clare.

My friend Mrs. Stenton, who has sent me some valuable criticisms on this appendix, suggests that I have laid rather too much stress upon the influence of family connexions. In 1215, as at other times of civil strife, families were divided, as they must always be when the ramifications of kindred are so intricate and widespread in society; and it would indeed be unfortunate if, in the interpretation of political movements, the argument from connexions of this kind were pressed without caution. But the existence of close family ties does seem to me to have been a significant factor in forming a definite group of men personally hostile to King John.

Rot. litt. claus., i. 151*b*, 152*b*. John de Laci had to promise to pay a fine of 7,000 marks for having the rest of his lands (*Rot. de oblatis et finibus*, pp. 494, 495).

[1] Stapleton, *Rotuli Scacc. Normanniae*, ii, p. cxix. That he was still a minor in 1211 appears from an entry in the *Rotulus de prestitis* for this year (ed. Hardy, p. 243): 'Iohanni filio Roberti super pat' suum ij marc. lib. Bartholomeo magistro suo'.

[2] Farrer, *Honors and Knights' Fees*, iii. 289, .

[3] *Rot. litt. claus.*, i. 91*b*, 100, 112; *Book of Fees*, i. 125, 'heres Ricardi de Munfichet'.

[4] Avelina was sister of Richard de Montfichet, and according to Matthew Paris, a lady of great beauty. See *G. E. C. Complete Peerage*, ed. Vicary Gibbs, i. 355.

Table to illustrate the connexion between some of the Twenty-Five.

(The names of the barons who were among the twenty-five are printed in italics)

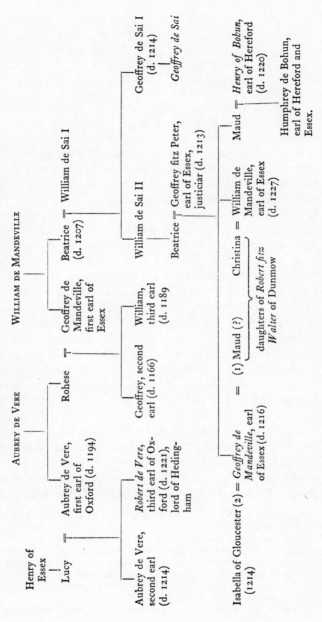

A Note on Stephen Langton's 'familia'

LANGTON's relations with his household of officials and clerks were intimate. Gerald of Wales gives us a glimpse of him talking about ecclesiastical problems with them,[1] and two of them, his brother Simon (who acted as his proctor in the negotiations with King John and afterwards at Rome) and Elias of Dereham were probably influenced by their feelings of loyalty to him when in 1215–17 they took so active a part in the activities of Louis of France. Unhappily little is known about Stephen's household. Simon, who returned to England in 1227, and Elias, who from 1222 was busy as canon of Salisbury until his death in 1245, were among the archbishop's executors (see above, p. 160). The other executors, Alexander of Stavensby, bishop of Lichfield and Coventry, Henry of Sandford, bishop of Rochester, and Thomas of Freckenham clearly belonged or had belonged to the group. The last named appears in 1218 as the archbishop's official,[2] that is to say, he presided over his court and was his right-hand man in diocesan administration. Henry of Sandford was doubtless elected bishop of Rochester at the archbishop's instance[3]; moreover, he had been archdeacon of Canterbury until his elevation in 1227, and is known to have had an intense admiration for Stephen (see above, p. 18). Alexander of Stavensby became bishop of Lichfield in 1224 after a disputed election and was consecrated by Honorius III at Rome.[4] He was chosen in preference to a monk of Coventry and was perhaps suggested by the archbishop. He was active during the next few months against Fawkes de Breauté, as later on behalf of Hubert de Burgh. In short, he played a thoroughly Langtonian part. I have

---

[1] *Opera*, iv. 75. [2] Patent Rolls, 1216–25, p. 148 (April 1218).

[3] The monks of Rochester had to seek the *licentia eligendi* from the archbishop, not from the king. Edmund of Hadenham gives a detailed account of the election of Henry of Sandford; Wharton, *Anglia Sacra*, i. 347, 348. The election of the archdeacon of Canterbury was made by invocation of the Holy Spirit, i.e. by unanimous agreement, which suggests co-operation with the archbishop. In 1214, when the precentor of St. Paul's, another learned secular, was elected, the archbishop is said to have been present.

[4] Stubbs, *Registrum Sacrum Anglicanum*, p. 56; *Annales Monastici*, iii. 90.

suggested above (p. 103 n.) that Gervase of Melkeley may have been the clerk mentioned by Pope Innocent when he refers to the two clerks 'A and G', sent to Rome by the archbishop in 1214. It is possible that the other was Alexander of Stavensby.

It may be suggested with rather more plausibility that Alexander was the archbishop's chancellor, the head of his secretariat. For early in 1224 when the earl of Chester and others sent Robert Passelew and Robert of Kent to Rome to represent their point of view, the interests of the archbishop and the justiciar were upheld by John Houghton, archdeacon of Bedford and Master A., the archbishop's chancellor.[1] Now Master Alexander of Stavensby was consecrated as bishop of Lichfield on 14 April at Rome. It looks as though the chancellor and the bishop, both in Rome about this time, were identical. The new bishop's active share in the proceedings of the summer, during the siege of Bedford, would thus be explained. However this may be, it is certain that, after the archbishop's death, Alexander, Henry of Rochester and John Houghton co-operated as King Henry's agents in Rome against the confirmation of Walter of Eynsham, the monk elected by his fellow-monks of Christ Church, Canterbury, as Stephen's successor.[2]

Stephen styled himself in his charters and letters 'Stephanus Dei gratia Cantuar' archiepiscopus, totius Anglie primas et sancte Romane ecclesie cardinalis'.[3] This form appears in an interesting French charter of 20 January 1215, which is entered on the dorse of the Charter Roll 16 John m. 5., obviously because it safeguarded royal rights which might be affected by the confirmation of the archbishop's right of advowson in the bishopric of Rochester.[4] Numerous acts of Stephen are to be found scattered among manuscript collections. They ought to be brought together. I may note a monition to the faithful in the province of Canterbury to subscribe to the building of Salisbury cathedral, with a promise of

---

[1] Annals of Dunstable in *Annales Monastici*, iii. 89: 'sed archidiacono Bedefordie et magistro A. cancellario archiepiscopi viriliter resistentibus, frustrata est spes eorum'. It is curious to find that in 1209 Stephen's *senescallus*, whom he sent to interview the king, was named Alexander; annals of Waverley, ibid., ii. 263.

[2] *Roger of Wendover*, iv. 171, 185; *Gervase of Canterbury* (ii. 115 ff.) gives a long and important account of the actual election by the monks. For the significance of the opposition to it by the court and the bishops cf. above, pp. 82, 111 n.

[3] *Register of S. Osmond*, ii. 57, &c.   [4] *Rotuli chartarum*, p. 209.

thirty days' indulgence,[1] an act uniting the church of Tenham to the archdeaconry of Canterbury (1227),[2] and a Harleian charter, 74 A. 14, of the year 1226, with the archbishop's seal. The seal is described by Mr. W. de G. Birch.[3] The obverse has a full-length figure of the archbishop, in vestments, lifting up the right hand in benediction, and holding the pastoral staff in the left hand. 'Stephanus Dei gracia Cantuariensis archiepiscopus'. The reverse is a smaller painted oval counterseal, depicting, it is of interest to find, the murder of Becket. The words are

Mors expressa foris tibi vita sit intus amoris.

A reference in the printed *Layettes du Trésor des Chartes* (i. 68, no. 118) might suggest the existence in the Archives Nationales (J. 254) of correspondence of Langton and John, archbishop of Tours. Monsieur Ch-V. Langlois has kindly given me the facts. J. 254 A, no. 44 is a letter, 13 June 1299, in which are included five documents extracted from the 'Registra cartarum Campanie'. The fourth of these is a *vidimus* delivered by Stephen, archbishop of Canterbury, without date. Only three lines come from Stephen's chancery, viz.:

Omnibus Christi fidelibus. Nouerit uniuersitas uestra nos uidisse litteras sigillatas sigillo Henrici bone memorie quondam comitis Trecensis palatini.

I suspect that the archbishop left his breviary to Elias of Dereham; for nearly a century later it was in the possession of another canon of Salisbury, Henry de la Wyle, the chancellor of the church. Among the books left to the cathedral by Henry's will, 2 June 1327, was 'Breviarium secundum Stephanum de Langton'.[4]

---

[1] Historical MSS. Commission: Report on Various Collections, i. 377 (dean and chapter of Salisbury).

[2] Eighth Report of the Historical MSS. Commission (1881) Appendix, p. 330*a* (Register D, Christ Church, Canterbury).

[3] *Catalogue of Seals in the Department of Manuscripts in the British Museum*, i. (1887), p. 160, no. 1196.

[4] Hist. MSS. Commission: Various Collections, i. 376. Henry de la Wyle was himself a scholar, a Merton man who commented on Aristotle. See Brodrick, *Memorials of Merton College* (1885), p. 185. He left books to Merton. His commentary on the *De Anima* survives in Magdalen College MS., no. 63, f. 58.

INDEX

(*Note.*—The names of medieval writers and chroniclers are usually indexed under their Christian names, as more convenient for reference.)